EMERSON'S ANTISLAVERY WRITINGS

RALPH WALDO EMERSON

EMERSON'S ANTISLAVERY WRITINGS

EDITED BY
Len Gougeon and Joel Myerson

YALE UNIVERSITY PRESS
New Haven and London

Designed by Jill Breitbarth and set in Janson type
by. DEKR Corporation, Woburn, Massachusetts.
Printed in the United States of America by
Sheridan Books, Ann Arbor, Michigan.

Library of Congress Cataloging-in-Publication Data
Emerson, Ralph Waldo, 1803–1882.
Emerson's antislavery writings / Ralph Waldo Emerson ;
edited by Len Gougeon and Joel Myerson.
p.   cm.
Includes bibliographical references and index.
ISBN 0-300-05970-1 (cloth: alk. paper)
ISBN 0-300-09402-7 (pbk.: alk. paper)
1. Antislavery movements—United States.   I. Title.
E449.E55   1995
973'.0496—dc20   94-24866   CIP

A catalogue record for this book
is available from the British Library.

The paper in this book meets the guidelines for
permanence and durability of the Committee
on Production Guidelines for Book Longevity
of the Council on Library Resources.

10 9 8 7 6 5 4 3 2

Contents

Contents

ACKNOWLEDGMENTS

Len Gougeon prepared the Historical Introduction and assumed primary responsibility for the texts from printed sources. Joel Myerson prepared the Textual Commentary and took primary responsibility for the texts from manuscript sources. Both of us checked and contributed to each other's work. Manuscript material is presented here by permission of the Ralph Waldo Emerson Memorial Association and of the Houghton Library of Harvard University. We thank Elizabeth Hurwit and Faith Short for editing the book. Individually, we would like to make the following acknowledgments.

During my many years of research on the topic of Emerson and antislavery I have accumulated debts to several institutions and individuals. For access to materials as well as friendly assistance I wish to express my thanks to the Trustees and staffs of the Houghton Library, Harvard University; the Schlesinger Library, Radcliffe College; the Boston Public Library; the Boston Athenaeum; the New York Public Library; the Library of Congress, Washington, D.C.; the Essex Institute, Salem, Massachusetts; the Massachusetts Historical Society; the American Antiquarian Society, Worcester,

Massachusetts; the curators of the Sophia Smith Collection, Smith College Library, Northampton, Massachusetts; and especially Marcia Moss and the staff of the Concord Free Public Library.

I would like to express my gratitude to Robert Gross for his kindness and generosity in providing me with copies of numerous petitions from the people of Concord to the federal and state governments and for sharing his knowledge and insights regarding reform in Concord. I would also like to thank my graduate assistant, Joyce Knott, for her many hours of producing typescripts of accounts and records of numerous abolition meetings from nineteenth-century newspapers; my department secretary, Rose Pedley, who, as usual, provided invaluable assistance and encouragement; the Faculty Research Committee of the University of Scranton for various travel and research grants, without which this project could not have been completed; the staff of the Harry and Jeanette Weinberg Memorial Library of the University of Scranton for their continuous help and support; and the many friends and colleagues who offered both moral support and advice.

Finally, I would like to thank my wife, Deborah, and my children, Elliott, Nadia, and Wesley, for their continuing support and enthusiasm for both Emerson and me.

L. G.

As usual, the University of South Carolina fully supported my research. I am grateful to the Research and Productive Scholarship Committee for a travel grant; to the Faculty Advisory Committee of the English Department for awarding me a semester's leave; and to the Interlibrary Loans division of the Thomas Cooper Library for obtaining scarce materials for me. Both Trevor Howard-Hill and Bert Dillon, chairs of the English Department, were supportive. Thanks are due Armida Gilbert, Jennifer Hynes, Alfred G. Litton, Robert Trogdon, and especially Alan Brasher for help in preparing and proofing the manuscript for this book. Nat Lewis proved a diligent newspaper researcher. For various types of assistance I wish to acknowledge Ronald A. Bosco, Ward Briggs, Lawrence Buell, Rodney G. Dennis, James Justus, Ralph H. Orth, Albert J. von Frank, and Douglas Emory Wilson.

And, of course, to Greta, my thanks for love and patience.

J. M.

Historical Background

Len Gougeon

> What is a man born for but to be a Reformer.
> —*"Man the Reformer," 1841*

From the earliest stages of his public career, Ralph Waldo Emerson envisioned himself as a reformer—not a mere specialized philanthropist who sought to mitigate one or two evils in a sea of corruption but "a Re-maker of what man has made; a renouncer of lies; a restorer of truth and good, imitating that great Nature which embosoms us all!"[1] As a means toward this noble end, in the first stage of his career as preacher, and then later as lecturer and writer, Emerson relied largely on the power of moral suasion. He felt, as most Unitarian moralists did, that the reform of society must always begin with the reform of individuals. Any effort to impose moral improvement on society through the passage of laws, restrictions, or prohibitions was doomed to failure because morality is a matter of the heart and all such impositions inevitably leave the heart untouched and unconverted. In addition, single-issue moral reform efforts like abolition missed the point that moral reform must always seek the renewal of the entire individual, not just the eradication of an isolated sin. Morality is not, after all, piecemeal.

In this matter Emerson was greatly influenced by William Ellery Channing, a teacher whom Emerson came to admire while a divinity student at Harvard. In an 1827 letter to his brother William, Emerson remarks that he is "glad [that] when God touches with fire such minds as Channing I feel the swift contagion that issues from such as he & stimulates the young to purposes of great & awful effort."[2] Channing was among the first Unitarian clergymen to consistently promote social reform. His searing condemnation of the institution of slavery, and those who supported it, in his work *Slavery* (1835) brought down upon him the censure of the conservative Unitarian establishment.[3] Emerson, however, found the work admirable and described it in his journal as one of the "perfectly genuine works of the times."[4] In his study Channing holds that only those directly involved in the institution—slaves and slaveholders—can eradicate the evil of slavery, and "none of us are anxious to take the office from their hands." He goes on to assert that slavery would soon disappear "were the obligation to remove it thoroughly understood and deeply felt." In Channing's view, the responsibility of those not directly involved in the institution is to offer "prayers and persuasions" to effect this reform.[5]

Because of this emphasis on individual responsibility, universal rather than partial reform, and the importance of moral suasion, Channing generally eschewed organized efforts at social reform. He once noted, "Our danger is that we shall substitute the consciences of others for our own, that we shall paralyze our faculties through dependence on foreign guides."[6] Emerson, who would eventually become the most famous, or infamous, spokesperson for self-reliance in the United States, shared Channing's observations and for this and other reasons was at first quite reluctant to participate in the greatest organized reform movement of his age, abolition.

Emerson's journals show that virtually from the very beginning of his recorded intellectual life he wrestled with the moral problem of American slavery. In his "Wide World" journal, written in 1822 while he was a teenage Harvard undergraduate, he describes a dream where he witnesses African men, women, and children being captured and enslaved by "men dressed in foreign garb." The pitiful scene evokes both his sympathy and concern and he states, "I launched my skiff to follow the boats and redeem the captives." Unfortunately, the would-be deliverer cannot reach them, but he comes "near enough to hear the piercing cry of the chained victims" who "were sold for a price and compelled to labour all the day long and scourged with whips until they fell dead in the fields, and found rest in the grave." Emerson follows this description of his dream with a rumination on "why Providence suffers the land of its richest productions to be thus defiled" by the crime of slavery (*JMN*, 2:41–42). After completing his theological training at Harvard and receiving his approbation to preach in 1826, Emerson often touched on the horror of slavery in his sermons, especially, as Ralph Rusk puts it, "when he needed examples of man's inhumanity to man."[7]

Opposition to slavery developed very early in North America. Among the early Puritans, Samuel Sewell—prominent diarist, legislator, and judge—published a strong attack on the institution in *The Selling of Joseph* (1700), one of the first antislavery tracts published in America. The first secular abolitionist organization, the Society for the Relief of Free Negroes Held in Bondage, was established in Philadelphia in 1775.[8] Several of the Founding Fathers, including Ben Franklin, George Washington, Thomas Jefferson, and John Adams, expressed antislavery sentiments at one time or another.[9] But strong organized opposition to the institution did not come about until the 1830s, during what Henry Steele Commager refers to as the Era of Reform, when a number of reform movements took shape in America. Some prompted religious freedom, women's rights, penal and prison reform, and peace, but none became as strong or as successful as the abolition movement.[10]

On 1 January 1831 William Lloyd Garrison founded the *Liberator* in Boston. It was destined to become one of the most famous antislavery journals (and regular reading in the Emerson household). The *Liberator* advocated a program of immediate emancipation without compensation to the slaveholder and without foreign colonization of the freedmen, both of which were the most extreme positions then held by antislavery reformers.[11] Soon thereafter, in 1832, Garrison joined with others to found the New England Anti-Slavery Society. Opposition to the abolitionists by a conservative majority was strong from the outset, and antiabolition riots were common throughout the 1830s.[12] The abolitionists were seen by many as unruly radicals who threatened the economic status quo, sowed sectional discord, and sought to undermine the firm foundations of constitutional government. Indeed, some abolitionists gladly played the role of radical and defied convention in both personal appearance and conduct, wearing long beards, unkempt hair, and outlandish dress.[13] Others, like Garrison, dressed conservatively but espoused extreme anti-institutional positions.

The abolitionists persisted in their cause with a religious fervor despite bitter and often violent opposition. Many women joined the movement (including Emerson's wife, Lidian) to express solidarity with the oppressed slaves.[14] Encouraged by the success of the British abolitionists in emancipating the slaves of the British West Indies in 1833, the American movement gained strength.

In the 1840s the abolition movement continued to grow; the expansion of slave territory through the annexation of Texas in 1845 gave rise to concerns about the increasing power of the slave states. The acquisition of vast new territories as a result of the Mexican War (1846–1848) increased these concerns substantially. Many feared that the traditional political balance between slave and free states, ensured by the Missouri Compromise since 1820, would be lost. It now appeared that the federal system could become dominated by proslavery forces. The Mexican War and related events served to precipitate Thoreau's famous tax protest and his one-night incarceration in the Concord jail. It also gave renewed energy to the abolitionists' "no union with slaveholders" movement, which sought to dissolve the union between slave and free states.[15] The situation reached a climax in 1850 with the passage of the Compromise of 1850, a package of federal legislation designed to resolve sectional differences once and for all. Daniel Webster, the famous senator from Massachusetts, supported the historic legislative effort in the hopes of preserving peace and the Union, but the opposite resulted. Because the compromise included the infamous Fugitive Slave Law, which required the return of all escaped slaves—even if they had been successful in establishing residence in a free state—it was uniformly rejected by abolitionists and many others. These defiant moralists refused to become slave catchers to satisfy what they considered an immoral federal statute. This "filthy enactment," as Emerson called it, virtually guaranteed sectional strife and political conflict. The inevitable culmination came in the spring of 1861 with the firing on Fort Sumter and the outbreak of the Civil War.

Before 1844, Emerson's response to the problem of reform in general and slavery in particular was to emphasize the power of moral suasion in converting the stony hearts of men, a course that his mentor, Channing, undoubtedly approved of. Even after making the revolutionary transition from Unitarian to Transcendentalist—and exchanging his pulpit for the lectern, which he called the new pulpit of the age—Emerson continued to address the subject of social reform, especially slavery, as a matter of individual morality. His early public pronouncements on the topic consistently reflect this philosophical inclination.

Emerson delivered his first antislavery address sometime in the second half of November 1837, in the vestry of the Second Church in Concord. Although he had consistently eschewed single-issue reforms up to this time, historical events compelled a response—a pattern that would be repeated frequently in the coming decades.

From 1834 to 1837, conflict over the slavery issue became more and more intense throughout the Northern states.[16] Perhaps not surprisingly, increased agitation brought mob violence directed against the abolitionists. The mobs sought to silence the antislavery activists. Indeed, this desire to suppress public discussion of the increasingly volatile slavery issue was reflected at the highest levels of government. After a boatload of abolitionist tracts from New York was impounded by the Charlestown postmaster, then seized and burned by a mob in 1835, Pres. Andrew Jackson declared that such information was incendiary and recommended that a law be passed to prohibit the circulation of antislavery information through the federal mails. In a similar effort at suppression the following year, the House of Representatives adopted a gag rule, which provided that all antislavery petitions be tabled without discussion. Violent antiabolition agitation reached a climax with the dramatic murder of Elijah P. Lovejoy, an abolitionist publisher, at the hands of an angry mob in Alton, Illinois, on 7 November 1837.[17] This event, which was extensively reported in newspapers throughout the North, shocked not only abolitionists and their immediate supporters but also those who, up to this time, had been on the periphery of the antislavery issue. Moralistic social reformers like Emerson and Channing saw the event as yet another grievous assault on the very principle of free speech. This impression was no doubt deepened when the Boston authorities denied Channing and others permission to use Faneuil Hall "in order that there might be an expression of public sentiment in regard to the late ferocious assault on the liberty of the press at Alton."[18]

Emerson, who by this time had begun to feel considerable discomfort, even guilt, over his own failure to grapple more directly with the slavery problem (*JMN*, 5:437), was shocked by the Alton affair. After describing Lovejoy in his journal as an authentic hero who was willing "to die for humanity & the rights of free speech & opinion" (*JMN*, 5:437), he decided to take a public stand. If moral suasion was to have its effect, if the hearts of those in need of moral regeneration were to be touched, then the principle of free speech must be preserved at all costs. Its preservation was for Emerson the sine qua non of reform. Without it no amelioration of personal or social ills was possible.

The only record of Emerson's presentation on this auspicious occasion appears as a brief, fragmentary outline in his journal (*JMN*, 12:151–152) and in a short passage quoted in James Elliot Cabot's *Memoir of Ralph Waldo Emerson*.[19] Both the journal outline and the Cabot passage show that Emerson's concern is with the need to preserve the principle of free speech.

If the motto on all palace-gates is "Hush," the honorable ensign to our town-halls should be "Proclaim." I account this a matter of grave importance, because symptoms of an overprudence are showing themselves around us. I regret to hear that all the churches but one, and almost all the public halls in Boston, are closed against the discussion of this question. Even the platform of the lyceum, hitherto the freest of all organs, is so bandaged and muffled that it threatens to be silent. But, when we have distinctly settled for ourselves the right and wrong of this question, and have covenanted with ourselves to keep the channels of opinion open, each man for himself, I think we have done all that is incumbent on most of us to do. Sorely as we may feel the wrongs of the poor slave in Carolina or in Cuba, we have each of us our hands full of much nearer duties.

Regarding the abolitionist, Emerson states, "Let him not exaggerate by his pity and his blame the outrage of the Georgian or Virginian, forgetful of the vices of his own town and neighborhood, of himself. Let our own evils check the bitterness of our condemnation of our brother, and, whilst we insist on calling things by their right names, let us not reproach the planter, but own that his misfortune is at least as great as his sin."

Not surprisingly, given the crisis atmosphere of the times and the undoubtedly high expectations of abolitionists in Emerson's audience, the speech was something of a disappointment to his listeners. Cabot's comment on the performance is revealing. "To the abolitionists," he says, "this tone appeared rather cool and philosophical, and some of his friends tried to rouse him to a fuller sense of the occasion. He was insufficiently alive, they told him, to the interests of humanity, and apt to allow his disgust at the methods or the manners of the philanthropists to blind him to the substantial importance of their work."[20]

Despite the ambivalence that he felt about such public protests, events drew Emerson into making another just six months later. The format this time was an open letter to Pres. Martin Van Buren concerning the forcible removal of the Cherokee Indians from their lands in the South to a western wilderness. Emerson's wife expressed the concern of many regarding this action in a letter to her sister dated 23 April 1838. "If you see no papers and few people, you do not know I suppose, that in one month from to-day the Cherokees old & young—sick and well—are to be forcibly dragged from their homes by *harpy* government-contractors;—and conveyed without regard to their comfort health or even life during the journey—into the wilderness beyond the Missi[ssi]ppi. This is done by

Congress on the strength of a treaty obtained by fraud of a few individual Cherokees." Lidian adds that "yesterday after church, a meeting of the Concord people was held to consider whether any thing could be done by them to arrest this terrible deed—and in any case to wash their hands of it by a Memorial to congress protesting against it as an act of awful iniquity. Mr. Emerson made the first address; stating the case and reading to the assembly of 'Appeal of the Cherokees'—He also expressed his sentiments on the subject very decidedly."[21] Garrison's *Liberator* carried several articles about the situation. The "Appeal of the Cherokees" and the "Plunder of the Cherokees," articles that appeared in the edition of 6 April 1838, are typical in describing the outrage in blunt and immediate terms. An earlier issue, dated 23 March 1838, included the sharply titled "Brutality of the Administration toward the Cherokees," whose author asserted that "the pretended treaty, on which the Cherokees are to be forced from their lands, *was never assented to by more than one hundred of the 18,000 individuals composing the tribe.*"

On the day after his public statement in Concord on the Cherokee situation and at the behest of his fellow citizens, Emerson penned his letter to President Van Buren expressing shock and dismay at the impending action of the government. He sent it to John Reed, a member of Congress from Massachusetts, who arranged for its publication in the *Washington Daily National Intelligencer* on 14 May 1838. The letter was shortly reprinted in several places, including the *Liberator* (22 June 1838). This exceptional foray into the realm of public protest roused many abolitionists to hope that Emerson would take a more prominent and active role in their cause, but he himself was no more satisfied with this latest effort than with his speech in November. In his journal he recorded the following reflection.

Yesterday went the letter to V[an]. B[uren]. a letter hated of me. A deliverance that does not deliver the soul. . . . This stirring in the philanthropic mud, gives me no peace. . . . I fully sympathise, be sure, with the sentiment I write, but I

accept it rather from my friends than dictate it. It is not my
impulse to say it & therefore my genius deserts me, no muse
befriends, no music of thought or of word accompanies. Bah!
(*JMN*, 5:479)

There were many reasons for Emerson's aversion to such public
reform activity, not the least of which was his temperament. He
also harbored a lingering suspicion of organizations. Lidian, an
antislavery activist herself by this time, was aware of both feelings.
She notes in the letter to her sister referred to above, "Mr. Emerson
very unwillingly takes part in public movements like that of yesterday preferring individual action." Many years later she remembered
the event again and observed in a letter to her daughter Ellen, "Your
father is not combative. . . . Yet he exercised great moral combat-
iveness in writing to the Pres. of the U.S. in defense of the Cherokee
Indians. It was against the grain he did it; and he said it was hardly
fit for him to suspend his true vocation to become their champion."[22]
Emerson had not resolved for himself the question of racial
inferiority, either. Like many other moralists and reformers, he was
not yet convinced that blacks and other minorities were altogether
equal in their ability to compete in society.[23] If they were not self-
reliant, any effort to establish their social equality through external
agitation and moral suasion would be for naught. This thorny
question would plague him for some years.
Furthermore, Emerson was not at all comfortable at this early
juncture with many of the persons who were the loudest and most
conspicuous proponents of abolition, which he still saw as only a
partial reform. In one journal entry, he refers to abolitionists as "an
altogether odious set of people, whom one would be sure to shun
as the worst of bores & canters" (*JMN*, 9:120).
Lastly, Emerson had not yet determined what role to play in
bringing about social reform. As Lidian pointed out, he tended to
see specific public protests as apart from his true vocation. Throughout his career Emerson saw himself as a "scholar poet" (*L*, 1:435).
It was primarily through his artistic and philosophical vocation that

he felt he could best serve society and ameliorate its ills. Becoming a stump orator for abolition would certainly not be in keeping with this role.

Perhaps with this more poetic goal in mind, at the same time that Emerson penned his letter to the president he also copied several lines from Charles Sprague's "Centennial Ode" which reflected the plight of the Cherokees, beginning with the lines, "Alas for them their day is over, / Their fires are out by hill & shore." He had originally used these same lines in memorializing the Indians of Concord in his "Historical Discourse" three years earlier. The situation, around the time of King Philip's War, was somewhat similar and Emerson notes in his "Discourse," "It is the misfortune of Concord to have permitted a disgraceful outrage upon the friendly Indians settled within its limits, in February, 1676, which ended in their forcible expulsion from the town."[24] History, it seems, was repeating itself.

After writing to Van Buren, Emerson would not return to the forum of public protest until 1 August 1844. During the interval he would experience a baptism of fire into the realm of public debate following the presentation of his highly controversial "Divinity School Address" at Harvard in July 1838. When the furor aroused by the speech subsided, Emerson again pursued his lecturing career, often touching on the general topic of reform but remaining outside the fray. He had apparently decided to avoid any direct involvement with specific social reform enterprises and to "let the republic alone until the republic comes to me" (JMN, 5:479).

The persistence of this attitude and the residual influence of the Unitarian emphasis on individualism in all matters of social reform were evident in several of the presentations and publications that Emerson produced in this period. In January 1839, in a lecture titled "The Protest," he expressed his concern that the current generation of reformers, various as they were, suffered from a certain myopia in fixing on one particular sin rather than the full spectrum of moral reform. "Every reformer is partial and exaggerates some one grievance. You may feel that there is somewhat ridiculous in his tenacious oppugnation of some one merely local and as it were cutaneous disorder as if he dreamed, good simple soul, that were this one great wrong righted a new era would begin."[25]

One year later Emerson returned to this subject in "Reforms," the sixth lecture in his series in Boston at the Masonic Temple. He begins his presentation with the observation that "nothing has more remarkably distinguished the Present Age than the great harvest of projects it has yielded for the reform of domestic, social, civil, literary, and ecclesiastical institutions" (*EL*, 3:256)—a situation that he generally applauds. His concern here, however, like Channing's earlier, is that such reform efforts not displace the central ethical responsibility of the individual soul. He therefore cautions his audience to "accept the reforms but accept not the person of the reformer nor his law. Accept the reform but be thou thyself sacred, intact, inviolable, one whom leaders, one whom multitudes cannot drag from thy central seat. If you take the reform as the reformer brings it to you he transforms you into an instrument" (*EL*, 3:260). Emerson essentially advises each citizen to follow his or her own conscience, even if others see it as doing nothing. Speaking in a distinctly personal tone, he assures reformers, "Though I sympathize with your sentiment and abhor the crime you assail yet I shall persist in wearing this robe, all loose and unbecoming as it is, of inaction, this wise passiveness until my hour comes when I can see how to act with truth as well as to refuse" (*EL*, 3:266).

Emerson addressed the topic of reform once again the following year in "Man the Reformer," which he delivered to the Mechanics' Apprentices' Library Association in Boston on 25 January 1841. He liked the lecture well enough to have it published in the *Dial* (April 1841) and later in *Nature, Addresses, and Lectures* (1849). In this piece Emerson presents a philosophy of reform that emphasizes the need for individuals to improve society by manifesting an enlightened and virtuous attitude in all of the daily functions of life. Primarily, people should simplify their lives and depend less on trade, an activity that often corrupts. As in his earlier presentations, Emerson here asserts that the truest reformers are circumspect in their virtue and that authentic reform will come only with the promulgation of love throughout society. Faith is a key ingredient.

"The power, which is at once spring and regulator in all efforts of reform, is faith in Man, the conviction that there is an infinite worthiness in him which will appear at the call of worth, and that all particular reforms are the removing of some impediment" (*CW*, 1:156). Ultimately, in Emerson's view, "love would put a new face on the weary old world in which we dwell as pagans and enemies," and he offers Christ as an example of a world reformer who made use of this great power as "a lover of mankind" (*CW*, 1:159).

In addition to exhorting would-be reformers to take a more comprehensive view of society's needs, Emerson, like the good preacher he always was, sometimes chided those hypocritical few who sought to pluck the mote out of another's eye without seeing the beam in their own. Thus, for example, in his famous essay "Self-Reliance," first published in 1841 in the volume then titled simply *Essays*, we find the following harsh statement directed squarely at certain abolitionists, as well as other self-serving reformers.

> If an angry bigot assumes this bountiful cause of Abolition, and comes to me with his last news from Barbadoes, why should I not say to him, 'Go love thy infant; love thy woodchopper: be good-natured and modest: have that grace; and never varnish your hard, uncharitable ambition with this incredible tenderness for black folk a thousand miles off. Thy love afar is spite at home.' Rough and graceless would be such greeting, but truth is handsomer than the affectation of love. Your goodness must have some edge to it—else it is none. (*CW*, 2:30)

Throughout the essay Emerson insists on the need for individuals to redeem themselves first; they should tend to the needs and obligations of their own immediate existence and not be distracted by specious enterprises to impose reform on others. Beyond the philosophical principal that informs Emerson's criticism here is his observation that many of the abolition agitators, like the famous British reformer George Thompson, were often rude, hypocritical, or both in their single-minded pursuit of abolition goals. Indeed, after entertaining Thompson at a breakfast in his home, Emerson recorded the following in his journal:

> Thompson the Abolitionist is inconvertible; what you say or what might be said would make no impression on him. He belongs I fear to that great class of the Vanity-stricken. An inordinate thirst for notice cannot be gratified until it has found in its gropings what is called a Cause that men will bow to; tying him self fast to that, the small man is then at liberty to consider all objections made to him as proofs of folly & the devil in the objector, & under that screen, if he gets a rotten egg or two, yet his name sounds through the world and he is praised & praised. *(JMN,* 5:91)

Edward Emerson, to explain his father's obvious antipathy in statements such as this, would later observe, "Persons reputed high-minded and generous were eagerly assailed by competing advocates of measures for the regeneration of man, varying much in their wisdom, and usually woefully partial. . . . Many of these pilgrims were unpresentable, rude and tedious; few had any eyes and heart for Nature, and almost all were without any sense of humor" *(W,* 3:349). Eventually, Ralph Waldo's opinion of the abolitionists changed dramatically, but in the 1830s and early 1840s he preferred to keep these self-styled idealists at arm's length.

Emerson's early thinking on the question of social reform generally and abolition in particular is summed up in his lecture "New England Reformers," which he delivered at Amory Hall in Boston on 3 March 1844. In this address Emerson once again observed that the movement toward reform in American society was growing and was reflected in a variety of areas, including temperance, nonresistance, abolition, and socialism. While Emerson saw some of these causes as silly, citing "a society for the protection of ground-worms, slugs and mosquitos" *(CW,* 3:150), he felt that most gave positive evidence of the "gradual casting off of material aids; and the indication of a growing trust in the private self-supplied powers of the individual." Still, many reformers did not yet recognize the underlying significance of this affirmation of the universal human impulse toward good. Such reformers, unfortunately, remain "partial; they are not equal to the work they pretend. They lose their way; in the assault on the kingdom of darkness, they expend all their energy on some accidental evil, and lose their sanity and power of benefit" (*CW*, 3:154). Also they are not fully aware of the importance of "the new and renewing principle of love" as the positive counterpoint to property and material corruption. Clearly, Emerson continued to feel considerable frustration with these well-intentioned souls; he observes somewhat caustically that "when we see an eager assailant of one of these wrongs, a special reformer, we feel like asking him, What right have you, sir, to your one virtue? Is virtue piecemeal? This is a jewel amidst the rags of a beggar" (*CW*, 3:155).

As in his earlier addresses on reform, Emerson here maintains that "if partiality was one fault of the movement party, the other defect was their reliance on Association" (*CW*, 3:155). He then reminds the associationists that "no society can ever be so large as one man"; and while unions are possible, "this union must be inward, and not one of covenants, and is to be reached by a reverse of the methods they use. The union is only perfect when all the uniters are isolated" (*CW*, 3:155, 156, 157). Predictably, the expression of these views garnered mixed reactions from the abolitionists. On the one hand, they applauded Emerson's attention to, and affirmation of, the need for authentic reform in American society. On the other hand, Emerson's criticism of some abolitionists—and, more important, his consistent emphasis on the need for universal rather than particular reform, as well as his corresponding emphasis on individual rather than associated efforts—cut to the very heart of their movement.

Emerson's further insistence that individuals follow their own judgement in promoting the ends of reform seemed to many abolitionists to promote an unconscionable passivity in the face of blatant evil. As early as 1838, Ellis Gray Loring—a friend of Emerson's from their Boston Latin School days and subsequently a prominent lawyer and abolitionist—told Emerson that he was "some times *thought* to teach, that, in the great struggles between right and wrong going on in society, we may safely & innocently stand neuter, altogether;—gratifying mere tastes, so they be elegant, intellectual tastes,—this is surely a misconstruction of your words."[26] Similarly, Maria Weston Chapman, one of the leading female abolitionists in Boston, drafted an article in 1844 in which she expressed her concerns about the Concord bard's views and his impact on potential reformers. Not surprisingly, she associates Emerson's views with those of his mentor, William Ellery Channing.

> [Emerson's] character being rather contemplative than active, at least according to popular acceptation of those words, he has been a philosophical speculator rather than a reformer. His wisdom has therefore made fools of some, & his naturalness [has] been the occasion of affectation in others. Hundreds of young persons have made him their excuse for avoiding the Anti Slavery battle & talking about the clear light; just as thousands have refused their aid to the cause because Dr. Channing wrote essays against associations.[27]

Although neither Loring nor Chapman could have known it, a great change was about to occur in Emerson's approach to the problem of American slavery. Historical events and the powerful influence of community, family, and friends contributed substantially to the change.

Concord was a hotbed of antislavery activity throughout the 1830s. Its newspapers, the *Yeoman's Gazette* and the *Concord Freeman*, vied with each other in running numerous articles and items supporting abolition. Antislavery orators were so common in the town that in 1838 Emerson remarked, "In Concord every third man lectures on slavery" (*JMN*, 5:505). A women's antislavery society was established in Concord around 1835, and Lidian, as well as the Thoreau women, were active members from early on. In addition to Lidian, Emerson's Aunt Mary Moody Emerson was an early convert to abolitionism, and his mother, Ruth, frequently joined her daughter-in-law and son in signing some of the many antislavery petitions that circulated through Concord in the 1830s and 1840s. Other abolitionists in Emerson's immediate family were his brother Charles (who in 1835 delivered a lengthy lecture on slavery in

Concord, in which he called for immediate emancipation—the more radical position even among abolitionists at the time) and Emerson's step-grandfather, the Reverend Ezra Ripley, a leading member of the community and someone whom Ralph Waldo admired greatly. Ripley was an early supporter of the Middlesex Anti-Slavery Society and provided both encouragement and the occasional use of his church for their quarterly meetings.[28]

Despite his consistent emphasis on the importance of the individual, Emerson was responsive to the influence and concerns of his immediate community regarding social issues. The record shows that he often joined his neighbors in expressing positions on national affairs, especially slavery. Thus, in addition to speaking at the town meeting to protest the removal of the Cherokees and sending his open letter to Martin Van Buren at the behest of that group, Emerson (along with 490 other male citizens) signed a petition to the U.S. Congress stating "that the treaty under color of which [the Cherokees] are to be removed beyond the Mississippi . . . [is] an atrocious fraud, [and] we most solemnly remonstrate against its execution. Believing that to deprive them of their lands without their consent is an outrage upon justice and humanity, a violation of all the principles of free government, and of the solemn obligation of the U. States to this dependent people, we most earnestly protest against it." The women of Concord, including Lidian Emerson, signed six separate versions of the same petition.[29]

Emerson and his townspeople specifically aimed to preserve the delicate political balance between slaveholding states and free states that had been established by the Missouri Compromise of 1820. If the slaveholders gained a majority, then the unlimited expansion of slavery would be virtually guaranteed, given the economics of the institution. Emerson was therefore greatly disturbed when Texas, after declaring its independence from Mexico, petitioned on 4 August 1837 for annexation to the United States. The entry of Texas into the Union as a slaveholding state would substantially increase the power and influence of the slaveholders. On 3 October 1837 Emerson joined Ezra Ripley and other citizens of Concord in signing a petition to the U.S. Congress that contained the following protest, among others.

> Although the independence of Texas has been recognized by this government, yet, it has not been acknowledged by Mexico, and is now forcibly resisted by that power:—therefore its annexation to the Union, might involve this nation in a war with Mexico. Against any measure, tending to such a result, we remonstrate. While we do not claim for Congress, the power to *abolish* slavery in the several States, we are opposed to its *further extension* by that body, hence, are decidedly hostile to the annexation of Texas to the Union, with a Constitution which expressly sanctions slavery, and encourages the slave trade between that country and the United States.

In January 1838 Emerson signed yet another petition to Congress arguing for the rejection of "all proposals for the annexation of Texas to this Union." A year later the women of Concord, including Lidian and Ruth Emerson, forwarded a similar petition. Despite such efforts, which were in keeping with Emerson's feeling that Massachusetts should "resist the annexation with tooth & nail" (*JMN*, 9:74) and that "the great & governing sentiment of the State is anti-slavery & anti-Texas" (*JMN*, 9:180), momentum for Texas annexation grew. In the spring of 1844 President Tyler was urging Congress to approve the measure, and eventual approval seemed all but inevitable.

It must have seemed to Emerson at this critical time that the emphasis on universal reform and individual action, which he favored, had so far failed not only to diminish slavery but even to contain it. Slavery threatened to dominate the Union and control its future development. Perhaps because of this acute concern, as well as the strong influence of family and friends within the Concord community, Emerson put aside his reservations. When the women of Concord invited him to speak at their annual celebration of emancipation in the British West Indies on 1 August 1844, he accepted. It had been seven years since Emerson last spoke publicly on the topic of slavery and six since his protest on behalf of the Cherokees.

Apparently he felt, when faced with the potentially unlimited expansion of slavery, that the republic had finally come to him. The topic this time would be the institution of slavery itself, not the issue of free speech or reform. In preparing for the presentation, Emerson was determined to master his subject thoroughly. He read and digested such lengthy and seminal works as *The History of the Rise, Progress, and Accomplishment of the Abolition of the African Slave Trade by the British Parliament* (1808, 1839) by Thomas Clarkson and *Emancipation in the West Indies: A Six Month's Tour in Antigua, Barbadoes, and Jamaica, in the Year 1837* (1838) by James A. Thome and J. Horace Kimball, and he borrowed a number of legal studies, records, and reports from his Boston friend Ellis Gray Loring. Emerson's extensive study of these sources had a profound effect on his understanding of slavery and changed forever his approach to the eradication of the evil.[30]

From Thome and Kimball, Emerson garnered firsthand accounts of the actual horrors of slavery—accounts of the dungeons that were attached to every plantation house, pregnant women who were punished on the treadmill if they did not work, and a twelve-year-old boy who was made to strip his own mother and publicly beat her. From Clarkson he learned of the British reformer's determined efforts to gather accounts and facts about the abominations of the slave trade from sailors and slavers on the Liverpool waterfront. From both sources, he developed a sense of the moral courage and unbounded faith of those who finally triumphed over this most heinous of human crimes, and discovered the almost immediate ameliorative effects of emancipation upon the slaves in the West Indies. The accounts fortified his sometimes beleaguered faith in the essential goodness of humanity in an age of growing skepticism and also eradicated most of his lingering doubts about the equality of blacks and their ability to compete successfully in a free society. In his address, for example, he refers to "the annihilation of the old indecent nonsense about the nature of the negro" and repeated a British politician's statement: "We have already gained one victory:

we have obtained for these poor creatures the recognition of their human nature, which, for a time, was most shamefully denied them." In the same vein, just six months earlier Emerson signed a petition calling on Massachusetts both to propose an amendment to the U.S. Constitution outlawing slavery and to eliminate all state laws and constitutional provisions "making any distinctions among citizens on account of color."

From the legal materials borrowed from Loring, Emerson acquainted himself with legal arguments and principles that had historically been brought against the institution of slavery. Collectively, these works moved Emerson immensely and provided the impetus for what would be one of his most comprehensive, intellectual, and emotional statements on slavery and reform.

Not everyone in Concord was sympathetic to the abolition movement. On the day of the address, Conservative officials in the town refused to allow Emerson to speak in any of the local churches. Nathaniel Hawthorne generously offered the use of his spacious front lawn at the Old Manse, but rain prevented an outdoor meeting. At last, the group settled for the courthouse. Upon arriving, the principals discovered that the same officials now refused permission to ring the church bell to call the townspeople to the meeting. Henry Thoreau defiantly rang the bell on his own accord.

In his presentation Emerson displayed a new respect for associated abolitionists, which must have surprised and delighted many in his audience, given his earlier criticisms. He had developed a new regard for abolitionists in general. Factors in this turnabout no doubt included the strong abolitionist feelings in his own family and community, as well as the antislavery activities of such friends and associates as William Henry Furness, Theodore Parker, and Samuel Joseph May. Emerson was apparently now prepared, in the face of disturbing national developments, to accept the notion that slavery was such a special and aggressive evil that organized and focused opposition was necessary. In stark contrast to his oft-stated criticisms of the myopia and partiality of the abolitionist movement, Emerson states, "I will say further, that we are indebted mainly to this movement, and to the continuers of it, for the popular discussion of every point of practical ethics, and a reference of every question to the absolute standard"; and he applauds the "free and daring discussions of [their] assemblies."

To say that the speech was a great success and a delight to abolitionists would be a gross understatement. Firsthand accounts of the well-attended gathering refer to tears flowing down the cheeks of "sturdy men as well as tenderhearted women" when Emerson described the infinite wrongs done to blacks. Another account describes the address as "full of ardent life" and "infused with a fine enthusiasm."[31] Virtually all abolitionists saw the speech as a declaration of Emerson's commitment to their cause. It was praised in the pages of the *Liberator*, *Herald of Freedom*, *Emancipator*, and elsewhere. John Greenleaf Whittier, the most highly regarded abolitionist poet of the age, told Emerson in a letter, "That you join with us in supporting the great *idea* which underlies our machinery of conventions and organizations, I have little doubt after reading thy Address."[32] Despite some residual concerns about accepting such a public role, Emerson himself was pleased enough with the piece to allow its publication in pamphlet form in both the United States and England.

The address was a major step forward for Emerson. It brought him into firm contact with a group whom he had mostly avoided, and he forged thereby a de facto alliance with them. Some were surprised by this development. A reporter for the *Boston Courier* observed, "Before we saw notice of this celebration, we were not aware that Mr. Emerson had sufficiently identified himself with the abolitionists, as a party, to receive such a distinguished token of their confidence." It was an observation that other segments of the community would also make. Although Emerson himself occasionally felt some discomfort over his new associates (around this time he wrote in his journal, "I do not and can not forsake my vocation for abolitionism" [*JMN*, 9:64n]), he never rejected them, and throughout the remainder of the decade he drew closer to the movement and its leading figures. There can be little doubt that on 1 August 1844, Ralph Waldo Emerson made the transition from philosophical antislavery to active abolitionism.

After 1 August, Emerson's reform activities became more frequent and public. In his address he had insisted that the state of Massachusetts provide protection for freeborn black citizens who, as crew members of Massachusetts ships, had been illegally arrested and detained under the slave laws of South Carolina, Georgia, and Louisiana. In response to such abuses, the Massachusetts General Court sent Emerson's neighbor and friend Samuel Hoar to South Carolina to look after the interests of such people. A short time after arriving, Hoar and his daughter Elizabeth (once a fiancé of Emerson's deceased brother Charles) were driven from Charleston by an angry mob with the tacit approval of local authorities.

Emerson was outraged by the event. On 17 December he sent a letter to Horace Greeley's *New-York Daily Tribune* praising Hoar for his courage under extraordinary circumstances and explaining the details of his expulsion (*L,* 7:620). The following month he attended a protest meeting in Concord that dealt with both Hoar's expulsion and the annexation question. He also signed yet another petition, in this case "a remonstrance" against the proposed annexation of Texas, and he apparently made a speech at the Concord meeting wherein he condemned South Carolina as a state that "has excluded every gentleman, every man of honor, every man of humanity, every free man from its territory" (*JMN,* 9:173–174). In February 1845 Emerson, Lidian, and his mother, Ruth, joined several Concord neighbors in petitioning the Massachusetts state legislature to cease the illegal detention of individuals as slaves "in the territories of the United States and in the District of Columbia." They also asked the legislature "to authorize the governor to provide counsel for the defense of such citizens of this commonwealth as have been or may be arrested in any of the territories of the United States, or in the District of Columbia, charged with violating any laws of such Territory or District, by aiding the escape of slaves." In addition, the petition called for the state of Massachusetts to seek a Supreme Court ruling on the constitutionality of such laws. Rather than being discouraged by the Hoar affair, were Emerson and other citizens of Concord apparently energized by it.

This mounting reform activity led Emerson to experience some mixed feelings about his increasingly public role as reformer, which he saw as drawing him away from his vocation as poet, scholar, and "generalizer." In his journal he remarks that society possesses recognizable evils whose "remedying is not a work for a society but for me to do." He adds, "I also feel the evil for I am covetous and I do not prosecute the reform because I have another task nearer" (*JMN*, 9:85). Despite such nearer tasks and an occasional feeling of ambivalence, Emerson remained receptive to opportunities to express himself on the burning issue of the day. And so, when invited in August 1845 to celebrate once again the anniversary of West Indian emancipation with a public address, he accepted.

Emerson delivered his second major antislavery speech on 1 August 1845 before a large audience at an all-day gathering of abolitionists of Middlesex and Suffolk counties held in a grove in Waltham, Massachusetts. The *Liberator* (8 August 1845) indicates that "large delegations from Boston and Concord, and considerable numbers from other places in the vicinity" attended. Speakers of the day included William Henry Channing, Emerson's friend and a longtime abolitionist whom he would soon address poetically in his "Ode to W. H. Channing"; William I. Bowditch, a prominent abolitionist; and Henry Wilson, a member of the Massachusetts legislature who later became a senator and vice president of the United States. Another occupant of the speaker's platform whom Emerson later recalled in his journal was Jonathan Walker, a sea captain who had been branded and jailed for a year in the South for the crime of transporting escaping slaves to the Bahamas. According to the *New-York Daily Tribune* (7 August 1845), the audience was also treated to some lines written for the occasion by James Russell Lowell.

In a stirring speech Emerson emphasizes the deleterious effects of racism in preventing a vigorous prosecution of the antislavery cause among the general public in the North. "The objection of an inferiority of race," says Emerson, is summarized in the word "Niggers." "They who say it and they who hear it, think it the voice of nature and fate pronouncing against the Abolitionist and Philanthropist." Emerson rejects this position outright and argues ardently for the dignity and the freedom of the oppressed. As with his address the year before, this one was reported in detail in the *New-York Daily Tribune*, *National Anti-Slavery Standard*, and *Liberator*, and Emerson's growing reputation as an abolitionist received yet another significant boost.

The next month Emerson attended the Middlesex Convention in Concord, which was called to express, once again, opposition to Texas annexation. After adjourning in Concord, the convention met again in Cambridge on 21 October. This time Emerson bore a letter to the assembly from John Greenleaf Whittier congratulating Emerson on his strong public stand against annexation and welcoming his "manly voice" to the chorus of opposition. Later printed in the *Emancipator* (1 October 1845), the letter undoubtedly contributed further to Emerson's stature as an abolitionist.

In November Emerson was able to strike another personal and public blow against racism and intolerance by refusing to lecture before the New Bedford Lyceum because of its recent exclusion of blacks from full membership. He probably first heard of the lyceum's new policy from his Concord neighbor and abolition activist Mary Merrick Brooks. Brooks was kept apprised of events in New Bedford by Caroline Weston, a friend and fellow abolitionist. After confirming the existence of the Lyceum's racist policy, Emerson sent the New Bedford group a polite yet firm letter rejecting their offer to lecture there and indicating that this policy, "by excluding others, I think ought to exclude me." He subsequently granted permission for his letter to be published, and it appeared in the *Liberator* (16 January 1846), along with a similar letter from Charles Sumner.

In the same month as the New Bedford episode, Emerson signed another Concord petition to Congress against the annexation; despite this eleventh-hour effort, Texas formally entered the Union on 29 December 1845. War with Mexico now appeared certain. Many abolitionists felt that the only way to protect the North from the contagion of the South was through separation, and "no union with slaveholders" became a prominent call. Emerson disagreed strongly with this position, which he saw as a negative one and as evidence of the pernicious influence of skepticism toward the possibilities of reform. Regardless of these objections, he continued to attend public events that associated him with the abolitionists. One was the funeral of Charles Turner Torrey, an abolitionist martyr who died in a Maryland prison, where he had been incarcerated for aiding escaping slaves. The funeral took place on 11 May 1846, eight days after the United States formally declared war on Mexico over the annexation issue; the timing undoubtedly lent a special poignancy to the occasion. In June, with the moral catastrophe of the Mexican War under way, Emerson composed his well-known "Ode Inscribed to W. H. Channing," in which he asserted that "Things are in the saddle, / And ride mankind." But he did not feel that separating the North from the South would improve the moral tone of either side. Instead, what was needed, as he had suggested in 1841, was an ameliorating infusion of love. "Let man serve law for man; / Hire for friendship, live for love, / For truth's and harmony's behoof."

With this Transcendental hope in mind, Emerson delivered another antislavery address a month later, on 4 July 1846, in Dedham, Massachusetts. The affair, sponsored by the Massachusetts Anti-Slavery Society, was designed to raise money to support antislavery lectures in the state. Emerson's participation was expected to help the organization to achieve its financial goals, and he furthered the ends of abolition both directly and indirectly by his presence. William Lloyd Garrison, James Freeman Clarke, and Wendell Phillips, all luminaries within the abolition ranks, joined him on the platform.

Emerson spoke of the "despair [which] has crept over Massachusetts, and over New England" in response to national events. He encouraged a positive and hopeful response to the ills of the day and castigated those who remained inert in the face of such astounding challenges to goodness, justice, and morality. He also applauded "the growth of the abolition party" and the activities of "these brave men and brave women pursuing their resolute course from year to year, through mobs, through favor, through neglect."

Although Emerson no doubt felt that he had made some inroads against despair and negativism with his presentation at Dedham, his optimism was dealt a substantial blow toward the end of the month by Thoreau's overnight incarceration in the Concord jail. Thoreau had refused to pay his poll tax as a personal protest against slavery and the Mexican War. He was released the next day, but Thoreau's action upset Emerson, who saw it as a purely negative gesture springing from the gloomy view "that the world is no longer a subject for reform." Emerson considered that such an attitude could have no positive conclusion or result. "This prison is one step to suicide" (*JMN*, 9:445, 447).

Perhaps to affirm his own positive activism, Emerson delivered his third address celebrating the anniversary of West Indian emancipation on 1 August 1846, shortly after penning his journal comments on Thoreau. Although no account of the speech survives, the *Liberator* (7 August 1846) provides a brief description: "Then there was the calm philosophical Emerson, closely scrutinizing, nicely adjusting the scales telling us the need be of all things."

Emerson's hopeful equilibrium was jolted somewhat in the fall of 1846 when a runaway slave on the ship *Ottoman* was seized as the vessel reached port in Boston. The slave was eventually returned to his master in Louisiana because the ship owners apparently feared legal reprisals and loss of commerce. The incident elicited expressions of outrage from Boston abolitionists, and a protest meeting was held at Faneuil Hall. The speakers at the meeting included Charles Sumner, Wendell Phillips, and Theodore Parker. Emerson, who had been invited to address the assembly, was unable to attend but did send a letter to the "Kidnapping Committee," which the group later published in a report. In his letter Emerson expressed in cogent terms his shock and disgust that such an outrage against freedom and justice could occur in Massachusetts.

This event and other national developments associated with the Mexican War depressed Emerson and diminished for a time his habitual optimism. In part as therapy for his depression, he decided to travel, and on 5 October 1847 he set sail for England and his first foreign lecture tour. He did not return until July 1848. During his tour Emerson was impressed with the unflagging efforts of the Chartists to achieve social reform in England. Indeed, revolution seemed to be in the air throughout Europe. Emerson recorded in his journal, "I fancied when I heard the times were anxious & political that there is to be a Chartist revolution on Monday next, and an Irish revolution in the following weeks, that the right scholar would feel,—now was the hour to test his genius." Under such circumstances, the poet-scholar assumed the role of a poet-reformer, whose "kingdom is at once over & under those perturbed regions. Let him produce its Charter now, & try whether it cannot win a hearing, & make felt its infinite superiority today, even today" (*JMN*, 10:310–311).

Emerson seems also by this time to have forgone completely his earlier reservations about the odiousness of some reformers. Provided the cause is just, much can be tolerated. "Shame to the fop of philosophy," he observes, "who suffers a little vulgarity of speech & of character to hide from him the true current of Tendency, & who abandons his true position of being priest & poet of those impious & unpoetic doers of God's work" (*JMN*, 10:326).

Emerson apparently came back refreshed from his British tour. The poet Ellery Channing observed in his journal, "It was after his English visit that he became so much happier and more joyous . . . & also assumed a more public life & habit."[33] Possibly because of this change, when William Lloyd Garrison invited Emerson to speak once again at the annual celebration of emancipation in the British West Indies, he accepted.

Emerson's last antislavery lecture of the decade was delivered on 3 August 1849 in Worcester, Massachusetts. More than five thousand people attended; they came from all over the state, and there were also delegations from Connecticut, Rhode Island, and New Hampshire. According to the *Liberator* account (17 August 1849), it was one of the largest abolition gatherings ever held in the commonwealth, and, as usual, Concord was well represented. The account also indicates that the meeting was not uniformly appreciated by the populace because it was "held under the auspices of the Massachusetts A. S. Society," whose members were often regarded as "fanatics," "madmen," "incendiaries," "disorganizers," "traitors," "comeouters," and "infidels." Clearly, abolitionism remained on the radical fringe of social reform in the eyes of many conservatives. By 1849, however, Emerson's association with these fanatics was firmly established. Throughout the 1840s he had come to know and respect some of the most prominent people in the movement, including Lucretia Mott, Wendell Phillips, and William Lloyd Garrison. In a letter to his friend Samuel Ward, written from Philadelphia in 1843, Emerson calls Mott "a noble woman" (*L*, 7:523). He admired Phillips as one of the most eloquent speakers on the American scene (*JMN*, 9:136–137). His earliest comments on Garrison, in 1839, describe him as "a man of great ability in conversation, of a certain longsightedness in debate which is a great excellence . . . and an eloquence of illustration which contents that ear & the mind." He also remarks approvingly on "his clearness from any taint of private end" (*JMN*, 7:281). Emerson's bond with these and other major abolitionists deepened over the years as the movement became more prominent and as developments on the national scene brought increased dangers to those who spoke for freedom. At times Emerson felt genuine pity for stalwart souls who, like Elijah Lovejoy, found themselves threatened and outnumbered. The typical Northerner, Emerson once remarked, "is surrounded with churches & Sunday schools & is hypocritical. How gladly, . . . if he dared, he would seal the lips of these poor men & poor women who speak for [the slave]." In a summary judgment of Garrison in 1844–1845, Emerson states simply, "I cannot speak of that gentleman without respect" (*JMN*, 9:132–133, 134). Although he occasionally criticized the actions or attitudes of Phillips and Garrison, he always held them in high regard. He frequently responded positively to requests from Phillips, Garrison, and others to make antislavery presentations. Sometimes he opted merely to join them on the platform to show his support for a noble cause.

The abolitionists for their part were delighted to have Emerson so firmly aligned with their cause after the 1844 emancipation address. As early as 1838, in a headnote to the Cherokee letter in the *Liberator* (22 June 1838), Garrison remarked: "The bold, energetic and independent tone of the following letter is worthy of the highest admiration. It ought to be printed in every newspaper, and sent to every family in the United States: Can it be possible that the mind and heart which gave it birth are unaffected by the woes of the slaves! We hope not." Garrison must have seen Emerson's 1844 address as the fulfillment of this early prayer. He praised the presentation in the *Liberator*, as did Nathaniel Rogers in the *Herald of Freedom*. One abolitionist recalled years later that Phillips was "wont for years to keep it on hand for distribution."[34] Maria Chapman probably summed up the reactions accurately when she said, in the draft article alluded to earlier, that "the abolitionists have been greatly cheered & strengthened by the words of Emerson." Abolitionists remained consistently appreciative of Emerson's many years of antislavery involvement.

In his lecture at Worcester Emerson showed the hopefulness of spirit that Ellery Channing described. He remained convinced that the amelioration of society's ills was inevitable and that the great work of reform was well under way. Once again he used a public occasion to praise his abolitionist colleagues: "It is the glory of these preachers of freedom that they have strengthened the moral sense, that they have anticipated this triumph which I look upon as inevitable, and which it is not in man to retard." Emerson's tone throughout the speech is bright and confident. Only a short time later, however, the passage of the Fugitive Slave Law and other legislation shocked and outraged the moralists of the North and introduced a decade of conflict and strife that greatly intensified Emerson's role as a social reformer.

Most citizens of Massachusetts, including Emerson, were taken by surprise when on 7 March 1850 Daniel Webster threw his considerable support behind the various legislative measures known collectively as the Compromise of 1850. These measures were designed to resolve the growing tensions between slaveholding and free states. Many people felt that the most disturbing measure was the infamous Fugitive Slave Law, which provided for the return of runaway slaves who had successfully escaped to the free states. With Webster's help the bill was passed on 18 September 1850. Emerson wondered how this "filthy enactment" could have been "made in the 19th Century, by people who could read & write."

His position, shared by virtually all abolitionists, is succinctly stated: "I will not obey it, by God" (*JMN*, 11:412), The first two attempts to enforce the law in Boston, against William and Ellen Craft and later against "Shadrach" (Fredric Jenkins, or Wilkins), failed. The second instance, in February 1851, involved a daring raid on the federal courthouse by Shadrach's supporters.

These unprecedented events were enough to convince Emerson that the authorities in Boston were serious about enforcement. Unable to attend the annual meeting of the Middlesex Anti-Slavery Society in Concord on 3 April 1851, Emerson provided a letter for the occasion (dated 18 March 1851), which constitutes the first public expression of his views on the matter. Despite his earlier misgivings about Thoreau's collision with the legal establishment, his reaction to the Compromise of 1850 was unequivocal: Break the law at every opportunity and register a constant protest "by voice and by pen . . . against the detestable statute of the last congress."

On the same day as the Middlesex meeting a fugitive slave named Thomas Sims was captured in Boston. This time the federal agents and their Boston cohorts, after deploying a formidable force, successfully returned their hapless victim to the bondage from which he had escaped. New England abolitionists were astounded by this act of officially sanctioned cruelty. Emerson vowed in his journal to "make no secret of my intention to keep [the citizens of Massachusetts] informed of the baseness of their accustomed leaders" (*JMN*, 11:354). Very shortly he was provided with an opportunity to exercise his new resolve. On 26 April 1851 thirty-five citizens of Concord invited him to speak on the recent distressing events in Boston. He accepted and on 3 May delivered his first address on the Fugitive Slave Law.

The speech is easily the most acerbic of his career. The cause of his ire is the general failure of morality and virtue in Boston and the nation, but the chief villain of the piece is Daniel Webster. Emerson had once greatly admired Webster and had been enthralled by his oratory and his powerful physical presence. But Webster's support of the compromise constituted for Emerson the greatest perfidy imaginable at a time when moral courage and committed leadership would have made all the difference. Emerson is unsparing in his attack. The "fame [of Webster] ends in this filthy law," and the once distinguished representative of Massachusetts has become "the head of the slavery party in this country."

Emerson's speech won immediate approval from abolitionist supporters and others. Charles Sumner, who would soon replace Webster as senator from Massachusetts, "rejoiced" in the presentation and asked Emerson to repeat it throughout Middlesex County in support of John Gorham Palfrey's run for Congress on the Free Soil ticket. It is a measure of the depth of Emerson's concern that he agreed to do so. Emerson well knew that political campaigning inevitably exposes one to the ridicule and venom of the opposing side. When he delivered his address in Cambridge, the *Liberator* (23 May 1851) reported that "a considerable body of students from Harvard College did what they could to disturb the audience and insult the speaker, by hisses and groans, interspersed with cheers for Webster, Clay, Filmore, Everett, and 'Old Harvard!' " The account added that "Mr. Emerson's refinement of character, scholarship, and mild and dignified deportment, could not save him from their noisy, yet feeble, insults."

A writer for the *Boston Semi-Weekly Advertiser* (23 May 1851) also took notice of Emerson's attacks on Webster and the Fugitive Slave Law. After a defense of Webster's position came a warning against the extremes of Emerson's views. "All that was urged against the law by Mr. Emerson . . . would have applied equally well to *any* law providing for the surrender of fugitives," from which it follows that agitators like Mr. Emerson "are doing their utmost to increase an excitement *ostensibly* against this particular law, but *really* against the provision of the Constitution, on which it was founded." Therefore, "if the doctrines of his lecture were sustained and enforced in the Free States, the Union would be infallibly severed."

Palfrey lost the election by a narrow margin, and Emerson retreated temporarily from the steamy realm of political polemics. In May 1852 he welcomed the Hungarian freedom fighter Louis Kossuth to Concord and grumbled in his journals about the shabbiness of American politics. The national parties held their conventions in the summer, and Emerson found the chief figures to be little better than "low conspirators" when compared to former leaders like George Washington (*JMN*, 13:63). Of course, not all American politicians fell into this category. A year after Palfrey's defeat, Emerson was pleased to attend a dinner in honor of Sen. John Parker Hale of New Hampshire, a leader of the Free Soilers and recent unsuccessful candidate for president. In the remarks he prepared for the occasion, Emerson noted that despite recent events, "the senator has not failed in his part. Justice has been done to his merits. And yet I cannot help adding a word of homage because they are so signal, & because I wish to extend my thanks to the like merits of others besides himself" (*JMN*, 14:411). Later in the year he was sufficiently inspired to contribute a poem, "Freedom," to an antislavery gift book entitled *Autographs for Freedom*, which was sold to raise money for Fredrick Douglass's newly established antislavery newspaper.

Emerson was eventually drawn back into the firestorm of national politics by the debate over the Kansas-Nebraska Bill in the spring of 1854. This measure, passed into law on 30 May, effectively nullified the Missouri Compromise of 1820, which specifically excluded slavery from the territories of the Louisiana Purchase north of the line 36° 30', thus making vast new areas available for the creation of additional slave states.

Emerson was greatly disturbed by the debate over the measure, as were other abolitionists. On 7 March 1854, the fourth anniversary of Webster's perfidy, he delivered his second speech on the Fugitive Slave Law at an antislavery gathering at the Tabernacle in New York City. Although measurably less acerbic than in his previous speech, Emerson nevertheless included an extensive and bitter condemnation of Daniel Webster, as well as an object lesson on the need for moral self-reliance in an age of deteriorating social values. Legal agreements like the Missouri Compromise and other social compacts are frail instruments in times of moral crisis because "covenants are of no use without honest men to keep them." Emerson also used the opportunity to argue against common notions of black inferiority, which inhibited reform.

The mighty Webster, dead now for two years, had his defenders still. After the Tabernacle gathering, the *Boston Bee* published an article accusing Emerson of "assailing the great who are dead from the meanest of all causes—a sordid envy." He has "long been the center of a system, composed of a few hundred ridiculous fools and lazy fellows, who deserve, each, a sound scourging for their impudence in daring to stay in a world where they are just so many nuisances, and of no earthly use whatever,—a parcel of selfish flunkies." Emerson "has been made the idol of this collection of human vermin because he is the most ridiculous and the wealthiest of the entire gang. . . . Emerson has houses, stocks, and others of those things that are desired by the carnal-minded." Not since the Palfrey campaign had the gentle bard been exposed to such undiluted vitriol, but the attack was a sign of the times.

An article in the *Boston Transcript* was less caustic. The writer refers to Emerson as "the great dreamer" who, "like Fine Ear in the fairy tale, lies upon the greensward and listens to the motion of each blade of grass, to the blossoming of flowers, hears the green leaves opening to the sunshine and the whole harmony of Nature's song, and then tells us—but not often in language which all men comprehend—what he has heard the grass, and flowers and green leaves say."

Around this time Emerson began keeping his "WO Liberty" notebook, devoted exclusively to abolition, slavery, and liberty (*JMN*, 14:373–430). This notebook contains drafts of seven antislavery speeches, and materials copied from earlier journals. The antislavery issue had clearly become a central concern of Emerson's intellectual life. Possibly he intended to use his WO Liberty notebook in preparing a book on liberty. If so, the publication of John Stuart Mill's *On Liberty* in 1859 may have preempted Emerson's effort.[35]

National affairs took a turn for the worse in May 1854, when Anthony Burns, another fugitive slave, was arrested in Boston. Under heavy security, Burns was brought before Commissioner Edward G. Loring, who heard the case and ordered that the victim be returned to his owner in Virginia. Boston citizens were in an uproar over the decision, but with the help of a large contingent of federal troops the order was carried out. Those who attempted to interfere forcibly—Wendell Phillips, Theodore Parker, and Thomas Wentworth Higginson among them—were arrested and charged with treason.[36]

Emerson was alternately outraged and dismayed by this gross act of injustice, and he began work on another major antislavery address (*JMN*, 14:420–423). He also offered support to those battling on the front lines. In June he wrote to Charles Sumner to thank him for his "brave temperate & sound Speeches" against the Kansas-Nebraska Act (*L*, 4:444). When the Fourth of July rolled around, few abolitionists were in a mood to celebrate. Lidian covered the front gate with black bunting to demonstrate her feeling that the country was "wholly lost to any sense of righteousness."[37] On the same day Thoreau delivered his powerful address "Slavery in Massachusetts" at an abolition gathering in Framingham, Massachusetts.[38]

In September Emerson began making arrangements to present his new antislavery lecture. He delivered it in Boston, on 25 January 1855, and then in Worcester, New York, Philadelphia, Syracuse, and other places. Not since his Fugitive Slave Law address of 1851 had Emerson given an antislavery lecture so many times. He undoubtedly felt that the times demanded it.

In the lecture Emerson asserts, "Whilst I insist on the doctrine of the independence and the inspiration of the individual, I do not cripple but exalt the social action," and he adds with obvious relish, "It is so delicious to act with great masses to great aims." Emerson's continued and pronounced involvement in the abolition movement indicated a dramatic change in his philosophy of social reform from the early 1840s—this change did not go unnoticed. In an article in the *Christian Inquirer*, reprinted in the *National Anti-Slavery Standard* (17 February 1855), a commentator states: "Mr. Emerson has given a fine anti-slavery lecture, and another on American character. Both lectures were full of pith and point, but neither contained anything of the old Transcendentalism. No more feeling in the skies, after the absolute, but sharp observations on human life and manners.

Never was such a change, apparently, as from the Emerson of '45 to the Emerson of '55." Emerson has left the "upper sphere" and now "talks about English men and Americans, about slavery and politics. . . . People say 'He is no more a philosopher, but a practical man.' "

Emerson's lecture was well received by his many abolitionist friends. According to the *Boston Daily Evening Traveller* (26 January 1855), he "was listened to throughout with breathless interest, and frequently applauded." Wendell Phillips later described the speech as "one of the greatest and bravest ever made in the city of Boston, or in New England." Emerson, said Phillips, "showed himself to be a man, whom literary fame had never tempted to a wrong, and whom the opinions of his fellow-citizens never fettered" (*National Anti-Slavery Standard*, 3 February 1855). Emerson's association with the abolitionists at this critical time was important to them, but it was not universally appreciated in Boston. After the antislavery series was completed, the *Boston Pilot* ran an article in which the abolitionist gathering was termed a meeting of the "Attend-to-the-business-of-others-and-neglect-your-own-Society." "Denunciation and blasphemy by the wholesale . . . is no longer a strange thing" at these meetings, nor is "treason," and the writer criticizes both Garrison and Emerson, the latter for failing to provide "a fair estimate of the slaveholder's case."

According to the *National Anti-Slavery Standard* (10 February 1855) article on Emerson's speech as delivered in New York, "the audience was large, and, we may say, in truth, that the speaker fulfilled the best anticipations of his friends." An earlier *Standard* reporter suggested somewhat ruefully that "not many of the wise, or learned, or influential, as men account these things, have joined themselves" to the abolitionist cause (3 February 1855). Emerson was a welcome exception.

Despite his enthusiasm, Emerson was sensitive to public criticism, which was frequently directed against him. He was well aware throughout his career that an idealist would always find himself criticized, even derided, by the more "practical" individuals in the society. It is therefore not surprising that he comments in his journal around this time, "Judges, Bank Presidents, Railroad men, men of fashion, lawyers universally all take the side of slavery," and "What a poor blind devil are you to break your shins for a bit of moonshine against this goodwill of the whole community" (*JMN*, 14:404). This fool of virtue peddled his moonshine and carried on the struggle, regardless of this predictable wrath of the established elite.

The national situation worsened in the spring of 1856 with the outbreak of warfare in Kansas between the proslavery and antislavery settlers there. The fighting was bloody, and destruction of lives and property extensive. In the context of heated congressional debates on the problem, Charles Sumner delivered his famous "Crime against Kansas" speech, in which he bitterly denounced the "slave oligarchy"—those who supported the proslavery partisans. Senator Andrew P. Butler of South Carolina was one of those severely criticized in this acerbic address; Butler's nephew, Preston Brooks, responded to the speech by assaulting Sumner as he later sat at his Senate desk on 22 May 1856. The senator was severely injured by his assailant, who was himself a representative from South Carolina. It would take Sumner three years to recover from his wounds.

Emerson and other friends and supporters of the Massachusetts senator were shocked and enraged by this latest episode of Southern barbarism. Emerson spoke at a meeting in Concord four days after the attack. In a short but powerful address he expressed his exasperation with the blatant cruelty and aggression of the slaveholding South. The differences between the slave states and the free had never been more painfully clear. The future looked dark indeed. "I do not see," said Emerson, "how a barbarous community and a civilized community can constitute one state. I think we must get rid of slavery, or we must get rid of freedom." The seriousness of Emerson's concern is evident in a letter that he penned a short time later to his brother William. "What times are these," he writes, and "how they make our studies impertinent, & even ourselves the same!" The bold aggression of the South had become a threat to freedom everywhere in the Union; "I am looking into the map to see where I shall go with my children when Boston & Massachusetts surrender to the slave-trade." Looking forward to the upcoming national elections, he observes, "If the Free States do not obtain the government next fall, which our experience does not entitle us to hope, nothing seems left, but to form at once a Northern Union, & break the old" (*L*, 5:23).

In June a meeting was held in Concord to raise funds for free-state immigrants in Kansas. Emerson probably spoke at this meeting. He donated fifty dollars to the cause, and the following month he joined several fellow citizens in signing a letter to the governor of Massachusetts asking for protection of Massachusetts citizens in Kansas.

In September another Kansas relief meeting was held, this time in Cambridge. It was sponsored by the Middlesex County Kansas Aid Committee, and Emerson was invited to speak. In his presentation he referred to firsthand reports of atrocities committed against innocent citizens in Kansas and urged his listeners to "give largely, lavishly" to provide Sharpe's rifles and other equipment to protect the unfortunates and to turn back the aggressive forces of the pro-slavery party. In Emerson's view, the time had come to meet force with force.

In the spring of 1857 the most celebrated of the Kansas freedom fighters, John Brown, traveled to Concord, where Thoreau introduced him to Emerson. Immediately taken by the commitment and sincerity of this rugged foe of slavery, Emerson invited him to stay the following night in his home. Their relationship would endure until Brown's dramatic demise on the eve of the Civil War.

The warfare in "bleeding Kansas" went on. In addition, the spring of 1858 brought the infamous Dred Scott decision, in which the U.S. Supreme Court declared that blacks were "so far inferior that they had no rights which the white man was bound to respect."[39] Emerson became convinced that the North must take measures to protect itself from the growing infection of slavery. He recorded in his journal the observation that slavery should be treated like the disease that it was. "We intend to set & to keep a *cordon sanitaire* all around the infected district, & by no means suffer the pestilence to spread" (*JMN*, 14:197).

In May 1859 John Brown stayed with the Emersons when he

returned to Concord to raise money for his cause. He spoke at the Town Hall, and Emerson, together with many other leading citizens, attended. As late as October, Emerson was still collecting money for Brown, but on the fifteenth of that month Brown staged his abortive attack on the federal arsenal at Harpers Ferry, Virginia. This event came as a great surprise to many, including Emerson, who praised Brown's courage but condemned the attack. As he told his brother William, Brown "is a true hero, but he lost his head there" (*L*, 5:178).

After John Brown's arrest, Emerson solicited support for his legal defense. On 8 November, in his lecture "Courage," he spoke of Brown as "that new saint . . . who, if he shall suffer, will make the gallows like the cross" (*W*, 7:427). Shortly thereafter, he joined several others in addressing a meeting in Boston "for the Relief of the Family of John Brown." In his speech on this occasion Emerson depicts Brown as a patriot and a hero, someone who, in an age of skepticism and moral enervation, maintains "a perfect Puritan faith." The two instruments of change that Brown believed in deeply, according to Emerson, are "the Golden Rule and the Declaration of Independence."

Very few in the Boston area shared Emerson's enthusiasm for Brown. Soon after the meeting on 2 December 1859, a *Boston Post* writer complained about the "anti-slavery fanatics" who supported John Brown rather than the Constitution of the United States. Wendell Phillips, Ralph Waldo Emerson, and others must not be "permitted to falsely assume to proclaim the sentiments of Boston in relation to recent deplorable events in Virginia." The conscientious and law-abiding citizens of the commonwealth must open their eyes and "see where these mad speculators of the Wendell Phillips school in public affairs are leading them." Such criticism notwithstanding, Emerson, Thoreau, Bronson Alcott, and others were adamant in their public support of Brown.[40] On the day of his execution, 2 December 1859, they arranged and participated in a memorial service in Concord. There were local objections, but the ceremonies were held anyway.[41]

On 6 January 1860 Emerson spoke once again on behalf of John

Brown, this time at a meeting in Salem, Massachusetts, to raise money for the support of his family—a pressing and immediate concern. Brown's daughters were staying with the Emersons and attending school in Concord at the time. In his speech Emerson emphasizes Brown's courage and commitment to a sublime cause. Brown was a virtuous man of action, and "all people, in proportion to their sensibility and self-respect, sympathize with him."

The Harpers Ferry raid caused more repercussions in Concord. Franklin Sanborn, one of the Secret Six who collaborated with Brown, was summoned to appear before a congressional committee investigating the raid. Fearing for his safety, he refused, and on 3 April 1860 agents from the Mason Committee came to Concord to arrest him. An alarm was raised and several townspeople, including Emerson, turned out to defend Sanborn. After a brief scuffle the agents were driven away.[42] The next day, Emerson, Thoreau, and others spoke at a meeting to protest this outrage. At another meeting, on 5 April, Emerson and Thoreau spoke again. The second gathering resulted in a plan to form a vigilance committee, which would protect the citizens of Concord from further abuses by the agents of the slave power. It must have seemed to many that Concord itself was no longer safe from the Southern contagion.

In November Abraham Lincoln was elected president of the United States without a single Southern electoral vote. Emerson rejoiced at the event, which he considered "the pronunciation of the masses of America against Slavery" (*JMN*, 4:363). In December South Carolina dissolved its ties to the Union and was soon followed by ten other states; together they eventually formed the Confederate States of America. Abolitionists generally applauded the secessions. Garrison wrote in the *Liberator* (14 January 1861) that "at last the covenant with death is annulled, and the agreement with hell broken. The people of the North should recognize the fact that the Union is dissolved, and act accordingly." Emerson also welcomed the breakup of the Union and saw it as a giant step toward the eventual abolition of slavery. He observes in his journal, "The furious slaveholder does not see that the one thing he is doing, by night & by day, is, to destroy slavery. They who help & they who hinder are all equally diligent in hastening its downfall. Blessed be the inevitabilities" (*JMN*, 15:91).

Others were not so delighted. Conservatives in the Boston area and elsewhere held the abolitionists responsible for this tragic development and, consequently, a great deal of animosity and violence was directed against them. At the same time, on the national level, a substantial effort was being made to placate the South and preserve the Union through compromise. The abolitionists opposed all such measures and were determined to agitate vigorously for the abolition of slavery despite vehement opposition. Emerson recognized the importance of moral fortitude at this critical moment and recorded in his journal the following: "Do the duty of the day. Just now the supreme duty of all thinking men is to assert freedom. Go where it is threatened, & say, 'I am for it, & do not wish to live in the world a moment longer than it exists'" (*JMN*, 15:111). An opportunity for Emerson to assert freedom was soon forthcoming. When Wendell Phillips invited him to speak at the annual meeting of the Massachusetts Anti-Slavery Society at Tremont Temple in Boston on 24 January 1861, he accepted, despite the likelihood that antiabolition agitators would try to break up the meeting.

Indeed, the meeting was raucous. Attacks on abolitionists had become so violent that Phillips had taken to carrying a revolver. The pro-Union rowdies who swarmed into the meeting were determined to disrupt it, and the local police were prepared to stand idly by and watch chaos erupt. According to the *Liberator* account (1 February 1861), when Emerson was introduced he received three resounding cheers for the Union, followed by groans, outcries, and catcalls. Because of the commotion he had to wait before beginning his presentation. In his talk Emerson insisted that there should be no compromises on the moral issues dividing North and South. "As to concessions, we have none to make. The monstrous concession made at the formation of the Constitution is all that can ever be asked; it has blocked the civilization and humanity of the times up to this day."

This sentiment, while greatly appreciated by Emerson's abolitionist cohorts, elicited a volley of hisses, groans, and yells to "put him out" and "dry up" from the rowdies. Calls for order were ignored, and the police refused to act. The tumult eventually became so loud and threatening that Emerson was forced to withdraw, and the meeting ended with the police clearing the galleries.

The experience served only to reinforce Emerson's commitment to the abolitionist cause, no matter the cost. For an individual universally known for his gentleness and sensitivity, this was a considerable commitment. The following journal entry reflects Emerson's state of mind.

> Phillips has the supreme merit in this time, that he & he alone stands in the gap & breach against the assailants. Hold up his hands. He did me the honor to ask me to come to the meeting at Tremont Temple, &, esteeming such invitation a command, though sorely against my inclination & habit, I went, and, though I had nothing to say, showed myself. If I were dumb, yet I would have gone & mowed & muttered or made signs. The mob roared whenever I attempted to speak, and, after several beginnings, I withdrew. (*JMN*, 15:111)

On 12 April 1861 Fort Sumter was fired on, beginning the bloodiest war in U.S. history. Many abolitionists, including Emerson, were surprised by the attack. Most apparently thought that the South would, and should, secede, but few believed that the newly formed Confederacy would be brazen enough to assail the North. In his journal Emerson wrote "this revolution is the work of no man, but the effervescence of nature . . . nothing that has occurred but has been a surprise, & as much to the leaders as to the hindmost. And not an abolitionist, not an idealist, can say without effrontery, I did it" (*JMN*, 15:405). Emerson welcomed the war as an opportunity to rid the nation, once and for all, of the plague of slavery.

The quick victory that Emerson and others had expected and hoped for did not materialize. The Union defeat at the first battle of Bull Run in July 1861 was a shocking revelation of Southern strength and determination. Everyone realized that it would be a long and costly struggle. Emerson never doubted that the war was being fought over slavery, even though Lincoln officially defined the purpose of the war as the preservation of the Union. From the very beginning Emerson and other abolitionists insisted that emancipation should be declared the immediate aim. In his "American Civilization" address delivered in Boston on 12 November 1861 and later published in the *Atlantic Monthly*, he states, "The war for the Union is broader than any state policy of sectional interest; but, at last, the Union is not broad enough, because of slavery; and we must come to emancipation, with compensation to loyal states. This is a principle. Everything else is an intrigue."[43]

For the first eighteen months of the war, Lincoln was disinclined to declare emancipation a goal because without a significant battlefield victory, such a policy would suggest desperation. Also, he was concerned about alienating the Border States (Missouri, Kentucky, Delaware, and Maryland)—all slave states that had chosen to remain in the Union. The technical victory of the Union forces at Antietam in the fall of 1862, however, provided Lincoln with the opportunity to issue his Preliminary Emancipation Proclamation. Emerson was delighted with Lincoln's long-awaited action, and on 12 October 1862 he celebrated the event in Boston with his own emancipation address. In it Emerson offers extensive praise of Lincoln for taking the considerable risks involved. "Against all timorous counsels," Lincoln "had the courage to seize the moment." When the proclamation took effect, on 1 January 1863, Emerson joined a large celebration at the Boston Music Hall. For this auspicious event he composed an occasional poem, "Boston Hymn," which he presented to a large and appreciative audience.

As the war progressed, Emerson contributed to the Northern effort in a number of ways. He spoke at fund-raisers for black orphans and for the newly formed Massachusetts Fifty-fourth Regiment, the first official all-black regiment in the Union army. On behalf of the latter he once again attacked racial prejudice. In June 1863 he served on the Committee of Visitation for West Point and was impressed by the intelligence and self-reliance of the young cadets. The commander of the Fifty-fourth, Col. Robert Gould Shaw, and many of his black troops were killed in a poorly planned and ultimately tragic attack on Fort Wagner, at Morris Island, South Carolina. Emerson memorialized them in his touching poem "Voluntaries," which appeared in the *Atlantic Monthly* in October 1863.

As the conflict dragged on, some war-weary Northerners raised the possibility of a negotiated settlement. There was also considerable talk that year about the likelihood of British and French intervention to impose a settlement. The British textile industry suffered from the interdiction of cotton shipments by the Northern blockade of Southern ports. Also, the British ruling class was generally critical of the Northern position during the war, and tensions between the two countries were at an all-time high in 1863.[44] Emerson was sensitive to the possibility that a negotiated settlement would come about and leave slavery in place. In his view, such an outcome would give the lie to all the sacrifices already made. Fearing such a moral catastrophe, Emerson composed and delivered "Fortune of the Republic," one of the most powerful addresses of his career. He repeated the lecture in several places between December 1863 and February 1864. In it he attacked, in sometimes biting language, the moral lethargy and gross materialism of the British as reflected in their willingness to accommodate the barbarism of slavery in order to preserve their cotton trade. He also attacked Clement Vallandigham and the Copperheads, and all other accommodationists who would cast aside the tremendous sacrifices of lives and property to bring a speedy but immoral end to the war. Emerson felt that much was at risk but also that much could be gained. The struggle would not—indeed, could not—be lost for lack of faith. The skepticism that had allowed slavery to flourish could not now be permitted to rescue it from the brink of annihilation.

Fortunately, the immediate crisis passed, Lincoln was reelected with a mandate to finish the job he had begun, and Union victories in the field throughout 1864 and the spring of 1865 eventually brought about the surrender of Robert E. Lee on 9 April 1865. The victory that Emerson had so long awaited was at hand. But the death of President Lincoln a mere six days later substantially diminished the euphoria that Emerson and others felt. On 19 April 1865 a memorial service was held in Concord in Lincoln's honor.

Emerson spoke, offering unreserved praise for the stricken president. "There, by his courage, his justice, his even temper, his fertile counsel, his humanity, he stood a heroic figure in the center of a heroic epic. He is the true history of the American people in his time" (W, 11:335). The death of Lincoln was but one more sacrifice demanded in the struggle against evil. In the time allotted him, in Emerson's view, he served his purpose well.

In late July Emerson was provided with an opportunity to celebrate, with unmixed feelings, the moral triumph of the North. The occasion was the annual commencement at his alma mater. In his "Harvard Commemoration Speech" (21 July 1865) Emerson expressed his belief that "the war gave back integrity to this erring and immoral nation" and that the sacrifices were well worth the result.

The costly conflict had ended, and with the passage of the Thirteenth Amendment in 1865, the heinous institution of slavery was utterly destroyed. Emerson's long abolition campaign was over. The succeeding years brought new challenges as the ugly forces of racism and segregation rushed in to fill the void left by slavery, and Emerson occasionally took the platform to do battle for civil rights and social equality. For the most part, however, that war was fought by another generation of reforming idealists, many of whom remembered Emerson's unflagging commitment to social justice and the sublime notion that every person was "born . . . to be a reformer."

Because most of the materials in this collection have not been generally available until now, scholars have for the most part depended on Emerson's early writings—"Man the Reformer" (1841), "Lecture on the Times" (1841), and "New England Reformers" (1844)—all readily accessible in the standard editions of Emerson's works, for establishing an understanding of his views on reform, particularly the antislavery movement. As a result, a distinctly conservative image of Emerson's attitude toward social reform has prevailed over the years. A brief overview of relevant scholarship perhaps suffices to make the point.

In a popular study, *The Age of Jackson* (Boston: Little, Brown, 1945), Arthur M. Schlesinger, Jr., indicates that the Transcendentalists tended to remain aloof from the everyday affairs of social reform and politics. "From their book-lined studies or their shady walks in cool Concord woods," he says, "the hullabaloo of party politics [appeared] unedifying and vulgar." He suggests that "for the typical Transcendentalist the flinching from politics perhaps expressed a failure they were seeking to erect into a virtue. The exigencies of responsibility were exhausting: much better to demand perfection and indignantly reject the half loaf than wear out body and spirit in vain grapplings with overmastering reality." According to Schlesinger, for Transcendentalists "the headlong escape into perfection left responsibility far behind for a magic domain where the mystic sentiment and gnomic utterance exorcised the rude intrusions of the world" (p. 382). Schlesinger calls politics Emerson's "greatest failure. He would not succumb to verbal panaceas, neither would he make the ultimate moral effort of Thoreau and cast off all obligation to society. Instead he lingered indecisively, accepting without enthusiasm certain relations to government but never confronting directly the implications of acceptance" (p. 384).

Several years later Stanley Elkins presented essentially the same indictment of Emerson in his *Slavery: A Problem in American Institutional and Intellectual Life* (Chicago: University of Chicago Press, 1959). Elkins depicts Emerson and other Transcendentalists as virtually detached from mundane affairs. In a section entitled "Intellectuals without Responsibility," he states that "the thinkers of Concord, who in the later thirties and forties would create an intellectual attitude at least coherent enough to be given a name—'Transcendentalism'—were men without connections. . . . They took next to no part in politics at all" (p. 147). He asserts, regarding Emerson and others, that "not only did these men fail to analyze slavery itself as an institution, but they failed equally to consider and exploit institutional means for subverting it. . . . Their relationship with abolition societies was never anything but equivocal" (p. 168).

George Frederickson furthers this notion of aloofness in his influential book *The Inner Civil War: Northern Intellectuals and the Crisis of the Union* (New York: Harper and Row, 1965). According to

Frederickson, Emerson was totally oblivious of his social environment until the eruption of the Civil War, which finally threatened "his ideal of the detached scholar-philosopher" (p. 176). Frederickson insists that "Emerson . . . had always shunned social commitments and public activity, even to the point of avoiding town affairs in the village of Concord." With the outbreak of the war, however, he became "an influential and active citizen" (pp. 178–179).

Even specific studies of Transcendentalists and their society frequently reiterate these erroneous assumptions. Taylor Stoehr, in his *Nay-Saying in Concord: Emerson, Alcott, and Thoreau* (Hamden, Conn.: Archon, 1979), gives the impression that Emerson and other Transcendentalists were removed from the major reform movements of their day. He states that, "compared to the communitists and other reformers, the transcendentalists were like a band of monks sitting cross-legged on the floor, indistinguishable in their chant" (p. 19). According to Stoehr, "The truth is that Emerson, Alcott, and Thoreau, rather than say aye or nay, were more likely to abstain entirely. Theirs was the most conservative attitude of all, neither approving nor as philosophers would say it, standing out of the way. The universe could be trusted to unfold without taking a vote" (p. 20).

Anne Rose, in her *Transcendentalism as a Social Movement, 1830–1850* (New Haven: Yale University Press, 1981), makes a similar assertion. "Of the original transcendentalists . . . only Emerson publicly opposed slavery with any regularity, but the same philosophical bent which made him a powerful speaker ran against the grain of the most important development of the decade, antislavery politics" (pp. 219–220). Indeed, like Elkins and the others, Rose sees Emerson as a detached philosopher, and she notes, "There was an abstraction in his approach to slavery which made his occasional musings on agencies of abolition—providence, commercial progress, purchase, disunion—comparatively desultory" (p. 219).

These representations of Emerson as an individual with a limited or tepid interest in matters of social reform constitute a well-established strain of Emerson scholarship. Oliver Wendell Holmes, in his 1884 biography, *Ralph Waldo Emerson*, which was published in the prestigious Houghton Mifflin series American Men of Letters, depicted Emerson as a social conservative who "had never been identified with the abolitionists" (p. 304). According to the Holmes account, Emerson theorized about reform occasionally at most and certainly never became an active reformer himself. Later biographers and commentators restated this position uncritically with the result that, ironically, the view is now widely accepted, largely on the basis of its frequent reiteration. With the appearance of the documents in this volume, however, the image of Emerson as aloof philosopher and conservative social commentator will have to be reevaluated. Although arguments about Emerson's philosophy of social reform will undoubtedly continue, at least the record of his thoughts and actions on slavery and abolition will now be available to inform this important debate.

LETTER TO
MARTIN VAN BUREN

23 April 1838

Concord, Massachusetts, April 23, 1838[1]

Sir: The seat you fill places you in a relation of credit and dearness to every citizen. By right and natural position, every citizen is your friend. Before any acts, contrary to his own judgment or interest, have repelled the affections of any man, each may look with trust and loving anticipations to your government. Each has the highest right to call your attention to such subjects as are of a public nature, and properly belong to the Chief Magistrate; and the good Magistrate will feel a joy in meeting such confidence. In this belief, and at the instance of a few of my friends and neighbors, I crave of your patience, through the medium of the press, a short hearing for their sentiments and my own; and the circumstance that my name will be utterly unknown to you will only give the fairer chance to your equitable construction of what I have to say.

Sir, my communication respects the sinister rumors that fill this part of the country concerning the Cherokee people. The interest always felt in the aboriginal population—an interest naturally growing as that decays—has been heightened in regard to this tribe. Even to our distant State, some good rumor of their worth and civility has arrived. We have learned with joy their improvement in social arts. We have read their newspapers. We have seen some of them in our schools and colleges. In common with the great body of the American People, we have witnessed with sympathy the painful endeavors of these red men to redeem their own race from the doom of eternal inferiority, and to borrow and domesticate in the tribe the inventions and customs of the Caucasian race.[2] And notwithstanding the unaccountable apathy with which, of late years, the Indians have been sometimes abandoned to their enemies, it is not to be doubted that it is the good pleasure and the understanding of all humane persons in the Republic, of the men and the matrons sitting in thriving independent families all over the land, that they shall be duly cared for, that they shall taste justice and love from all to whom we have delegated the office of dealing with them.

The newspapers now inform us that in December, 1835, a treaty, contracting for the exchange of the entire Cherokee territory, was pretended to be made by an agent on the part of the United States with some persons appearing on the part of the Cherokees; that the fact afterwards[3] transpired that these individual Indians did by no means represent the will of the nation; and that, out of eighteen thousand souls composing the nation, fifteen thousand six hundred and sixty-eight have protested against the so-called treaty. It now appears that the Government of the United States choose to hold the Cherokees to this sham treaty, and the proceeding to execute the same.[4] Almost the entire Cherokee nation stand up and say, "This is not our act. Behold us! Here are we. Do not mistake that handful of deserters for us." And the President and his Cabinet, the Senate and the House of Representatives, neither hear these men nor see them, and are contracting to put this nation into carts and boats, and to drag them over mountains and rivers to a wilderness at a vast distance beyond the Mississippi. And a paper, purporting to be an army order, fixes a month from this day as the hour for this doleful removal.

In the name of God, sir, we ask you if this is so? Do the newspapers rightly inform us? Men and women, with pale and perplexed faces, meet one another in streets and churches here, and ask if this be so? We have inquired if this be a gross misrepresentation from the party opposed to the Government and anxious to blacken it with the People. We have looked into newspapers of different parties, and find a horrid confirmation of the tale. We are slow to believe it. We hoped the Indians were misinformed, and their remonstrance was premature, and would turn out to be a needless act of terror. The piety, the principle, that is left in these United States—if only its coarsest form, a regard to the speech of men—forbid us to entertain it as a fact. Such a dereliction of all faith and virtue, such a denial of justice, and such deafness to screams for mercy, were never heard of in times of peace, and in the dealing of a nation with its own allies and wards, since the earth was made. Sir, does the Government think that the People of the United States are become savage and mad? From their minds are the sentiments of love and of a good nature wiped clean out? The soul of man, the justice, the mercy, that is the heart's heart in all men, from Maine to Georgia, does abhor this business.

In speaking thus the sentiments of my neighbors and my own, perhaps I overstep the bounds of decorum. But would it not be a higher indecorum coldly to argue a matter like this? We only state the fact, that a crime is projected that confounds our understandings by its magnitude—a crime that really deprives us as well as the Cherokees of a country; for how could we call the conspiracy that should crush these poor Indians our Government, or the land that was cursed by their parting and dying imprecations our country, any more? You, sir, will bring down that renowned chair in which you sit into infamy if your seal is set to this instrument of perfidy; and the name of this nation, hitherto the sweet omen of religion and liberty, will stink to the world.

You will not do us the injustice of connecting this remonstrance with any sectional or party feeling. It is in our hearts the simplest commandment of brotherly love. We will not have this great and solemn claim upon national and human justice huddled aside under the flimsy plea of its being a party act. Sir, to us the questions upon which the Government and the People have been agitated during the past year, touching the prostration of the currency and of trade, seem motes in the comparison. The hard times, it is true, have brought this discussion home to every farmhouse and poor man's table in this town, but it is the chirping of grasshoppers, beside the immortal question whether justice shall be done by the race of civilized to the race of savage man; whether all the attributes of reason, of civility, of justice, and even of mercy, shall be put off by the American People, and so vast an outrage upon the Cherokee nation, and upon human nature, shall be consummated.

One circumstance lessens the reluctance with which I intrude on your attention: my conviction that the Government ought to be admonished of a new historical fact, which the discussion of this question has disclosed, namely, that there exists in a great part of the Northern People a gloomy diffidence of the *moral* character of the Government. On the broaching of this question, a general expression of despondency, of disbelief that any good will accrue from a remonstrance on an act of fraud and robbery, appeared in those men to whom we naturally turn for aid and counsel. Will the American Government steal? will it lie? will it kill? We asked triumphantly. Our wise men shake their heads dubiously. Our counsellors and old statesmen here say that, ten years ago, they would have staked their life on the affirmation that the proposed Indian measures could not be executed; that the unanimous country would put them down. And now the steps of this crime follow each other so fast, at such fatally quick time, that the millions of virtuous citizens whose agents the Government are, have no space to interpose, and must shut their eyes until the last howl and wailing of these poor tormented villages and tribes shall afflict the ear of the world.

I will not hide from you as an indication of this alarming distrust, that a letter addressed as mine is, and suggesting to the mind of the Executive the plain obligations of man, has a burlesque character in the apprehension of some of my friends. I, sir, will not beforehand treat you with the contumely of this distrust. I will at least state to you this fact, and show you how plain and humane people whose love would be honor regard the policy of the Government and what injurious inferences they draw as to the mind of the governors. A man with your experience in affairs must have seen

4

cause to appreciate the futility of opposition to the moral sentiment. However feeble the sufferer, and however great the oppressor, it is in the nature of things that the blow should recoil on the aggressor. For, God is in the sentiment, and it cannot be withstood. The potentate and the People perish before it; but with it and as its executors, they are omnipotent.

I write thus, sir, to inform you of the state of mind these Indian tidings have awakened here, and to pray with one voice more, that you, whose hands are strong with the delegated power of fifteen millions of men, will avert, with that might, the terrific injury which threatens the Cherokee tribe.

With great respect, sir, I am, your fellow-citizen,
Ralph Waldo Emerson.

"An Address . . . on . . . the Emancipation of the Negroes in the British West Indies"

1 August 1844

Friends and Fellow Citizens,[1]

We are met to exchange congratulations on the anniversary of an event singular in the history of civilization; a day of reason; of the clear light; of that which makes us better than a flock of birds and beasts: a day, which gave the immense fortification of a fact,—of gross history,—to ethical abstractions. It was the settlement, as far as a great Empire was concerned, of a question on which almost every leading citizen in it had taken care to record his vote; one which for many years absorbed the attention of the best and most eminent of mankind. I might well hesitate, coming from other studies, and without the smallest claim to be a special laborer in this work of humanity, to undertake to set this matter before you; which ought rather to be done by a strict cooperation of many well-advised persons; but I shall not apologize for my weakness. In this cause, no man's weakness is any prejudice; it has a thousand sons; if one man cannot speak, ten others can; and whether by the wisdom of its friends, or by the folly of the adversaries; by speech and by silence; by doing and by omitting to do, it goes forward. Therefore I will speak,—or, not I, but the might of liberty in my weakness. The subject is said to have the property of making dull men eloquent.

It has been in all men's experience a marked effect of the enterprise in behalf of the African, to generate an overbearing and defying spirit. The institution of slavery seems to its opponent to have but one side, and he feels that none but a stupid or a malignant person can hesitate on a view of the facts. Under such an impulse, I was about to say, If any cannot speak, or cannot hear the words of freedom, let him go hence,—I had almost said, Creep into your grave, the universe has no need of you! But I have thought better: let him not go. When we consider what remains to be done for this interest, in this country, the dictates of humanity make us tender of such as are not yet persuaded. The hardest selfishness is to be borne with. Let us withhold every reproachful, and, if we can, every indignant remark. In this cause, we must renounce our temper, and the risings of pride. If there be any man who thinks the ruin of a race of men a small matter, compared with the last decoration and completions of his own comfort,—who would not so much as part with his ice-cream, to save them from rapine and manacles, I think, I must not hesitate to satisfy that man, that also his cream and vanilla are safer and cheaper, by placing the negro nation on a fair footing, than by robbing them. If the Virginian piques himself on the picturesque luxury of his vassalage, on the heavy Ethiopian manners of his house-servants, their silent obedience, their hue of bronze, their turbaned heads, and would not exchange them for the more intelligent but precarious hired-service of whites, I shall not refuse to show him, that when their free-papers are made out, it will still be their interest to remain on his estate, and that the oldest planters of Jamaica are convinced, that it is cheaper to pay wages, than to own the slave.

The history of mankind interests us only as it exhibits a steady gain of truth and right, in the incessant conflict which it records, between the material and the moral nature. From the earliest monuments, it appears, that one race was victim, and served the other races. In the oldest temples of Egypt, negro captives are painted on the tombs of kings, in such attitudes as to show that they are on the point of being executed; and Herodotus, our oldest historian, relates that the Troglodytes hunted the Ethiopians in four-horse-

8

chariots.[2] From the earliest time, the negro has been an article of luxury to the commercial nations. So has it been, down to the day that has just dawned on the world. Language must be raked, the secrets of slaughter-houses and infamous holes that cannot front the day, must be ransacked, to tell what negro-slavery has been. These men, our benefactors, as they are producers of corn and wine, of coffee, of tobacco, of cotton, of sugar, of rum, and brandy, gentle and joyous themselves, and producers of comfort and luxury for the civilized world,—there seated in the finest climates of the globe, children of the sun,—I am heart-sick when I read how they came there, and how they are kept there. Their case was left out of the mind and out of the heart of their brothers. The prizes of society, the trumpet of fame, the privileges of learning, of culture, of religion, the decencies and joys of marriage, honor, obedience, personal authority, and a perpetual melioration into a finer civility, these were for all, but not for them. For the negro, was the slave-ship to begin with, in whose filthy hold he sat in irons, unable to lie down; bad food, and insufficiency of that; disfranchisement; no property in the rags that covered him; no marriage, no right in the poor black woman that cherished him in her bosom,—no right to the children of his body; no security from the humors, none from the crimes, none from the appetites of his master: toil, famine, insult, and flogging; and, when he sunk in the furrow, no wind of good fame blew over him, no priest of salvation visited him with glad tidings: but he went down to death, with dusky dreams of African shadow-catchers and Obeahs[3] hunting him. Very sad was the negro tradition, that the Great Spirit, in the beginning, offered the black man, whom he loved better than the buckra[4] or white, his choice of two boxes, a big and a little one. The black man was greedy, and chose the largest. "The buckra box was full up with pen, paper, and whip, and the negro box with hoe and bill; and hoe and bill for negro to this day."

But the crude element of good in human affairs must work and ripen, spite of whips, and plantation-laws, and West Indian interest. Conscience rolled on its pillow, and could not sleep. We sympathize very tenderly here with the poor aggrieved planter, of whom so

9

many unpleasant things are said; [but if we saw the whip applied to old men, to tender women; and, undeniably, though I shrink to say so,—pregnant women set in the treadmill for refusing to work, when, not they, but the eternal law of animal nature refused to work;—if we saw men's backs flayed with cowhides, and "hot rum poured on, superinduced with brine or pickle, rubbed in with a cornhusk, in the scorching heat of the sun;"—if we saw the runaways hunted with blood-hounds into swamps and hills; and, in cases of passion, a planter throwing his negro into a copper of boiling cane-juice,—if we saw these things with eyes, we too should wince. They are not pleasant sights. The blood is moral: the blood is anti-slavery: it runs cold in the veins: the stomach rises with disgust, and curses slavery.] Well, so it happened; a good man or woman, a country-boy or girl, it would so fall out, once in a while saw these injuries, and had the indiscretion to tell of them. The horrid story ran and flew; the winds blew it all over the world. They who heard it, asked their rich and great friends, if it was true, or only missionary lies. The richest and greatest, the prime minister of England, the king's privy council were obliged to say, that it was too true. It became plain to all men, the more this business was looked into, that the crimes and cruelties of the slave-traders and slave-owners could not be overstated. The more it was searched, the more shocking anecdotes came up,—things not to be spoken. Humane persons who were informed of the reports, insisted on proving them. Granville Sharp was accidentally made acquainted with the sufferings of a slave, whom a West Indian planter had brought with him to London, and had beaten with a pistol on his head so badly, that his whole body became diseased, and the man useless to his master, who left him to go whither he pleased.[5] The man applied to Mr. William Sharp,[6] a charitable surgeon, who attended the diseases of the poor. In process of time, he was healed. Granville Sharp found him at his brother's, and procured a place for him in an apothecary's shop. The master accidentally met his recovered slave, and instantly endeavored to get possession of him again. Sharp protected the slave. In consulting with the lawyers, they told Sharp the laws were against him. Sharp would not believe it; no prescription on earth could ever render such iniquities legal. 'But the decisions are against you, and Lord Mansfield, now chief justice of England, leans to the decisions.'[7] Sharp instantly sat down and gave himself to the study of English law for more than two years, until he had proved that the opinions relied on of Talbot and Yorke, were incompatible with the former English decisions, and with the whole spirit of English law.[8] He published his book in 1769, and he so filled the heads and hearts of his advocates, that when he brought the case of George Somerset,[9] another slave, before Lord Mansfield, the slavish decisions were set aside, and equity affirmed. There is a sparkle of God's righteousness in Lord Mansfield's judgment, which does the heart good. Very unwilling had that great lawyer been to reverse the late decisions; he suggested twice from the bench, in the course of the trial, how the question might be got rid of: but the hint was not taken; the case was adjourned again and again, and judgment delayed. At last judgment was demanded, and on the 22d June, 1772, Lord Mansfield is reported to have decided in these words; "Immemorial usage preserves the memory of *positive law*, long after all traces of the occasion, reason, authority, and time of its introduction, are lost; and in a case so odious as the condition of slaves, must be taken strictly; (tracing the subject to natural principles, the claim of slavery never can be supported.) The power claimed by this return never was in use here. We cannot say the cause set forth by this return is allowed or approved of by the laws of this kingdom; and therefore the man must be discharged."[10]

This decision established the principle that the "air of England is too pure for any slave to breathe," but the wrongs in the islands were not thereby touched. Public attention, however, was drawn that way, and the methods of the stealing and the transportation from Africa, became noised abroad. The Quakers got the story. In their plain meeting-houses, and prim dwellings, this dismal agitation got entrance. They were rich: they owned for debt, or by inheritance, island property; they were religious, tender-hearted men and women; and they had to hear the news, and digest it as they could. Six Quakers met in London on the 6th July, 1783; William Dillwyn, Samuel Hoar, George Harrison, Thomas Knowles, John Lloyd,

Joseph Woods, "to consider what step they should take for the relief and liberation of the negro slaves in the West Indies, and for the discouragement of the slave-trade on the coast of Africa."[11] They made friends and raised money for the slave; they interested their Yearly Meeting; and all English and all American Quakers. John Woolman of New Jersey, whilst yet an apprentice, was uneasy in his mind when he was set to write a bill of sale of a negro, for his master.[12] He gave his testimony against the traffic, in Maryland and Virginia. Thomas Clarkson was a youth at Cambridge, England, when the subject given out for a Latin prize dissertation, was, "Is it right to make slaves of others against their will?"[13] He wrote an essay, and won the prize; but he wrote too well for his own peace; he began to ask himself, if these things could be true; and if they were, he could no longer rest. He left Cambridge; he fell in with the six Quakers. They engaged him to act for them. He himself interested Mr. Wilberforce in the matter.[14] The shipmasters in that trade were the greatest miscreants, and guilty of every barbarity to their own crews. Clarkson went to Bristol, made himself acquainted with the interior of the slaveships, and the details of the trade. The facts confirmed his sentiment, "that Providence had never made that to be wise, which was immoral, and that the slave-trade was as impolitic as it was unjust;" that it was found peculiarly fatal to those employed in it. More seamen died in that trade, in one year, than in the whole remaining trade of the country in two. Mr. Pitt and Mr. Fox were drawn into the generous enterprise.[15] In 1788, the House of Commons voted Parliamentary inquiry. In 1791, a bill to abolish the trade was brought in by Wilberforce, and supported by him, and by Fox, and Burke, and Pitt, with the utmost ability and faithfulness; resisted by the planters, and the whole West Indian interest, and lost. During the next sixteen years, ten times, year after year, the attempt was renewed by Mr. Wilberforce, and ten times defeated by the planters. The king, and all the royal family but one, were against it. These debates are instructive, as they show on what grounds the trade was assailed and defended. Every thing generous, wise, and sprightly is sure to come to the attack. On the other part, are found cold prudence, barefaced selfishness, and silent votes. But the nation was aroused to enthusiasm. Every horrid fact became known. In 1791, three hundred thousand persons in Britain pledged themselves to abstain from all articles of island produce. The planters were obliged to give way; and in 1807, on the 25th March, the bill passed, and the slave-trade was abolished.

The assailants of slavery had early agreed to limit their political action on this subject to the abolition of the trade, but Granville Sharp, as a matter of conscience, whilst he acted as chairman of the London Committee, felt constrained to record his protest against the limitation, declaring that slavery was as much a crime against the Divine law, as the slave-trade. The trade, under false flags, went on as before. In 1821, according to official documents presented to the American government by the Colonization Society, 200,000 slaves were deported from Africa.[16] Nearly 30,000 were landed in the port of Havana alone. In consequence of the dangers of the trade growing out of the act of abolition, ships were built sharp for swiftness, and with a frightful disregard of the comfort of the victims they were destined to transport. They carried five, six, even seven hundred stowed in a ship built so narrow as to be unsafe, being made just broad enough on the beam to keep the sea. In attempting to make its escape from the pursuit of a man-of-war, one ship flung five hundred slaves alive into the sea. These facts went into Parliament. In the islands, was an ominous state of cruel and licentious society; every house had a dungeon attached to it; every slave was worked by the whip. There is no end to the tragic anecdotes in the municipal records of the colonies. The boy was set to strip and to flog his own mother to blood, for a small offence. Looking in the face of his master by the negro was held to be violence by the island courts. He was worked sixteen hours, and his ration by law, in some islands, was a pint of flour and one salt herring a day. He suffered insult, stripes, mutilation, at the humor of the master: iron collars were riveted on their necks with iron prongs ten inches long; capsicum pepper was rubbed in the eyes of the females; and they were done to death with the most shocking levity between the master and manager, without fine or inquiry.

And when, at last, some Quakers, Moravians, and Wesleyan and Baptist missionaries, following in the steps of Carey and Ward in the East Indies,[17] had been moved to come and cheer the poor victim with the hope of some reparation, in a future world, of the wrongs he suffered in this, these missionaries were persecuted by the planters, their lives threatened, their chapels burned, and the negroes furiously forbidden to go near them. These outrages rekindled the flame of British indignation. Petitions poured into Parliament: a million persons signed their names to these; and in 1833, on the 14th May, Lord Stanley, minister of the colonies, introduced into the House of Commons his bill for the Emancipation.[18]

The scheme of the minister, with such modification as it received in the legislature, proposed gradual emancipation; that on 1st August, 1834, all persons now slaves should be entitled to be registered as apprenticed laborers, and to acquire thereby all the rights and privileges of freemen, subject to the restriction of laboring under certain conditions. These conditions were, that the praedials should owe three fourths of the profits of their labor to their masters for six years, and the nonpraedials for four years.[19] The other fourth of the apprentice's time was to be his own, which he might sell to his master, or to other persons; and at the end of the term of years fixed, he should be free.

With these provisions and conditions, the bill proceeds, in the twelfth section, in the following terms. "Be it enacted, that all and every person who, on the 1st August, 1834, shall be holden in slavery within any such British colony as aforesaid, shall upon and from and after the said 1st August, become and be to all intents and purposes free, and discharged of and from all manner of slavery, and shall be absolutely and forever manumitted; and that the children thereafter born to any such persons, and the offspring of such children, shall, in like manner, be free from their birth; and that from and after the 1st August, 1834, slavery shall be and is hereby utterly and forever abolished and declared unlawful throughout the British colonies, plantations, and possessions abroad."

The ministers, having estimated the slave products of the colonies in annual exports of sugar, rum, and coffee, at £1,500,000 *per annum*, estimated the total value of the slave-property at 30,000,000 pounds sterling, and proposed to give the planters, as a compensation for so much of the slaves' time as the act took from them, 20,000,000 pounds sterling, to be divided into nineteen shares for the nineteen colonies, and to be distributed to the owners of slaves by commissioners, whose appointment and duties were regulated by the Act. After much debate, the bill passed by large majorities. The apprenticeship system is understood to have proceeded from Lord Brougham, and was by him urged on his colleagues, who, it is said, were inclined to the policy of immediate emancipation.[20]

The colonial legislatures received the act of Parliament with various degrees of displeasure, and, of course, every provision of the bill was criticised with severity. The new relation between the master and the apprentice, it was feared, would be mischievous; for the bill required the appointment of magistrates, who should hear every complaint of the apprentice, and see that justice was done him. It was feared that the interest of the master and servant would now produce perpetual discord between them. In the island of Antigua, containing 37,000 people, 30,000 being negroes, these objections had such weight, that the legislature rejected the apprenticeship system, and adopted absolute emancipation. In the other islands the system of the ministry was accepted.

The reception of it by the negro population was equal in nobleness to the deed. The negroes were called together by the missionaries and by the planters, and the news explained to them. On the night of the 31st July, they met everywhere at their churches and chapels, and at midnight, when the clock struck twelve, on their knees, the silent, weeping assembly became men; they rose and embraced each other; they cried, they sung, they prayed, they were wild with joy, but there was no riot, no feasting. I have never read anything in history more touching than the moderation of the negroes. Some American captains left the shore and put to sea, anticipating insurrection and general murder. With far different thoughts, the negroes spent the hour in their huts and chapels. I will not repeat to you the well-known paragraph, in which Messrs. Thome and Kimball, the commissioners sent out in the year 1837 by the American Anti-slavery Society, describe the occurrences of that night in the island of Antigua. It has been quoted in every newspaper, and Dr. Channing has given it additional fame.[21] But I must be indulged in quoting a few sentences from the pages that follow it, narrating the behavior of the emancipated people on the next day.

"The first of August came on Friday, and a release was proclaimed from all work until the next Monday. The day was chiefly spent by the great mass of the negroes in the churches and chapels. The clergy and missionaries throughout the island were actively engaged, seizing the opportunity to enlighten the people on all the duties and responsibilities of their new relation, and urging them to the attainment of that higher liberty with which Christ maketh his children free. In every quarter, we were assured, the day was like a sabbath. Work had ceased. The hum of business was still: tranquillity pervaded the towns and country. The planters informed us, that they went to the chapels where their own people were assembled, greeted them, shook hands with them and exchanged the most hearty good wishes. At Grace Hill, there were at least a thousand persons around the Moravian Chapel who could not get in. For once the house of God suffered violence, and the violent took it by force. At Grace Bay, the people, all dressed in white, formed a procession, and walked arm in arm into the chapel. We were told that the dress of the negroes on that occasion was uncommonly simple and modest. There was not the least disposition to gaiety. Throughout the island, there was not a single dance known of, either day or night, nor so much as a fiddle played."[22]

On the next Monday morning, with very few exceptions, every negro on every plantation was in the field at his work. In some places, they waited to see their master, to know what bargain he would make; but, for the most part, throughout the islands, nothing painful occurred. In June, 1835, the ministers, Lord Aberdeen and Sir George Grey,[23] declared to the Parliament, that the system worked well; that now for ten months, from 1st August, 1834, no injury or violence had been offered to any white, and only one black had been hurt in 800,000 negroes: and, contrary to many sinister predictions, that the new crop of island produce would not fall short of that of the last year.

But the habit of oppression was not destroyed by a law and a day of jubilee. It soon appeared in all the islands, that the planters were disposed to use their old privileges, and overwork the apprentices; to take from them, under various pretences, their fourth part of their time; and to exert the same licentious despotism as before. The negroes complained to the magistrates, and to the governor. In the island of Jamaica, this ill blood continually grew worse. The governors, Lord Belmore, the Earl of Sligo, and afterwards Sir Lionel Smith, (a governor of their own class, who had been sent out to gratify the planters,) threw themselves on the side of the oppressed, and are at constant quarrel with the angry and bilious island legislature.[24] Nothing can exceed the ill humor and sulkiness of the addresses of this assembly.

I may here express a general remark, which the history of slavery seems to justify, that it is not founded solely on the avarice of the planter. We sometimes say, the planter does not want slaves, he only wants the immunities and the luxuries which the slaves yield him; give him money, give him a machine that will yield him as much money as the slaves, and he will thankfully let them go. He has no love of slavery, he wants luxury, and he will pay even this price of crime and danger for it. But I think experience does not warrant this favorable distinction, but shows the existence, beside the covetousness, of a bitterer element, the love of power, the voluptuousness of holding a human being in his absolute control. We sometimes observe, that spoiled children contract a habit of annoying quite wantonly those who have charge of them, and seem to measure their own sense of well-being, not by what they do, but by the degree of reaction they can cause. It is vain to get rid of them by not minding them: if purring and humming is not noticed, they squeal and screech; then if you chide and console them, they find the experiment succeeds, and they begin again. The child will sit in your arms contented, provided you do nothing. If you take a book and read, he commences hostile operations. The planter is the spoiled child of his unnatural habits, and has contracted in his indolent and luxurious climate the need of excitement by irritating and tormenting his slave.

Sir Lionel Smith defended the poor negro girls, prey to the licentiousness of the planters; they shall not be whipped with tamarind rods, if they do not comply with their master's will; he defended the negro women; they should not be made to dig the cane-holes, (which is the very hardest of the field-work;) he defended the Baptist preachers and the stipendiary magistrates, who are the negroes' friends, from the power of the planter. The power of the planters, however, to oppress, was greater than the power of the apprentice and of his guardians to withstand. Lord Brougham and Mr. Buxton declared that the planter had not fulfilled his part in the contract, whilst the apprentices had fulfilled theirs;[25] and demanded that the emancipation should be hastened, and the apprenticeship abolished. Parliament was compelled to pass additional laws for the defence and security of the negro, and in ill humor at these acts, the great island of Jamaica, with a population of half a million, and 300,000 negroes, early in 1838, resolved to throw up the two remaining years of apprenticeship, and to emancipate absolutely on the 1st August, 1838. In British Guiana, in Dominica, the same resolution had been earlier taken with more good will; and the other islands fell into the measure; so that on the 1st August, 1838, the shackles dropped from every British slave. The accounts which we have from all parties, both from the planters, and those too who were originally most opposed to the measure, and from the new freemen, are of the most satisfactory kind. The manner in which the new festival was celebrated, brings tears to the eyes. The First of August, 1838, was observed in Jamaica as a day of thanksgiving and prayer. Sir Lionel Smith, the governor, writes to the British Ministry, "It is impossible for me to do justice to the good order, decorum, and gratitude, which the whole laboring population manifested on that happy occasion. Though joy beamed on every countenance, it was throughout tempered with solemn thankfulness to God, and the churches and chapels were everywhere filled with these happy people in humble offering of praise."

The Queen, in her speech to the Lords and Commons, praised

the conduct of the emancipated population: and, in 1840, Sir Charles Metcalfe, the new governor of Jamaica, in his address to the Assembly, expressed himself to that late exasperated body in these terms.[26] "All those who are acquainted with the state of the island, know that our emancipated population are as free, as independent in their conduct, as well-conditioned, as much in the enjoyment of abundance, and as strongly sensible of the blessings of liberty, as any that we know of in any country. All disqualifications and distinctions of color have ceased; men of all colors have equal rights in law, and an equal footing in society, and every man's position is settled by the same circumstances which regulate that point in other free countries, where no difference of color exists. It may be asserted, without fear of denial, that the former slaves of Jamaica are now as secure in all social rights, as freeborn Britons." He further describes the erection of numerous churches, chapels, and schools, which the new population required, and adds that more are still demanded. The legislature, in their reply, echo the governor's statement, and say, "The peaceful demeanor of the emancipated population redounds to their own credit, and affords a proof of their continued comfort and prosperity."

I said, this event is signal in the history of civilization. There are many styles of civilization, and not one only. Ours is full of barbarities. There are many faculties in man, each of which takes its turn of activity, and that faculty which is paramount in any period, and exerts itself through the strongest nation, determines the civility of that age; and each age thinks its own the perfection of reason. Our culture is very cheap and intelligible. Unroof any house, and you shall find it. The well-being consists in having a sufficiency of coffee and toast, with a daily newspaper; a well-glazed parlor, with marbles, mirrors and centre-table; and the excitement of a few parties and a few rides in a year. Such as one house, such are all. The owner of a New York manor imitates the mansion and equipage of the London nobleman; the Boston merchant rivals his brother of New York; and the villages copy Boston. There have been nations elevated by great sentiments. Such was the civility of Sparta and the Dorian race, whilst it was defective in some of the chief elements of ours.[27] That of Athens, again lay in an intellect dedicated to beauty. That of Asia Minor in poetry, music, and arts; that of Palestine in piety; that of Rome in military arts and virtues, exalted by a prodigious magnanimity; that of China and Japan in the last exaggeration of decorum and etiquette. Our civility, England determines the style of, inasmuch as England is the strongest of the family of existing nations, and as we are the expansion of that people. It is that of a trading nation; it is a shopkeeping civility. The English lord is a retired shopkeeper, and has the prejudices and timidities of that profession. And we are shopkeepers, and have acquired the vices and virtues that belong to trade. We peddle, we truck, we sail, we row, we ride in cars, we creep in teams, we go in canals—to market, and for the sale of goods. The national aim and employment streams into our ways of thinking, our laws, our habits, and our manners. The customer is the immediate jewel of our souls. Him we flatter, him we feast, compliment, vote for, and will not contradict. It was or it seemed the dictate of trade, to keep the negro down. We had found a race who were less warlike, and less energetic shopkeepers than we; who had very little skill in trade. We found it very convenient to keep them at work, since, by the aid of a little whipping, we could get their work for nothing but their board and the cost of whips. What if it cost a few unpleasant scenes on the coast of Africa? That was a great way off; and the scenes could be endured by some sturdy, unscrupulous fellows, who could go for high wages and bring us the men, and need not trouble our ears with the disagreeable particulars. If any mention was made of homicide, madness, adultery, and intolerable tortures, we would let the church-bells ring louder, the church organ swell its peal, and drown the hideous sound. The sugar they raised was excellent: nobody tasted blood in it. The coffee was fragrant; the tobacco was incense; the brandy made nations happy; the cotton clothed the world. What! all raised by these men, and no wages? Excellent! What a convenience! They seemed created by providence to bear the heat and the whipping, and make these fine articles.

But unhappily, most unhappily, gentlemen, man is born with intellect, as well as with a love of sugar, and with a sense of justice, as well as a taste for strong drink. These ripened, as well as those. You could not educate him, you could not get any poetry, any wisdom, any beauty in woman, any strong and commanding character in man, but these absurdities would still come flashing out,— these absurdities of a demand for justice, a generosity for the weak and oppressed. Unhappily too, for the planter, the laws of nature are in harmony with each other: that which the head and the heart demand, is found to be, in the long run, for what the grossest calculator calls his advantage. The moral sense is always supported by the permanent interest of the parties. Else, I know not how, in our world, any good would ever get done. It was shown to the planters that they, as well as the negroes, were slaves; that though they paid no wages, they got very poor work; that their estates were ruining them, under the finest climate; and that they needed the severest monopoly laws at home to keep them from bankruptcy. The oppression of the slave recoiled on them. They were full of vices; their children were lumps of pride, sloth, sensuality and rottenness. The position of woman was nearly as bad as it could be, and, like other robbers, they could not sleep in security. Many planters have said, since the emancipation, that, before that day, they were the greatest slaves on the estates. Slavery is no scholar, no improver; it does not love the whistle of the railroad; it does not love the newspaper, the mailbag, a college, a book, or a preacher who has the absurd whim of saying what he thinks; it does not increase the white population; it does not improve the soil; everything goes to decay. For these reasons, the islands proved bad customers to England. It was very easy for manufacturers less shrewd than those of Birmingham and Manchester to see,[28] that if the state of things in the islands was altered, if the slaves had wages, the slaves would be clothed, would build houses, would fill them with tools, with pottery, with crockery, with hardware; and negro women love fine clothes as well as white women. In every naked negro of those thousands, they saw a future customer. Meantime, they saw further, that the slave-trade, by keeping in barbarism the whole coast of eastern Africa, deprives them of countries and nations of customers, if once freedom and civility, and European manners

21

could get a foothold there. But the trade could not be abolished, whilst this hungry West Indian market, with an appetite like the grave, cried, "More, more, bring me a hundred a day;" they could not expect any mitigation in the madness of the poor African war-chiefs. These considerations opened the eyes of the dullest in Britain. More than this, the West Indian estate was owned or mortgaged in England, and the owner and the mortgagee had very plain intimations that the feeling of English liberty was gaining every hour new mass and velocity, and the hostility to such as resisted it, would be fatal. The House of Commons would destroy the protection of island produce, and interfere on English politics in the island legislation: so they hastened to make the best of their position, and accepted the bill.

These considerations, I doubt not, had their weight, the interest of trade, the interest of the revenue, and, moreover, the good fame of the action. It was inevitable that men should feel these motives. But they do not appear to have had an excessive or unreasonable weight. On reviewing this history, I think the whole transaction reflects infinite honor on the people and parliament of England. It was a stately spectacle, to see the cause of human rights argued with so much patience and generosity, and with such a mass of evidence before that powerful people. It is a creditable incident in the history, that when, in 1789, the first privy-council report of evidence on the trade, a bulky folio, (embodying all the facts which the London Committee had been engaged for years in collecting, and all the examinations before the council,) was presented to the House of Commons, a late day being named for the discussion, in order to give members time,—Mr. Wilberforce, Mr. Pitt, the prime minister, and other gentlemen, took advantage of the postponement, to retire into the country, to read the report. For months and years the bill was debated, with some consciousness of the extent of its relations by the first citizens of England, the foremost men of the earth; every argument was weighed, every particle of evidence was sifted, and laid in the scale; and, at last, the right triumphed, the poor man was vindicated, and the oppressor was flung out. I know that England has the advantage of trying the question at a wide distance from the spot where the nuisance exists: the planters are not, excepting in rare examples, members of the legislature. The extent of the empire, and the magnitude and number of other questions crowding into court, keep this one in balance, and prevent it from obtaining that ascendancy, and being urged with that intemperance, which a question of property tends to acquire. There are causes in the composition of the British legislature, and the relation of its leaders to the country and to Europe, which exclude much that is pitiful and injurious in other legislative assemblies. From these reasons, the question was discussed with a rare independence and magnanimity. It was not narrowed down to a paltry electioneering trap, and, I must say, a delight in justice, an honest tenderness for the poor negro, for man suffering these wrongs, combined with the national pride, which refused to give the support of English soil, or the protection of the English flag, to these disgusting violations of nature.

Forgive me, fellow citizens, if I own to you, that in the last few days that my attention has been occupied with this history, I have not been able to read a page of it, without the most painful comparisons. Whilst I have read of England, I have thought of New England. Whilst I have meditated in my solitary walks on the magnanimity of the English Bench and Senate, reaching out the benefit of the law to the most helpless citizen in her world-wide realm, I have found myself oppressed by other thoughts. As I have walked in the pastures and along the edge of woods, I could not keep my imagination on those agreeable figures, for other images that intruded on me. I could not see the great vision of the patriots and senators who have adopted the slave's cause:—they turned their backs on me. No: I see other pictures—of mean men: I see very poor, very ill-clothed, very ignorant men, not surrounded by happy friends,—to be plain,—poor black men of obscure employment as mariners, cooks, or stewards, in ships, yet citizens of this our Commonwealth of Massachusetts,—freeborn as we,—whom the slave-laws of the States of South Carolina, Georgia, and Louisiana, have arrested in the vessels in which they visited those ports, and shut up in jails so long as the vessel remained in port, with the stringent addition, that if the shipmaster fails to pay the costs of this official arrest, and the board in jail, these citizens are to be sold for slaves, to pay that expense. This man, these men, I see, and no law to save them. Fellow citizens, this crime will not be hushed up any longer. I have learned that a citizen of Nantucket, walking in New Orleans, found a freeborn citizen of Nantucket, a man, too, of great personal worth, and, as it happened, very dear to him, as having saved his own life, working chained in the streets of that city, kidnapped by such a process as this. In the sleep of the laws, the private interference of two excellent citizens of Boston has, I have ascertained, rescued several natives of this State from these southern prisons. Gentlemen, I thought the deck of a Massachusetts ship was as much the territory of Massachusetts, as the floor on which we stand. It should be as sacred as the temple of God. The poorest fishing-smack, that floats under the shadow of an iceberg in the northern seas, or hunts the whale in the southern ocean, should be encompassed by her laws with comfort and protection, as much as within the arms of Cape Ann and Cape Cod. And this kidnapping is suffered within our own land and federation, whilst the fourth article of the Constitution of the United States ordains in terms, that, "The citizens of each State shall be entitled to all privileges and immunities of citizens in the several States." If such a damnable outrage can be committed on the person of a citizen with impunity, let the Governor break the broad seal of the State; he bears the sword in vain. The Governor of Massachusetts is a trifler:[29] the State-house in Boston is a play-house: the General Court is a dishonored body: if they make laws which they cannot execute. The great-hearted Puritans have left no posterity. The rich men may walk in State-street, but they walk without honor; and the farmers may brag their democracy in the country, but they are disgraced men. If the State has no power to defend its own people in its own shipping, because it has delegated that power to the Federal Government, has it no representation in the Federal Government? Are those men dumb? I am no lawyer, and cannot indicate the forms applicable to the case, but here is something which transcends all forms. Let the senators and representatives of the State, containing a population of a million freemen, go in a body before the Congress, and say, that they have a demand to make on them so imperative, that all functions of government must stop, until it is satisfied. If ordinary legislation cannot reach it, then extraordinary must be applied. The Congress should instruct the President to send to those ports of Charleston, Savannah, and New Orleans, such orders and such force, as should release, forthwith, all such citizens of Massachusetts as were holden in prison without the allegation of any crime, and should set on foot the strictest inquisition to discover where such persons, brought into slavery by these local laws, at any time heretofore, may now be. That first;—and then, let order be taken to indemnify all such as have been incarcerated. As for dangers to the Union, from such demands!—the Union is already at an end, when the first citizen of Massachusetts is thus outraged. Is it an union and covenant in which the State of Massachusetts agrees to be imprisoned, and the State of Carolina to imprison? Gentlemen, I am loath to say harsh things, and perhaps I know too little of politics for the smallest weight to attach to any censure of mine,—but I am at a loss how to characterize the tameness and silence of the two senators and the ten representatives of the State at Washington. To what purpose, have we clothed each of those representatives with the power of seventy thousand persons, and each senator with near half a million, if they are to sit dumb at their desks, and see their constituents captured and sold;— perhaps to gentlemen sitting by them in the hall? There is a scandalous rumor that has been swelling louder of late years,—perhaps it is wholly false,—that members are bullied into silence by southern gentlemen. It is so easy to omit to speak, or even to be absent when delicate things are to be handled. I may as well say what all men feel, that whilst our very amiable and very innocent representatives and senators at Washington, are accomplished lawyers and merchants, and very eloquent at dinners and at caucuses, there is a disastrous want of *men* from New England. I would gladly make exceptions, and you will not suffer me to forget one eloquent old man, in whose veins the blood of Massachusetts rolls, and who singly has defended the freedom of speech, and the rights of the

MEANS/ENDS

free, against the usurpation of the slave-holder. But the reader of Congressional debates, in New England, is perplexed to see with what admirable sweetness and patience the majority of the free States, are schooled and ridden by the minority of slave-holders. What if we should send thither representatives who were a particle less amiable and less innocent? I entreat you, sirs, let not this stain attach, let not this misery accumulate any longer. If the managers of our political parties are too prudent and too cold;—if, most unhappily, the ambitious class of young men and political men have found out, that these neglected victims are poor and without weight; that they have no graceful hospitalities to offer; no valuable business to throw into any man's hands, no strong vote to cast at the elections; and therefore may with impunity be left in their chains or to the chance of chains, then let the citizens in their primary capacity take up their cause on this very ground, and say to the government of the State, and of the Union, that government exists to defend the weak and the poor and the injured party; the rich and the strong can better take care of themselves. And as an omen and assurance of success, I point you to the bright example which England set you, on this day, ten years ago.

There are other comparisons and other imperative duties which come sadly to mind,—but I do not wish to darken the hours of this day by crimination; I turn gladly to the rightful theme, to the bright aspects of the occasion.

This event was a moral revolution. The history of it is before you. Here was no prodigy, no fabulous hero, no Trojan horse, no bloody war, but all was achieved by plain means of plain men, working not under a leader, but under a sentiment. Other revolutions have been the insurrection of the oppressed; this was the repentence of the tyrant. It was the masters revolting from their mastery. The slave-holder said, I will not hold slaves. The end was noble, and the means were pure. Hence, the elevation and pathos of this chapter of history. The lives of the advocates are pages of greatness, and the connexion of the eminent senators with this question, constitutes the immortalizing moments of those men's lives. The bare enunciation of the theses, at which the lawyers and legislators arrived, gives a glow to the heart of the reader. Lord Chancellor Northington is the author of the famous sentence, "As soon as any man puts his foot on English ground, he becomes free."[30] "I was a slave," said the counsel of Somerset, speaking for his client, "for I was in America: I am now in a country, where the common rights of mankind are known and regarded." Granville Sharp filled the ear of the judges with the sound principles, that had from time to time been affirmed by the legal authorities. "Derived power cannot be superior to the power from which it is derived." "The reasonableness of the law is the soul of the law." "It is better to suffer every evil, than to consent to any." Out it would come, the God's truth, out it came, like a bolt from a cloud, for all the mumbling of the lawyers. One feels very sensibly in all this history that a great heart and soul are behind there, superior to any man, and making use of each, in turn, and infinitely attractive to every person according to the degree of reason in his own mind, so that this cause has had the power to draw to it every particle of talent and of worth in England, from the beginning. All the great geniuses of the British senate, Fox, Pitt, Burke, Grenville, Sheridan, Grey, Canning, ranged themselves on its side;[31] the poet Cowper wrote for it:[32] Franklin, Jefferson, Washington, in this country, all recorded their votes. All men remember the subtlety and the fire of indignation, which the Edinburgh Review contributed to the cause;[33] and every liberal mind, poet, preacher, moralist, statesman, has had the fortune to appear somewhere for this cause. On the other part, appeared the reign of pounds and shillings, and all manner of rage and stupidity; a resistance which drew from Mr. Huddlestone in Parliament the observation,[34] "That a curse attended this trade even in the mode of defending it. By a certain fatality, none but the vilest arguments were brought forward, which corrupted the very persons who used them. Every one of these was built on the narrow ground of interest, of pecuniary profit, of sordid gain, in opposition to every motive that had reference to humanity, justice, and religion, or to that great principle which comprehended them all."—This moral force perpetually reinforces and dignifies the friends of this cause. It gave that tenacity to their point which has insured ultimate triumph; and it gave that superiority in reason, in imagery, in eloquence, which makes in all countries anti-slavery meetings so attractive to the people, and has made it a proverb in Massachusetts, that, "eloquence is dog-cheap at the anti-slavery chapel?"

I will say further, that we are indebted mainly to this movement, and to the continuers of it, for the popular discussion of every point of practical ethics, and a reference of every question to the absolute standard. It is notorious, that the political, religious, and social schemes, with which the minds of men are now most occupied, have been matured, or at least broached, in the free and daring discussions of these assemblies. Men have become aware through the emancipation, and kindred events, of the presence of powers, which, in their days of darkness, they had overlooked. Virtuous men will not again rely on political agents. They have found out the deleterious effect of political association. Up to this day, we have allowed to statesmen a paramount social standing, and we bow low to them as to the great. We cannot extend this deference to them any longer. The secret cannot be kept, that the seats of power are filled by underlings, ignorant, timid, and selfish, to a degree to destroy all claim, excepting that on compassion, to the society of the just and generous. What happened notoriously to an American ambassador in England, that he found himself compelled to palter, and to disguise the fact that he was a slave-breeder, happens to men of state. Their vocation is a presumption against them, among well-meaning people. The superstition respecting power and office, is going to the ground. The stream of human affairs flows its own way, and is very little affected by the activity of legislators. What great masses of men wish done, will be done; and they do not wish it for a freak, but because it is their state and natural end. There are now other energies than force, other than political, which no man in future can allow himself to disregard. There is direct conversation and influence. A man is to make himself felt, by his proper force. The tendency of things runs steadily to this point, namely, to put every man on his merits, and to give him so much power as he naturally exerts—no more, no less. Of course, the timid and

28

base persons, all who are conscious of no worth in themselves, and who owe all their place to the opportunities which the old order of things allowed them to deceive and defraud men, shudder at the change, and would fain silence every honest voice, and lock up every house where liberty and innovation can be pleaded for. They would raise mobs, for fear is very cruel. But the strong and healthy yeomen and husbands of the land, the self-sustaining class of inventive and industrious men, fear no competition or superiority. Come what will, their faculty cannot be spared.

The First of August marks the entrance of a new element into modern politics, namely, the civilization of the negro. A man is added to the human family. Not the least affecting part of this history of abolition, is, the annihilation of the old indecent nonsense about the nature of the negro. In the case of the ship Zong, in 1781, whose master had thrown one hundred and thirty-two slaves alive into the sea, to cheat the underwriters, the first jury gave a verdict in favor of the master and owners: they had a right to do what they had done.[35] Lord Mansfield is reported to have said on the bench, "The matter left to the jury is,—Was it from necessity? For they had no doubt,—though it shocks one very much,—that the case of slaves was the same as if horses had been thrown overboard. It is a very shocking case." But a more enlightened and humane opinion began to prevail. Mr. Clarkson, early in his career, made a collection of African productions and manufactures, as specimens of the arts and culture of the negro; comprising cloths and loom, weapons, polished stones and woods, leather, glass, dyes, ornaments, soap, pipe-bowls, and trinkets. These he showed to Mr. Pitt, who saw and handled them with extreme interest. "On sight of these," says Clarkson, "many sublime thoughts seemed to rush at once into his mind, some of which he expressed;" and hence appeared to arise a project which was always dear to him, of the civilization of Africa,— a dream which forever elevates his fame. In 1791, Mr. Wilberforce announced to the House of Commons, "We have already gained one victory: we have obtained for these poor creatures the recognition of their human nature, which, for a time, was most shamefully denied them." It was the sarcasm of Montesquieu, "it would not do to suppose that negroes were men, lest it should turn out that whites were not;" for, the white has, for ages, done what he could to keep the negro in that hoggish state. His laws have been furies. It now appears, that the negro race is, more than any other, susceptible of rapid civilization. The emancipation is observed, in the islands, to have wrought for the negro a benefit as sudden as when a thermometer is brought out of the shade into the sun. It has given him eyes and ears. If, before, he was taxed with such stupidity, or such defective vision, that he could not set a table square to the walls of an apartment, he is now the principal, if not the only mechanic, in the West Indies; and is, besides, an architect, a physician, a lawyer, a magistrate, an editor, and a valued and increasing political power. The recent testimonies of Sturge, of Thome and Kimball, of Gurney, of Phillippo, are very explicit on this point, the capacity and the success of the colored and the black population in employments of skill, of profit, and of trust;[36] and, best of all, is the testimony to their moderation. They receive hints and advances from the whites, that they will be gladly received as subscribers to the Exchange, as members of this or that committee of trust. They hold back, and say to each other, that "social position is not to be gained by pushing."

I have said that this event interests us because it came mainly from the concession of the whites; I add, that in part it is the earning of the blacks. They won the pity and respect which they have received, by their powers and native endowments. I think this a circumstance of the highest import. Their whole future is in it. Our planet, before the age of written history, had its races of savages, like the generations of sour paste, or the animalcules that wriggle and bite in a drop of putrid water. Who cares for these or for their wars? We do not wish a world of bugs or of birds; neither afterward of Scythians, Caraibs, or Feejees.[37] The grand style of nature, her great periods, is all we observe in them. Who cares for oppressing whites, or oppressed blacks, twenty centuries ago, more than for bad dreams? Eaters and food are in the harmony of nature; and there too is the germ forever protected, unfolding gigantic leaf after leaf, a newer flower, a richer fruit, in every period, yet its next product is never to be guessed. It will only save what is worth saving; and it saves not by compassion, but by power. It appoints no police to guard the lion, but his teeth and claws; no fort or city for the bird, but his wings; no rescue for flies and mites, but their spawning numbers, which no ravages can overcome. It deals with men after the same manner. If they are rude and foolish, down they must go. When at last in a race, a new principle appears, an idea;— *that* conserves it; ideas only save races. If the black man is feeble, and not important to the existing races not on a parity with the best race, the black man must serve, and be exterminated. But if the black man carries in his bosom an indispensable element of a new and coming civilization, for the sake of that element, no wrong, nor strength, nor circumstance, can hurt him: he will survive and play his part. So now, the arrival in the world of such men as Toussaint,[38] and the Haytian heroes, or of the leaders of their race in Barbadoes and Jamaica, outweighs in good omen all the English and American humanity. The anti-slavery of the whole world, is dust in the balance before this,—is a poor squeamishness and nervousness: the might and the right are here: here is the anti-slave: here is man: and if you have man, black or white is an insignificance. The intellect,— that is miraculous! Who has it, has the talisman: his skin and bones, though they were of the color of night, are transparent, and the everlasting stars shine through, with attractive beams. But a compassion for that which is not and cannot be useful or lovely, is degrading and futile. All the songs, and newspapers, and money-subscriptions, and vituperation of such as do not think with us, will avail nothing against a fact. I say to you, you must save yourself, black or white, man or woman; other help is none. I esteem the occasion of this jubilee to be the proud discovery, that the black race can contend with the white; that, in the great anthem which we call history, a piece of many parts and vast compass, after playing a long time a very low and subdued accompaniment, they perceive the time arrived when they can strike in with effect, and take a master's part in the music. The civility of the world has reached that pitch, that their more moral genius is becoming indispensable, and the quality of this race is to be honored for itself. For this, they

EVOLUTION THE NATURAL ORDER

SELF-EMANCIPATION

PLATO
JUSTICE

have been preserved in sandy deserts, in rice-swamps, in kitchens and shoe-shops, so long: now let them emerge, clothed and in their own form.

There remains the very elevated consideration which the subject opens, but which belongs to more abstract views than we are now taking, this namely, that the civility of no race can be perfect whilst another race is degraded. It is a doctrine alike of the oldest, and of the newest philosophy, that, man is one, and that you cannot injure any member, without a sympathetic injury to all the members. America is not civil, whilst Africa is barbarous.

These considerations seem to leave no choice for the action of the intellect and the conscience of the country. There have been moments in this, as well as in every piece of moral history, when there seemed room for the infusions of a skeptical philosophy; when it seemed doubtful, whether brute force would not triumph in the eternal struggle. I doubt not, that sometimes a despairing negro, when jumping over the ship's sides to escape from the white devils who surrounded him, has believed there was no vindication of right; it is horrible to think of, but it seemed so. I doubt not, that sometimes the negro's friend, in the face of scornful and brutal hundreds of traders and drivers, has felt his heart sink. Especially, it seems to me, some degree of despondency is pardonable, when he observes the men of conscience and of intellect, his own natural allies and champions,—those whose attention should be nailed to the grand objects of this cause, so hotly offended by whatever incidental petulances or infirmities of indiscreet defenders of the negro, as to permit themselves to be ranged with the enemies of the human race; and names which should be the alarums of liberty and the watchwords of truth, are mixed up with all the rotten rabble of selfishness and tyranny. I assure myself that this coldness and blindness will pass away. A single noble wind of sentiment will scatter them forever. I am sure that the good and wise elders, the ardent and generous youth will not permit what is incidental and exceptional to withdraw their devotion from the essential and permanent characters of the question. There have been moments, I said, when men might be forgiven, who doubted. Those moments are past. Seen in masses, it cannot be disputed, there is progress in human society. There is a blessed necessity by which the interest of men is always driving them to the right; and, again, making all crime mean and ugly. The genius of the Saxon race, friendly to liberty; the enterprise, the very muscular vigor of this nation, are inconsistent with slavery. The Intellect, with blazing eye, looking through history from the beginning onward, gazes on this blot, and it disappears. The sentiment of Right, once very low and indistinct, but ever more articulate, because it is the voice of the universe, pronounces Freedom. The Power that built this fabric of things affirms it in the heart; and in the history of the First of August, has made a sign to the ages, of his will.

Anniversary of
West Indian Emancipation

1 August 1845

This occasion seems one of hope, not of sorrow and distrust.[1] While I sympathise with the feelings that have been expressed by others, I cannot but wish to recall the audience to the occasion that has brought us together, and look forward to the similar occasion which we hope to celebrate in our own land.[2]

What is the defence of Slavery? What is the irresistible argument by which every plea of humanity and reason has hitherto been borne down?

Is it a doubt of the equity of the negro's cause? By no means. Is it a doubt of the sincerity of the reformer? No; the Abolitionists are thought partial, credulous, tedious monomaniacs; bitter—but no man doubts their sincerity. Is it a stringent self-interest? No; this acts in certain places. It acts on the seaboard, and in great thoroughfares, where the Northern merchant or manufacturer exchanges hospitalities with the Southern planter, or trades with him, and loves to exculpate himself from all sympathy with those turbulent Abolitionists. But it acts only there—not on the Northern people at large. The farmers, for example, in this Country, or in this State, feel no pinch of self-interest to court the complacency of the Southerner. If Fitchburg stock is good[3]—if we can buy and sell land, and wood, and hay, and corn—if we can sell shoes, and tinware, and clocks, and carriages, and chairs—we don't care whether he likes or mislikes it. What, then, is the objection? I think there is but one single argument which has any real weight with the bulk of the Northern people, and which lies in one word—a word which I hear pronounced with triumphant emphasis in bar-rooms, in shops, in streets, in kitchens, at musters, and at cattle-shows. That word is *Niggers!*—a word which, cried by rowdy boys and rowdy men in the ear of this timid and sceptical generation, is reckoned stronger than heaven; it blows away with a jeer all the efforts of philanthropy, all the expostulations of pity, the cries of millions, now for hundreds of years—all are answered by this insulting appellation, "Oh, the Niggers!" and the boys straightway sing Jim Crow and jump Jim Crow in the streets and taverns.[4]

It is the objection of an inferiority of race.[5] They who say it and they who hear it, think it the voice of nature and fate pronouncing against the Abolitionist and the Philanthropist; that the *ya, ya* of the Negro, his laugh, and the imperfect articulation of his organs designate an imperfect race; and that the good-will of amiable enthusiasts in his behalf will avail him no more against this sentence of Nature than a pair of oars against the falling ocean at Niagara.

And what is the amount of this conclusion in which the men of New-England acquiesce? It is, that the Creator of the Negro has given him up to stand as a victim of a caricature of the white man beside him; to stoop under his pack, and to bleed under his whip. If that be the doctrine, then, I say, if He has given up his cause, He has also given up mine, who feel his wrong, and who in our hearts must curse the Creator who has undone him.

But no, it is not so; the Universe is not bankrupt: still stands the old heart firm in its seat, and knows that, come what will, the right is and shall be. Justice is for ever and ever. And what is the reply to this fatal allegation?

I believe there is a sound argument derived from facts collected in the United States and in the West Indies, in reply to this alleged hopeless inferiority of the colored race.[6] But I shall not touch it. I concern myself now with the morals of the system, which seem to scorn a tedious catalogue of particulars on a question so simple as this. The only reply, then, to this poor, sceptical ribaldry is the affirming heart. The sentiment of right, which is the principle of civilization and the reason of reason, fights against this damnable atheism. All the facts in history are fables, and untrustworthy, beside the dictates of the moral sentiment which speaks one and the same voice in all ages. And what says that to the injured Negro? If we listen to it, it assures us that in his very wrongs is his strength. The Persians have a proverb: "Beware of the orphan; for when the orphan sets a-crying, the throne of the Almighty is shaken from side to side." It is certain that, if it should come to question, all just men, all intelligent agents, must take the part of the black against the white man. Then I say, never is the planter safe; his house is a den; a just man cannot go there, except to tell him so. Whatever may appear at the moment, however contrasted the fortunes of the black and the white—though the one live in his hereditary mansion-house, and the latter in a shed; though one rides an Arabian horse, and the other is hunted by blood-hounds; though one eats, and the other sweats; one strikes, and the other dies—yet is the planter's an unsafe and unblest condition. Nature fights on the other side; and as power is always stealing from the idle to the busy hand, it seems inevitable that a revolution is preparing at no distant day to set these disjointed matters right.

See further, if you with me are believing and not unbelieving, if you are open to hope and not to despair, in what manner the moral power secures the welfare of the black man.

In the moral creation, it is appointed from everlasting, that the protection of the weak shall be in the illumination of the strong. It is in the order of things the privilege of superiority to give, to bestow, to protect, to love, to serve. This is the office and the source of power. It is power's power to do these things; and, on the other hand, it is the ruin of power to steal, to injure, and to put to death. The hope and the refuge of the weaker individual and the weaker races is here. It will not always be reputable to steal and to oppress. It will not always be possible. Every new step taken in the true order of human life takes out something of brutality and infuses something of good will. Precisely as it is the necessity of grass to grow, of the child to be born, of light to shine, of heat to radiate, and of matter to attract, so is it of man's race and of every race to rise and to refine. "All things strive to ascend, and ascend in their striving." And it will be as natural and obvious a step with the increased dominion of right reason over the human race, for the interests of the more amicable and pacific classes to be eagerly defended by the more energetic, as it is now for Trade to displace War.[7]

I know that this race have long been victims. They came from being preyed on by the barbarians of Africa to be preyed on by the barbarians of America. To many of them, no doubt, Slavery was a mitigation and a gain. Put the slave under negro drivers, and it is said these are more cruel than the white. Their fate now, as far as it depends on circumstances, depends on the raising of their masters. The masters are ambitious of culture and civility. Elevate, enlighten, civilize the semi-barbarous nations of South Carolina, Georgia, Alabama—take away from their debauched society the Bowie-knife, the rum-bowl, the dice-box, and the stews—take out the brute, and infuse a drop of civility and generosity, and you touch those selfish lords with thought and gentleness.

Instead of racers, jockies, duelists and peacocks, you shall have a race of decent and lawful men, incapacitated to hold slaves, and eager to give them liberty. . . . I hold it, then, to be the part of right reason, to hope and to affirm well of the destinies of this portion of the human family, and to accept the humane voices which in our times have espoused their cause, as only the forerunners of vast majorities in this country and in the race.

LETTER TO
WILLIAM ROTCH

17 November 1845

Concord, Nov. 17th, 1845.

W. J. Rotch, Esq., Secretary

Dear Sir:—If I come to New Bedford, I should be ready to fix, say the first Tuesday of March, and the second.[1] But I have to say, that I have indirectly received a report of some proceedings in your Lyceum, lately, which, by excluding others, I think ought to exclude me. My informant said, that the application of a colored person for membership by purchase of a ticket in the usual manner, had been rejected by a vote of the Lyceum; and this, for the first time. Now, as I think the Lyceum exists for popular education, as I work in it for that, and think that it should bribe and importune the humblest and most ignorant to come in, and exclude nobody, or, if any body, certainly the most cultivated,—this vote quite embarrasses me, and I should not know how to speak to the company. Besides, in its direct counteraction to the obvious duty and sentiment of New England, and of all freemen in regard to the colored people, the vote appears so unkind, and so unlooked for, that I could not come with any pleasure before the Society.

If I am misinformed, will you—if they are printed—have the goodness to send me the proceedings; or, if not printed, their purport; and oblige,

Yours respectfully,
R. W. Emerson

Antislavery
Speech at Dedham

4 July 1846

Mr. President:—I am struck, as others who have addressed you, with the singular spectacle which our recent politics exhibit.[1] In its connection with the Federal Government, a despair has crept over Massachusetts, and over New England, in regard to those objects which our people naturally love and aim at. The active, enterprising, intelligent, well-meaning, and substantial part of the people find themselves paralyzed and defeated everywhere, by the foreign and newly-arrived portion of the citizens, by the youthful, by the uneducated, and by the unscrupulous voters, and by those reckless persons who have assumed to lead these masses.[2]

The creators of wealth, the conscientious and responsible persons, those whose names are given in as fit for jurors, referees, for offices of trust, those whose opinion makes public opinion, and who, in any crisis of public danger, would be the class most relied on, find themselves degraded into observers; flung out neck and feet from all share in the action and counsels of the nation. On the occurrence of each new event, New England resolves itself, not into a revolutionary committee, no, but into a debating society.

There is no citizen, however private and sequestered, who, in the last months, can have failed to notice this inaction and apathy. I ask myself whether the people of Massachusetts are such snivelling nobodies as they appear? And from the best lights I get, here and elsewhere, I find some solution to the question, consistent with what good we know of them. At least, I think I understand it a little.

In this mercantile country, there is a thrift which lays its grasp on almost all the forcible and well-organized individuals. It makes the law of their actions. The Southerner said frankly, if not very civilly, through the mouth of John Randolph, "Gentlemen of the free States, we shall drive you to the wall: we have done it, and we shall keep you there."[3] The Northerner seemed not to hear him, and observers were at a loss to account for his tameness. The truth is, the Northerners have good blood in their veins, and are very well able to give as good as they get; but they are old traders, and make it a rule rarely to shoot their customers, and never until the bill is paid. It were easy for them to retort, "Gentlemen, we are not so deaf as you imagine. We can defend our honor, and are not more than others tender of our skin, but we *are* very tender of our mortgages: we own you: every acre of your plantations is virtually covered by bonds and securities held in New-York and Boston." Hence, though slaveholders are apt to have a bad temper, and vicious politics,—a strong desire to keep the peace, and a good humor with them, is felt not only by the financial authorities in State street and Wall street, but also by the cotton-spinners, the freighters, the shoe-dealers, the cabinet-makers, the printers, the booksellers, and by every description of Northern salesmen.

Thus of one great portion of our population the sincere opposition to the late mischievous measures is paralyzed. Another part of the people is the war-party, a ferocious minority, which no civilization has yet caused to disappear in any country; that mob, which every nation holds within it, of young and violent persons craving strong drink, craving blood, craving coarse animal excitement, at any cost. It is of no use to vote Slavery and the wars of Slavery to be damnable, if we go ahead of the sense and civilization of the people: the wolf will show his head very unexpectedly. It does very well for the English and American towns to exchange peace-tracts: Old Worcester sends such to New Worcester, Old Plymouth to

New Plymouth, Old York to New-York. It is all very pleasant and amiable. But war has not ceased in either country for a moment. If France, and England, and America are forced, by a keener self-interest, to keep the peace with each other, that does not hinder that some poor Algerines, Sikhs, Seminoles, or Mexicans, should be devoured by these peace-loving States at the same moment.[4] This war-party, this section of rowdy boys, older or younger, ever ready to throw up their caps at any prospect of a fight, are stimulated and trumpeted on by that needy band of profligate editors and orators, who find their selfish account in encouraging this brutal instinct.

If two classes do not exhaust the population, I might reckon a third class, whose conscientious action is overpowered by their repulsion to anything novel and irregular. Our people are respecters, not of essential, but of external law, decorum, routine, and official forms. I fear it is to a superstition which has killed the religion, to a parliamentariness or official form, that Governor Briggs and his dignified supporters have just now immolated the integrity of the State.[5]

But, Mr. President and friends, I am not here to accuse parties or persons. I much prefer the method of the sun to that of the north wind; and, amidst these causes of the political apathy of Massachusetts, and New England,—causes which really co-exist with a great deal of good-meaning and innocency of the crimes which we have permitted to be done,—I value as a redeeming trait, the growth of the abolition party, the true successors of that austere Church, which made nature and history sacred to us all in our youth. I often ask myself, what is to take the place, to the young people, of those restraining influences which the old Calvinism, or Puritanism, under whatever form, exerted on the youth of such as are as old, or almost as old, as I am. The young men seem left to a frivolous, external, Parisian manner of living. What can better supply that outward church they want, than this fervent, self-denying school of love and action, which, too, the blood of martyrs has already consecrated? When I have seen the phalanx of these brave men and brave women pursuing their resolute course from year to year, through mobs, through favor, through neglect, I have thought of the march of Napoleon's celebrated Guard, amidst the Cossacks and the snow-drifts.[6] Beausset, the Emperor's chamberlain, relates, that he has seen a detachment of twenty thousand men put to flight by the cry of a coward, "that the Cossacks were coming;" and, in their breaking of their own ranks, almost interrupting the march of four thousand warriors of the Imperial Guard, who, calm and intrepid, held on their way, through snows and through Cossacks, never stopping to inquire whether the sun still existed in that frightful cold. With the noblest purpose in the general defection and apathy the Abolitionists have been faithful to themselves.

The history of this party of freedom, seems to me one of the best symptoms, but it is only a symptom. I am glad, not for what it has done, but that the party exists. Not what they do, but what they see, seems to me sublime. They have seen, against all appearances, that the right will conquer, and though it has not with it the people of the world, it has the world itself, and the world's Builder; and they have thrown themselves unhesitatingly on that side.

I am a debtor, in common with all well-meaning persons, to this association. I think they have yet lessons to learn, and are learning them. I shall esteem them, as they cease to be a party, and come to rely on that which is not party, nor part, but which is the whole, and which as readily and irresistibly pours itself from one man, as from the most numerous co-operation. I hope to see those great men arise among us, who, like the west wind bring the sunshine with them; those conquering natures, which make the difference by their presence or absence; where they are, there is power; those who do not, as the men of talents we are wont to see, defer to the solemn nonsense of existing things but without an effort set them aside and repudiate them, because they are in the presence of and do share what is greater. There are other crimes besides Slavery and the Mexican war, and a more comprehensive faith, I hope, is coming, which will resolve all the parts of duty into a harmonious whole.

Letter to the
Kidnapping Committee

23 September 1846

Concord, September 23, 1846.

Dr. S. G. Howe, and Associates of the Committee of Citizens:[1]

If I could do or say any thing useful or equal to the occasion, I would not fail to attend the meeting on Thursday. I feel the irreparable shame to Boston of this abduction. I hope it is not possible that the city will make the act its own, by any color or justification. Our State has suffered many disgraces, of late years, to spoil our pride in it, but never any so flagrant as this, if the people of the commonwealth can be brought to be accomplices in this crime,— which, I assure myself, will never be. I hope it is not only not to be sustained by the mercantile body, but not even by the smallest portion of that class. If the merchants tolerate this crime,—as nothing will be too bad for their desert,—so it is very certain they will have the ignominy very faithfully put to their lips. The question you now propose, is a good test of the honesty and manliness of our commerce. If it shall turn out, as desponding men say, that our people do not really care whether Boston is a slave-port or not, provided our trade thrives, then we may, at least, cease to dread hard times and ruin. It is high time our bad wealth came to an end. I am sure, I shall very cheerfully take my share of suffering in the ruin of such a prosperity, and shall very willingly turn to the mountains to chop wood, and seek to find for myself and my children labors compatible with freedom and honor.

With this feeling, I am proportionably grateful to Mr. Adams and yourselves,[2] for undertaking the office of putting the question to our people, whether they will make this cruelty theirs? and of giving them an opportunity of clearing the population from the stain of this crime, and of securing mankind from the repetition of it, in this quarter, forever.

> Respectfully and thankfully,
> Your obedient servant,
> *R. W. Emerson.*

ANTISLAVERY REMARKS
AT WORCESTER

3 August 1849

It is beyond my power to express even the satisfaction which I feel in seeing this collection of the friends of freedom on a day so truly the subject of heartfelt joy to us and to all men.[1] There is no purer anniversary certainly, than this. There is no one in which all would more willingly sympathise. It is to me especially welcome in its observance. The true tone that belongs to us, as men, in view of this great evil of slavery, is one, not of fear but of congratulation.

I am accustomed to consider more the men than the abolitionists. It is perhaps the vice of my habit of speculation, that I am prone rather to consider the history of the race, the genius and energy of any nation, than to insist very much upon individual action.

I regret very much the miserable state of health which seems to forbid me to enter upon a subject to which I would willingly devote a few words; but I think the scope left for human exertion, for individual talent to be very small. I believe that we are to congratulate ourselves, as rational beings, that we are under the control of higher laws than any human will. We may congratulate ourselves on the impotence of the human will. We are to rejoice in the march of events, in the sequence of the centuries, the progress of the great universal human, and shall I not say, divine, genius, which overpowers all our vices as well as our virtues, and turns our vices to the general benefit. I believe that the ardor of our virtuous enthusiasm in behalf of the slave, and of our indignation at his oppressor, naturally blinds us a little to the fate that is involved alike in our freedom, and in the slaveholding system at the South.[2]

The course of history is one everywhere. It is a constant progress of amelioration. Like the amelioration in the pear-tree, or apple-tree, so well-known to botanists.[3] One must look to the planters of the South with the same feelings that he would regard the spider and the fly, the tiger and the deer. It is a barbarism. The people are barbarous. They are still in the animal state. They are not accountable like those whose eyes have once been opened to a Christianity that makes a return to evil impossible. Revolutions, as we say, never move backward. In our own history, this has been repeated over and over again.

For instance, look at that people from whom we came,—the Norwegians.[4] It is known to you that the people of Iceland were early Christianized and civilized. That system of piracy which was so universal in the Scandinavians of the Peninsula, universal among the Norwegians, Danes and Swedes, never found any countenance in Iceland. Only the rudest and most uncivilized of the Icelanders fell into the practice, and joined in the exploits of the Vikings. As early as in the 12th century, and in the beginning of the 13th, the union of the Hanse towns, the commercial towns of Germany, to protect themselves against the pirates, had a certain success, and the Norwegians, like the Icelanders, were compelled to abandon piracy. That which had been the employment of noblemen and gentlemen in that country, soon became disreputable, and was no longer permitted. It became disreputable, and was at once given up by the mass of the nation.

The same thing is happening with regard to slavery every day. You know very well who introduced slavery into this country; Christopher Columbus,—the foremost man in the world of his time. After his discovery, he sent back three ships loaded with slaves to Ferdinand and Queen Isabella, to pay the expense of the cargoes sent out. Soon after, Bartholomew Columbus, his brother, sent out other vessels loaded with slaves. This was in 1495. There may have been some wild hope of converting the cannibals, but it was to put an end to the abominable cruelty thus commenced, that some set about colonizing Hispaniola with African slaves.[5]

This progress of amelioration is very slow. Still we have gone forward a great way since that time. The people of the South are by their climate enervated. They have been demoralised by their vicious habits; still they are as innocent in their slaveholding as we are in our Northern vices. Yet it becomes essential, it becomes imperative, as man rises in the scale of civilization, as the ameliorating and expanding principles find effect in him;—it becomes as imperative that this institution should become discreditable, and should perish, as the old institutions which have gone before.

I consider the genius of this nation, the characterising element of it, to be self-government. Now just as long as the frame is feeble and small, and the belly is large, as it happens all over the Southern country, so long the large portion must depend upon the small portion. Tyrant and slave, will naturally be the relation between the parties. As soon as they are placed in positions where the national element, the element of the times as well as the element of this country, comes into play, such a relation cannot continue.

Mr. Wilmot! It would take millions of such men to make the 36th degree of latitude the line of slavery.[6] It is in the ordinance of the universe. Wherever a cooler climate, wherever frost—which is good alike for apples and for men—comes in, slavery cannot subsist.

I see the great and beautiful laws to which you and I are all subject, which I should be glad to unfold as they should be; but I must renounce it.[7] It should be praise enough for our friends who have carried forward this great work, friends to whom it seems to me always, the country is more and more indebted, that it is the glory of these preachers of freedom that they have strengthened the moral sense, that they have anticipated this triumph which I look upon as inevitable, and which it is not in man to retard. It is very natural to us all, perhaps, to exaggerate the importance of our services, but it is the order of Providence that we should conspire heartily in this work. In this connection, an old eastern verse occurs to me which expresses a sense which I have often wished to impress:

> 'Fool thou must be, though wisest of the wise,
> Then be the fool of virtue, not of vice.'[8]

LETTER TO
MARY MERRICK BROOKS

18 March 1851

New York, 18th March, 1851.

Dear Friend:[1]

I had more reasons than one to regret leaving home at this time, and, if my present engagements were not of two seasons' standing, I should have made every effort to relieve myself.[2] For your Liberty meeting, I think it has a certain importance just now; and, really, at this moment, it seems imperative that every lover of human rights should, in every manner, singly or socially, in private and in public, by voice and by pen—and, first of all, by substantial help and hospitality to the slave, and defending him against his hunters,— enter his protest for humanity against the detestable statute of the last Congress. I find it a subject of conversation in all cars and steamboats, and every where distributing society into two classes, according to the moral feasibility of individuals on one part, and their habitual docility to party leading on the other. I do not know how the majority of to-day will be found to decide. Sometimes people of natural probity and affection are so warped by the habit of party, and show themselves so unexpectedly callous and inhuman, that it seems we must wait for the Almighty to create a new generation, a little more keenly alive to moral impressions, before any improvement in institutions can be looked for. But, as far as I have observed, there is, on all great questions, a tide or undulation in the public mind—a series of actions and reactions. The momentary interest carries it to day; but, presently, the advocates of the liberal principle are victorious,—and the more entirely, because they had persisted unshaken under evil report. And, as justice alone satisfies every body, they are sure to prevail at last.

If the world has any reason in it, it is forever safe and successful to urge the cause of love and right. I know it is very needless to say this to you, and others like you, who cannot, if they would, help serving the truth, though all the world be gone to worship Mammon.[3] But it is the only answer I know how to make to our mathematical compatriots. So, wishing you a day of happy thoughts and sympathies on Thursday, I remain,

> Yours respectfully and gratefully,
> *R. W. Emerson.*

"ADDRESS TO THE CITIZENS OF CONCORD" ON THE FUGITIVE SLAVE LAW

3 May 1851

Fellow Citizens,[1]

I accepted your invitation to speak to you on the great question of these days, with very little consideration of what I might have to offer; for there seems to be no option. The last year has forced us all into politics, and made it a paramount duty to seek what it is often a duty to shun.

We do not breathe well. There is infamy in the air. I have a new experience. I wake in the morning with a painful sensation, which I carry about all day, and which, when traced home, is the odious remembrance of that ignominy which has fallen on Massachusetts, which robs the landscape of beauty, and takes the sunshine out of every hour. I have lived all my life in this State, and never had any experience of personal inconvenience from the laws, until now. They never came near me to my discomfort before. I find the like sensibility in my neighbors. And in that class who take no interest in the ordinary questions of party politics. There are men who are as sure indexes of the equity of legislation and of the sane state of public feeling, as the barometer is of the weight of the air; and it is a bad sign when these are discontented. For, though they snuff oppression and dishonor at a distance, it is because they are more

[handwritten annotation:] ← EXCEPT THOREAU AND ALCOTT !

impressionable: the whole population will in a short time be as painfully affected.

Every hour brings us from distant quarters of the Union the expression of mortification at the late events in Massachusetts, and at the behavior of Boston. The tameness was indeed shocking. Boston, of whose fame for spirit and character we have all been so proud; Boston, whose citizens, intelligent people in England told me, they could always distinguish by their culture among Americans; the Boston of the American Revolution, which figures so proudly in "John Adams's Diary," which the whole country has been reading;[2] Boston, spoiled by prosperity, must bow its ancient honor in the dust, and make us irretrievably ashamed. In Boston,—we have said with such lofty confidence,—no fugitive slave can be arrested;—and now, we must transfer our vaunt to the country, and say with a little less confidence,—no fugitive man can be arrested here;—at least we can brag thus until tomorrow, when the farmers also may be corrupted.

The tameness is indeed complete. It appears, the only haste in Boston, after the rescue of Shadrach last February,[3] was, who should first put his name on the list of volunteers in aid of the marshal. I met the smoothest of episcopal clergymen the other day, and allusion being made to Mr. Webster's treachery, he blandly replied, "Why, do you know I think *that* the great action of his life." It looked as if, in the city, and the suburbs, all were involved in one hot haste of terror,—presidents of colleges and professors, saints and brokers, insurers, lawyers, importers, manufacturers;—not an unpleasing sentiment, not a liberal recollection, not so much as a snatch of an old song for freedom, dares intrude on their passive obedience. The panic has paralysed the journals, with the fewest exceptions, so that one cannot open a newspaper, without being disgusted by new records of shame. I cannot read longer even the local good news. When I look down the columns at the titles of paragraphs, "Education in Massachusetts," "Board of Trade," "Art Union," "Revival of Religion," what bitter mockeries! The very convenience of property, the house and land we occupy, have lost their best value, and a man looks gloomily on his children, and thinks 'What have I done, that you should begin life in dishonor?' Every liberal study is discredited: Literature, and science appear effeminate and the hiding of the head. The college, the churches, the schools, the very shops and factories are discredited; real estate, every kind of wealth, every branch of industry, every avenue to power, suffers injury, and the value of life is reduced. Just now a friend came into my house and said, "If this law shall be repealed, I shall be glad that I have lived; if not, I shall be sorry that I was born." What kind of law is that which extorts language like this from the heart of a free and civilized people?

One intellectual benefit we owe to the late disgraces. The crisis had the illuminating power of a sheet of lightning at midnight. It showed truth. It ended a good deal of nonsense we had been wont to hear and to repeat, on the 19th April, the 17th June,[4] and the 4th July. It showed the slightness and unreliableness of our social fabric; it showed what stuff reputations are made of; what straws we dignify by office and title, and how competent we are to give counsel and help in a day of trial. It showed the shallowness of leaders; the divergence of parties from their alleged grounds; showed that men would not stick to what they had said: that the resolutions of public bodies, or the pledges never so often given and put on record of public men, will not bind them. The fact comes out more plainly, that you cannot rely on any man for the defence of truth, who is not constitutionally, or by blood and temperament, on that side. A man of a greedy and unscrupulous selfishness may maintain morals when they are in fashion: but he will not stick. However close Mr. Wolf's nails have been pared, however neatly he has been shaved, and tailored, and set up on end, and taught to say "Virtue and Religion," he cannot be relied on at a pinch: he will say, morality means pricking a vein. The popular assumption that all men loved freedom, and believed in the Christian religion, was found hollow American brag. Only persons who were known and tried benefactors are found standing for freedom: the sentimentalists went down stream. I question the value of our civilization, when I see that the public mind had never less hold of the strongest of all truths. The sense of injustice is blunted,—a sure sign of the shal-

OFFENDS HIS SENSE OF MORALITY

HONOR
TACTFULNESS
TRUTH
HONESTY
LOYALTY

lowness of our intellect. I cannot accept the railroad and telegraph in exchange for reason and charity. It is not skill in iron locomotives that marks so fine civility as the jealousy of liberty. I cannot think the most judicious tubing a compensation for metaphysical debility. What is the use of admirable law-forms and political forms, if a hurricane of party feeling and a combination of monied interests can beat them to the ground? What is the use of courts, if judges only quote authorities, and no judge exerts original jurisdiction, or recurs to first principles? What is the use of a Federal Bench, if its opinions are the political breath of the hour? And what is the use of constitutions, if all the guaranties provided by the jealousy of ages for the protection of liberty are made of no effect, when a bad act of Congress finds a willing commissioner?

The levity of the public mind has been shown in the past year by the most extravagant actions. Who could have believed it, if foretold, that a hundred guns would be fired in Boston on the passage of the Fugitive Slave bill?[5] Nothing proves the want of all thought, the absence of standard in men's minds more than the dominion of party. Here are humane people who have tears for misery, an open purse for want, who should have been the defenders of the poor man, are found his embittered enemies, rejoicing in his rendition,—merely from party ties. I thought none that was not ready to go on all fours, would back this law. And yet here are upright men, *compotes mentis*, husbands, fathers, trustees, friends, open, generous, brave, who can see nothing in this claim for bare humanity and the health and honor of their native state, but canting fanaticism, sedition, and "one idea." Because of this preoccupied mind, the whole wealth and power of Boston,—200,000 souls, and 180 millions of money,—are thrown into the scale of crime; and the poor black boy, whom the fame of Boston had reached in the recesses of a rice-swamp, or in the alleys of Savannah, on arriving here, finds all this force employed to catch him. The famous town of Boston is his master's hound. The learning of the Universities, the culture of elegant society, the acumen of lawyers, the majesty of the Bench, the eloquence of the Christian pulpit, the stoutness of Democracy, the respectability of the Whig party, are all combined to kidnap him.

MEANS/ENDS
KARMA

The crisis is interesting as it shows the self-protecting nature of the world, and of the divine laws. It is the law of the world as much immorality as there is, so much misery. The greatest prosperity will in vain resist the greatest calamity. You borrow the succour of the devil, and he must have his fee. He was never known to abate a penny of his rents. In every nation all the immorality that exists breeds plagues. Out of the corrupt society that exists we have never been able to combine any pure prosperity. There is always something in the very advantages of a condition which hurts it. Africa has its malformation; England has its Ireland; Germany its hatred of classes; France its love of gunpowder; Italy, its Pope; and America, the most prosperous country in the universe, has the greatest calamity in the universe, negro slavery.

Let me remind you a little in detail how the natural retributions act in reference to the statute which Congress passed a year ago. For these few months have shown very conspicuously its nature and impracticability.

It is contravened,

1. By the sentiment of duty. An immoral law makes it a man's duty to break it, at every hazard. For virtue is the very self of every man. It is therefore a principle of law, that an immoral contract is void, and that an immoral statute is void, for, as laws do not make right, but are simply declaratory of a right which already existed, it is not to be presumed that they can so stultify themselves as to command injustice.

It is remarkable how rare in the history of tyrants is an immoral law. Some color, some indirection was always used. If you take up the volumes of the "Universal History," you will find it difficult searching. The precedents are few. It is not easy to parallel the wickedness of this American law. And that is the head and body of this discontent, that the law is immoral. Here is a statute which enacts the crime of kidnapping,—a crime on one footing with arson and murder. A man's right to liberty is as inalienable as his right to life.

Pains seem to have been taken to give us in this statute a wrong pure from any mixture of right. If our resistance to this law is not right, there is no right. This is not meddling with other people's affairs: this is <u>hindering other people from meddling with us</u>. This is not going crusading into Virginia and Georgia after slaves, who, it is alleged, are very comfortable where they are:—that amiable argument falls to the ground: but this is befriending in our own state, on our own farms, a man who has taken the risk of being shot, or burned alive, or cast into the sea, or starved to death, or suffocated in a wooden box, to get away from his driver; and this man who has run the gauntlet of a thousand miles for his freedom, the statute says, you men of Massachusetts shall hunt, and catch, and send back again to the dog-hutch he fled from.

It is contrary to the primal sentiment of duty, and therefore all men that are born are, in proportion to their power of thought and their moral sensibility, found to be the natural enemies of this law. <u>The resistance of all moral beings is secured to it.</u> I had thought, I confess, what must come at last would come at first, a banding of all men against the authority of this statute. I thought it a point on which all sane men were agreed, that the law must respect the public morality. I thought that all men of all conditions had been made sharers of a certain experience, that in certain rare and retired moments they had been made to see how man is man, or what makes the essence of rational beings, namely, that, whilst animals have to do with eating the fruits of the ground, men have to do with rectitude, with benefit, with truth, with something which *is*, independent of appearances: and that this tie makes the substantiality of life, this, and not their ploughing or sailing, their trade or the breeding of families. I thought that every time a man goes back to his own thoughts, these angels receive him, talk with him, and, that, in the best hours, he is uplifted in virtue of this essence, into a peace and into a power which the material world cannot give: that these moments counterbalance the years of drudgery, and that this owning of a law, be it called morals, religion, or godhead, or what you will, constituted the explanation of life, the excuse and indemnity for the errors and calamities which sadden it. In long years consumed in trifles they remember these moments, and are consoled. I thought it was this fair mystery, whose foundations are hidden in eternity, which made the basis of human society, and of law; and that to pretend any thing else, as, that the acquisition of property was the end of living, was to confound all distinctions, to make the world a greasy hotel, and, instead of noble motives and inspirations, and a heaven of companions and angels around and before us, to leave us in a grimacing menagerie of monkeys and idiots. All arts, customs, societies, books, and laws, are good as they foster and concur with this spiritual element; all men are beloved as they raise us to it; all are hateful as they deny or resist it. The laws especially draw their obligation only from their concurrence with it.

I am surprised that lawyers can be so blind as to suffer the principles of law to be discredited. A few months ago, in my dismay at hearing that the Higher Law was reckoned a good joke in the courts, I took pains to look into a few law-books. I had often heard that the Bible constituted a part of every technical law-library, and that it was a principle in law that immoral laws are void. I found accordingly, that the great jurists, Cicero, Grotius, Coke, Blackstone, Burlamaqui, Montesquieu, Vattel, Burke, Mackintosh, Jefferson, do all affirm this.[6]

I have no intention to recite these passages I had marked:—such citation indeed seems to be something cowardly, for no reasonable person needs a quotation from Blackstone to convince him that white cannot be legislated to be black, and shall content myself with reading a single passage.

Blackstone admits the sovereignty "antecedent to any positive precept of the law of nature" among whose principles are, "that we should live honestly, should hurt nobody, and should render unto every one his due," etc. *"No human laws are of any validity, if contrary to this."* "Nay, if any human law should allow or enjoin us to commit a crime" (his instance is murder) "we are bound to transgress that human law; or else we must offend both the natural and divine."

Lord Coke held, that where an act of parliament is against common right and reason, the common law shall control it, and adjudge it to be void. Chief Justice Hobart, Chief Justice Holt, and Chief Justice Mansfield held the same.[7] Lord Mansfield in the case of the slave Somerset, wherein the dicta of Lords Talbot and Hardwicke had been cited to the effect of carrying back the slave to the West Indies, said, "I care not for the supposed *dicta* of judges, however eminent, if they be contrary to all principle." Even the Canon Law says, (in malis promissis non expedit servare fidem) "neither allegiance nor oath can bind to obey that which is wrong." Vattel is equally explicit. "No engagement (to a sovereign) can oblige or even authorize a man to violate the laws of nature." All authors who have any conscience or modesty, agree, that a person ought not to obey such commands as are evidently contrary to the laws of God. Those governors of places who bravely refused to execute the barbarous orders of Charles IX. to the famous St. Bartholomew's, have been universally praised; and the court did not dare to punish them, at least, openly. "Sire," said the brave Orte, governor of Bayonne, in his letter; "I have communicated your majesty's command to your faithful inhabitants and warriors in the garrison, and I have found there only good citizens, and brave soldiers; not one hangman: therefore, both they and I most humbly entreat your majesty, to be pleased to employ your arms and lives in things that are possible, however hazardous they may be, and we will exert ourselves to the last drop of our blood."[8]

The practitioners should guard this dogma well, as the palladium of the profession, as their anchor in the respect of mankind; against a principle like this, all the arguments of Mr. Webster are the spray of a child's squirt against a granite wall.

2. It is contravened by all the sentiments. How can a law be enforced that fines pity, and imprisons charity? As long as men have bowels, they will disobey. You know that the Act of Congress of September 18, 1850, is a law which every one of you will break on the earliest occasion. There is not a manly whig, or a manly democrat, of whom, if a slave were hidden in one of our houses from the hounds, we should not ask with confidence to lend his wagon in aid of his escape, and he would lend it. The man would be too strong for the partisan.

And here I may say that it is absurd, what I often hear, to accuse the friends of freedom in the north with being the occasion of the new stringency of the southern slave-laws. If you starve or beat the

orphan, in my presence, and I accuse your cruelty, can I help it?
In the words of Electra, in the Greek tragedy,

> "'Tis you that say it, not I. You do the deeds,
> And your ungodly deeds find me the words."[9]

Will you blame the ball for rebounding from the floor; blame the
air for rushing in where a vacuum is made or the boiler for exploding
under pressure of steam? These facts are after the laws of the world,
and so is it law, that, when justice is violated, anger begins. The
very defence which the God of Nature has provided for the innocent
against cruelty, is the sentiment of indignation and pity in the bosom
of the beholder. Mr. Webster tells the President, that "he has been
in the north, and he has found no man whose opinion is of any
weight who is opposed to the law." Ah! Mr. President, trust not
the information. The gravid old universe goes spawning on; the
womb conceives and the breasts give suck to thousands and millions
of hairy babes formed not in the image of your statute, but in the
image of the universe; too many to be bought off; too many than
that they can be rich, and therefore peaceable; and necessitated to
express first or last every feeling of the heart. You can keep no
secret, for, whatever is true, some of them will unseasonably say.
You can commit no crime, for they are created in their sentiments
conscious of and hostile to it; and, unless you can suppress the
newspaper, pass a law against bookshops, gag the English tongue
in America, all short of this is futile. This dreadful English speech
is saturated with songs, proverbs, and speeches that flatly contradict
and defy every line of Mr. Mason's statute.[10] Nay, unless you can
draw a sponge over those seditious ten commandments which are
the root of our European and American civilization; and over that
eleventh commandment, "Do unto others as you would have others
do to you," your labor is vain.

3. It is contravened by the written laws themselves, because the
sentiments, of course, write the statutes. Laws are merely declaratory of the natural sentiments of mankind and the language of all
permanent laws will be in contradiction to any immoral enactment:
And thus it happens here: statute fights against statute. By the law

of Congress, March 2, 1807, it is piracy and murder punishable with death, to enslave a man on the coast of Africa.[11] By law of Congress, September 1850, it is a high crime and misdemeanor punishable with fine and imprisonment to resist the re-enslaving of a man on the coast of America. Off soundings, it is piracy and murder to enslave him. On soundings, it is fine and prison not to re-enslave. What kind of legislation is this? What kind of Constitution which covers it? And yet the crime which the second law ordains is greater that the crime which the first law forbids under penalty of the gibbet. For it is a greater crime to re-enslave a man who has shown himself fit for freedom, that to enslave him at first, when it might be pretended to be a mitigation of his lot as a captive in war.

4. It is contravened by the mischiefs it operates. A wicked law can not be executed by good men, and must be by bad. Flagitious men must be employed, and every act of theirs is a stab at the public peace. It cannot be executed at such a cost, and so it brings a bribe in its hand. This law comes with infamy in it, and out of it. It offers a bribe in its own clauses for the consummation of the crime. To serve it, low and mean people are found by the groping of the government. No government ever found it hard to pick up tools for base actions. If you cannot find them in the huts of the poor, you shall find them in the palaces of the rich. Vanity can buy some, ambition others, and money others. The first execution of the law, as was inevitable, was a little hesitating; the second was easier; and the glib officials became, in a few weeks, quite practiced and handy at stealing men.

But worse, not the officials alone are bribed, but the whole community is solicited. The scowl of the community is attempted to be averted by the mischievous whisper, "Tariff and southern market, if you will be quiet; no tariff and loss of southern market, if you dare to murmur." I wonder that our acute people who have learned that the cheapest police is dear schools, should not find out that an immoral law costs more than the loss of the custom of a southern city.

The humiliating scandal of great men warping right into wrong was followed up very fast by the cities. New York advertised in southern markets, that it would go for slavery, and posted the names of merchants who would not. Boston, alarmed, entered into the same design. Philadelphia, more fortunate, had no conscience at all, and, in this auction of the rights of mankind, rescinded all its legislation against slavery. And the "Boston Advertiser" and the "Courier," in these weeks, urge the same course on the people of Massachusetts.[12] Nothing remains in this race of roguery, but to coax Connecticut or Maine to out-bid us all by adopting slavery into its constitution.

Economics

Great is the mischief of a legal crime. Every person who touches this business is contaminated. There has not been in our lifetime another moment when public men were personally lowered by their political action. But here are gentlemen whose believed probity was the confidence and fortification of multitudes, who, by fear of public opinion, or, through the dangerous ascendancy of southern manners, have been drawn into the support of this foul business. We poor men in the country who might once have thought it an honor to shake hands with them, or to dine at their boards, would now shrink from their touch, nor could they enter our humblest doors. You have a law which no man can obey, or abet the obeying, without loss of self-respect and forfeiture of the name of a gentleman. What shall we say of the functionary by whom the recent rendition was made? If he has rightly defined his powers, and has no authority to try the case, but only to prove the prisoner's identity, and remand him, what office is this for a reputable citizen to hold? No man of honor can sit on that bench. It is the extension of the planter's whipping-post: and its incumbents must rank with a class from which the turnkey, the hangman, and the informer are taken,—necessary functionaries, it may be, in a state, but to whom the dislike and the ban of society universally attaches.

Attacks the Judicial System and Judges

5. These resistances appear in the history of the statute, in the retributions which speak so loud in every part of this business, that I think a tragic poet will know how to make it a lesson for all ages.

Mr. Webster's measure was, he told us, final. It was a pacification, it was a suppression, a measure of conciliation and adjustment.

These were his words at different times: "there was to be no parleying more"; it was "irrepealable." Does it look final now? His final settlement has dislocated the foundations. The statehouse shakes like a tent. His pacification has brought all the honesty in every house, all scrupulous and good-hearted men, all women, and all children, to accuse the law. It has brought United States' swords into the streets, and chains round the courthouse. "A measure of pacification and union." What is its effect? To make one sole subject for conversation and painful thought throughout the continent, namely, slavery. There is not a man of thought or of feeling, but is concentrating his mind on it. There is not a clerk but recites its statistics; not a politician, but is watching its incalculable energy in the elections; not a jurist but is hunting up precedents; not a moralist but is prying into its quality; not an economist but is computing its profit and loss; Mr. Webster can judge whether this sort of solar microscope brought to bear on his law is likely to make opposition less.

The only benefit that has accrued from the law is its service to the education. It has been like a university to the entire people. It has turned every dinner-table into a debating club, and made every citizen a student of natural law. When a moral quality comes into politics, when a right is invaded, the discussion draws on deeper sources; general principles are laid bare, which cast light on the whole frame of society. And it is cheering to behold what champions the emergency called to this poor black boy; what subtlety, what logic, what learning, what exposure of the mischief of the law, and, above all, with what earnestness and dignity the advocates of freedom were inspired. It was one of the best compensations of this calamity.

But the Nemesis works underneath again. It is a power that makes noonday dark, and draws us on to our undoing; and its dismal way is to pillory the offender in the moment of his triumph. The hands that put the chain on the slave are in that moment manacled. Who has seen anything like that which is now done?

The words of John Randolph, wiser than he knew, have been ringing ominously in all echoes for thirty years,—words spoken in the heat of the Missouri debate. "We do not govern the people of the north by our black slaves, but by their own white slaves. We know what we are doing. We have conquered you once, and we can and will conquer you again. Aye, we will drive you to the wall, and when we have you there once more, we will keep you there, and nail you down like base money." These words resounding ever since from California to Oregon, from Cape Florida to Cape Cod, come down now like the cry of Fate, in the moment when they are fulfilled. By white slaves, by a white slave, are we beaten. Who looked for such ghastly fulfilment, or to see what we see? Hills and Hallets,[13] servile editors by the hundred, we could have spared. But him, our best and proudest, the first man of the north in the very moment of mounting the throne, irresistibly taking the bit in his mouth, and the collar on his neck, and harnessing himself to the chariot of the planters,—

The fairest American fame ends in this filthy law. Mr. Webster cannot choose but regret his loss. He must learn that those who make fame accuse him with one voice; that those who have no points to carry that are not identical with public morals and generous civilization, that the obscure and private who have no voice and care for none, so long as things go well, but who feel the disgrace of the new legislation creeping like a miasma into their homes, and blotting the daylight,—those to whom his name was once dear and honored, as the manly statesman to whom the choicest gifts of nature had been accorded, disown him: that he who was their pride in the woods and mountains of New England, is now their mortification,—they have torn down his picture from the wall, they have thrust his speeches into the chimney. No roars of New York mobs can drown this voice in Mr. Webster's ear. It will outwhisper all the salvos of the "Union Committee's" cannon. But I have said too much on this painful topic. I will not pursue that bitter history.

But passing from the ethical to the political view, I wish to place this statute, and we must use the introducer and substantial author of the bill as an illustration of the history.

I have as much charity for Mr. Webster, I think, as any one has.

I need not say how much I have enjoyed his fame. Who has not helped to praise him? Simply, he was the one eminent American of our time, whom we could produce as a finished work of nature. We delighted in his form and face, in his voice, in his eloquence, in his power of labor, in his concentration, in his large understanding, in his daylight statement, simple force; the facts lay like strata of a cloud, or like the layers of the crust of the globe. He saw things as they were, and he stated them so. He has been by his clear perception and statement, in all these years, the best head in Congress, and the champion of the interests of the northern seaboard.

But as the activity and growth of slavery began to be offensively felt by his constituents, the senator became less sensitive to these evils. They were not for him to deal with: he was the commercial representative. He indulged occasionally in excellent expression of the known feeling of the New England people: but, when expected and when pledged, he omitted to speak, and he omitted to throw himself into the movement in those critical moments when his leadership would have turned the scale. At last, at a fatal hour, this sluggishness accumulated to downright counteraction, and, very unexpectedly to the whole Union, on the 7th March, 1850, in opposition to his education, association, and to all his own most explicit language for thirty years, he crossed the line, and became the head of the slavery party in this country.

Mr. Webster perhaps is only following the laws of his blood and constitution. I suppose his pledges were not quite natural to him. Mr. Webster is a man who lives by his memory, a man of the past, not a man of faith or of hope. He obeys his powerful animal nature;—and his finely developed understanding only works truly and with all its force, when it stands for animal good; that is, for property. He believes, in so many words, that government exists for the protection of property. He looks at the Union as an estate, a large farm, and is excellent in the completeness of his defence of it so far. He adheres to the letter. Happily, he was born late,—after the independence had been declared, the Union agreed to, and the Constitution settled. What he finds already written, he will defend. Lucky that so much had got well written when he came. For he

[handwritten marginal note: CAN'T LET WEBSTER GET OFF THAT EASY]

has no faith in the power of self-government; none whatever in extemporising a government. Not the smallest municipal provision, if it were new, would receive his sanction. In Massachusetts, in 1776, he would, beyond all question, have been a refugee. He praises Adams and Jefferson; but it is a past Adams and Jefferson that his mind can entertain. A present Adams and Jefferson he would denounce. So with the eulogies of liberty in his writings,— they are sentimentalism and youthful rhetoric. He can celebrate it, but it means as much from him as from Metternich or Talleyrand.[14] This is all inevitable from his constitution. All the drops of his blood have eyes that look downward. It is neither praise nor blame to say that he has no moral perception, no moral sentiment, but, in that *region*, to use the phrase of the phrenologists, a hole in the head.[15] The scraps of morality to be gleaned from his speeches are reflections of the minds of others. He says what he hears said, but often makes signal blunders in their use.

The destiny of this country is great and liberal, and is to be greatly administered. It is to be administered according to what is, and is to be, and not according to what is dead and gone. The Union of this people is a real thing, an alliance of men of one stock, one language, one religion, one system of manners and ideas. I hold it to be a real and not a statute Union. The people cleave to the Union, because they see their advantage in it, the added power of each.

I suppose the Union can be left to take care of itself. As much real Union as there is, the statutes will be sure to express. As much disunion as there is, no statutes can long conceal. Under the Union I suppose the fact to be that there are really two nations, the north and the south. It is not slavery that severs them, it is climate and temperament. The south does not like the north, slavery or no slavery, and never did. The north likes the south well enough, for it knows its own advantages. I am willing to leave them to the facts. If they continue to have a binding interest, they will be pretty sure to find it out: if not, they will consult their peace in parting. But one thing appears certain to me, that, as soon as the Constitution ordains an immoral law, it ordains disunion. The law is suicidal, and cannot be obeyed. The Union is at an end as soon as an immoral law is enacted. And he who writes a crime into the statute-book digs under the foundations of the capitol to plant there a powder magazine, and lays a train.

Nothing seems to me more hypocritical than the bluster about the Union. A year ago we were all lovers of the Union, and valued so dearly what seemed the immense destinies of this country, that we reckoned an impiety any act that compromised them. But in the new attutude in which we find ourselves the personal dishonor which now rests on every family in Massachusetts, the sentiment is changed. No man can look his neighbor in the face. We sneak about with the infamy of crime, and cowardly allowance of it on our parts, and frankly, once for all, the Union, such an Union, is intolerable. The flag is an insult to ourselves. The Union,—I give you the sentiment of every decent citizen—The Union! O yes, I prized that, other things being equal; but what is the Union to a man self-condemned, with all sense of self-respect and chance of fair fame cut off, with the names of conscience and religion become bitter ironies, and liberty the ghastly mockery which Mr. Webster means by that word. The worst mischiefs that could follow from secession and new combination of the smallest fragments of the wreck, were slight and medicable to the calamity your Union has brought us.

It did not at first appear, and it was incredible, that the passage of the law would so absolutely defeat its proposed objects: but from the day when it was attempted to be executed in Massachusetts, this result has become certain, that the Union is no longer desireable. Whose deed is that?

I pass to say a few words to the question, What shall we do?

1. What in our federal capacity in our relation to the nation?

2. And what as citizens of a state?

I am an Unionist as we all are, or nearly all, and <u>I strongly share the hope of mankind in the power, and, therefore, in the duties of the Union; and I conceive it demonstrated,—the necessity of common sense and justice entering into the laws.</u>

REFORM
REMEDY

What shall we do? First, abrogate this law; then proceed to

confine slavery to slave states, and help them effectually to make an end of it. Or shall we, as we are advised on all hands, lie by, and wait the progress of the census? But will Slavery lie by? I fear not. She is very industrious, gives herself no holidays. No proclamations will put her down. She got Texas, and now will have Cuba, and means to keep her majority. The experience of the past gives us no encouragement to lie by.

Shall we call a new convention, or will any expert statesman furnish us a plan for the summary or gradual winding up of slavery, so far as the Republic is its patron? Where is the South itself? Since it is agreed by all sane men of all parties (or was yesterday) that slavery is mischievous, why does the South itself never offer the smallest counsel of her own? I have never heard in twenty years any project except Mr. Clay's.[16] Let us hear any project with candor and respect. Is it impossible to speak of it with reason and good nature? It is really the project fit for this country to entertain and accomplish. Every thing invites to emancipation. The grandeur of the design; the vast stake we hold; the national domain; the new importance of Liberia;[17] the manifest interests of the slave states; the religious effort of the free states; the public opinion of the world;—all join to demand it. It is said, it will cost a thousand millions of dollars to buy the slaves,—which sounds like a fabulous price. But if a price were named in good faith,—with the other elements of a practicable treaty in readiness, and with the convictions of mankind on this mischief once well awake and conspiring, I do not think any amount that figures could tell, founded on an estimate, would be quite unmanageable. Every man in the world might give a week's work to sweep this mountain of calamities out of the earth.

Nothing is impracticable to this nation, which it shall set itself to do. Were ever men so endowed, so placed, so weaponed? Their power of territory seconded by a genius equal to every work. By new arts the earth is subdued, roaded, tunneled, telegraphed, gas-lighted; vast amounts of old labor disused; the sinews of man being relieved by sinews of steam. We are on the brink of more wonders.

The sun paints: presently we shall organize the echo, as now we do the shadow. Chemistry is extorting new aids. The genius of this people, it is found, can do anything which can be done by men. These thirty nations are equal to any work, and are every moment stronger. In twenty-five years, they will be fifty millions. Is it not time to do something besides ditching and draining, and making the earth mellow and friable? Let them confront this mountain of poison,—bore, blast, excavate, pulverize, and shovel it once for all, down into the bottomless Pit. A thousand millions were cheap.

But grant that the heart of financiers, accustomed to practical figures, shrinks within them at these colossal amounts, and the embarrassments which complicate the problem. Granting that these contingencies are too many to be spanned by any human geometry, and that these evils are to be relieved only by the wisdom of God working in ages,—and by what instruments,—whether Liberia, whether flax-cotton, whether the working out this race by Irish and Germans, none can tell, or by what scourges God has guarded his law; still the question recurs, What must we do? One thing is plain, we cannot answer for the Union, but we must keep Massachusetts true. It is of unspeakable importance that she play her honest part. She must follow no vicious examples. Massachusetts is a little State. Countries have been great by ideas. Europe is little, compared with Asia and Africa. Yet Asia and Africa are its ox and its ass. Europe, the least of all the continents, has almost monopolized for twenty centuries the genius and power of them all. Greece was the least part of Europe. Attica a little part of that,—one tenth of the size of Massachusetts. Yet that district still rules the intellect of men. Judaea was a petty country. Yet these two, Greece and Judaea, furnish the mind and the heart by which the rest of the world is sustained. And Massachusetts is little, but, if true to itself, can be the brain which turns about the behemoth. I say Massachusetts, but I mean Massachusetts in all the quarters of her dispersion; Massachusetts, as she is the mother of all the New England states, and as she sees her progeny scattered over the face of the land, in the farthest south and the uttermost west.

The immense power of rectitude is apt to be forgotten in politics. But they who have brought this great wrong on the country have not forgotten it. They avail themselves of the known probity and honor of Massachusetts, to endorse the statute. The ancient maxim still holds that never was any injustice effected except by the help of justice. The great game of the government has been win the sanction of Massachusetts to the crime. Hitherto they have succeeded only so far as to win Boston to a certain extent. The behaviour of Boston was the reverse of what it should have been: it was supple and officious, and it put itself into the base attitude of pander to the crime. It should have placed obstruction at every step. Let the attitude of the state be firm. Let us respect the Union to all honest ends. But also respect an older and wider union, the law of nature and rectitude. Massachusetts is as strong as the universe, when it does that. We will never intermeddle with your slavery,—but you can in no wise be suffered to bring it to Cape Cod and Berkshire. This law must be made inoperative. It must be abrogated and wiped out of the statute book; but, whilst it stands there, it must be disobeyed.

We must make a small State great, by making every man in it true. It was the praise of Athens, "she could not lead countless armies into the field, but she knew how with a little band to defeat those who could." Every Roman reckoned himself at least a match for a province. Every Dorian did. Every Englishman in Australia, in South Africa, in India, or in whatever barbarous country their forts and factories have been set up,—represents London, represents the art, power, and law of Europe. Every man educated at the northern schools carries the like advantages into the south. For it is confounding distinctions to speak of the geographic sections of this country as of equal civilization. Every nation and every man bows, in spite of himself, to a higher mental and moral existence; and the sting of the late disgraces is, that this royal position of Massachusetts was foully lost, that the well-known sentiment of her people was not expressed. Let us correct this error. In this one fastness, let truth be spoken, and right done. Here let there be no confusion in our ideas. Let us not lie, nor steal, nor help to steal; and let us not call stealing by any fine names, such as "union" or "patriotism." Let us know, that not by the public, but by ourselves, our safety

71

must be bought. That is the secret of southern power, that they rest not in meetings, but in private heats and courages. It is very certain from the perfect guaranties in the Constitution, and the high arguments of the defenders of liberty, which the occasion called out, that there is sufficient margin in the statute and the law for the spirit of the magistrate to show itself, and one, two, three occasions have just now occurred and passed, in either of which, if one man had felt the spirit of Coke or Mansfield or Parsons,[18] and read the law with the eye of freedom, the dishonor of Massachusetts had been prevented, and a limit set to these encroachments forever.

The Fugitive Slave Law

7 March 1854

I do not often speak to public questions.[1] They are odious and hurtful and it seems like meddling or leaving your work. I have my own spirits in prison,—spirits in deeper prisons, whom no man visits, if I do not. And then I see what havoc it makes with any good mind this dissipated philanthropy. The one thing not to be forgiven to intellectual persons is not to know their own task, or to take their ideas from others and believe in the ideas of others. From this want of manly rest in their own, and foolish acceptance of other people's watchwords, comes the imbecility and fatigue of their conversation. For they cannot affirm these from any original experience, and, of course, not with the natural movement and whole power of their nature and talent, but only from their memory, only from the cramp position of standing for their teacher.—They say, what they would have you believe, but which they do not quite know.

My own habitual view is to the well-being of students or scholars, and it is only when the public event affects them, that it very seriously affects me. And what I have to say is to them. For every man speaks mainly to a class whom he works with, and more or less fitly represents. It is to them I am beforehand related and engaged,—in this audience or out of this audience,—to them and not to others. And yet when I say the class of scholars and students,—that is a class which comprises in some sort all mankind,—comprises every man in the best hours of his life:—and in these days not only virtually, but actually. For who are the readers and thinkers of 1854?

Owing to the silent revolution which the newspaper has wrought, this class has come in this country to take in all classes. Look into the morning trains, which, from every suburb carry the businessmen into the city, to their shops, counting-rooms, work-yards, and warehouses. With them, enters the car the humble priest of politics, philosophy, and religion in the shape of the newsboy. He unfolds his magical sheets, two pence a head his bread of knowledge costs, and instantly the entire rectangular assembly fresh from their breakfast, are bending as one man to their second breakfast. There is, no doubt, chaff enough, in what he brings, but there is fact and thought and wisdom in the crudeness from all regions of the world.

Now I have lived all my life without suffering any known inconvenience from American slavery. I never saw it; never heard the whip; I never felt the check on my free speech and action; until the other day when Mr. Webster by his personal influence brought the Fugitive Slave law on the country. I say Mr. Webster, for though the bill was not his, yet it is notorious that he was the life and soul of it, that he gave all he had, it cost him his life. And under the shadow of his great name, inferior men sheltered themselves, and threw their ballots for it, and made the law. I say inferior men; there were all sorts of what are called brilliant men, accomplished men, men of high office, a President of the United States, senators, and of eloquent speech, but men without self-respect, without character, and it was droll to see that office, age, fame, talent, even a repute for honesty, all count for nothing. They had no opinions, they had no memory for what they had been saying like the Lord's prayer, all their lifetime; they were only looking to what their great captain did, and if he jumped, they jumped,—if he stood on his head, they did. In ordinary, the supposed sense of their district and state is their guide, and this keeps them to liberty and justice. But it is always a little difficult to decipher what this public sense is:

74

and when a great man comes, who knots up into himself the opinions and wishes of his people, it is so much easier to follow him as an exponent of this. He, too, is responsible, they will not be. It will always suffice to say,—I followed him. I saw plainly that the great show their legitimate power in nothing more than in their power to misguide us. I saw that a great man, deservedly esteemed and admired for his powers and their general right direction, was able, fault of the total want of stamina in public men, when he failed, to break them all with him, to carry parties with him.

It showed much. It ended a great deal of nonsense we had been accustomed to hear and to repeat, on the 22nd December,[2] 19th April, 17th June, and 4th July. It showed what reputations are made of; what straw we dignify by office and title, and how competent they are to give counsel and help in a day of trial: the shallowness of leaders; showed the divergence of parties from their alleged grounds, and that men would not stick to what they had said: that the resolutions of public bodies, and the pledges never so often given and put on record, of public men,— will not bind them. The fact comes out more plainly, that you cannot rely on any man for the defence of truth who is not constitutionally, or by blood and temperament, on that side.

[margin note: REPEATED]

In what I have to say of Mr. Webster I do not confound him with vulgar politicians of his own time or since. There is always base ambition enough, men who calculate on the immense ignorance of masses of men;—that is their quarry and farm,—they use the constituencies at home only for their shoes. And of course they can drive out from the contest any honorable man. The low can best win the low, and all men like to be made much of. There are those too who have power and inspiration only to do ill. Their talent or their faculty deserts them when they undertake anything right.

Mr. Webster had a natural ascendancy of aspect and carriage, which distinguished him over all his contemporaries. His countenance, his figure, and his manners, were all in so grand a style, that he was, without effort, as superior to his most eminent rivals, as they were to the humblest, so that his arrival in any place was an event which drew crowds of people, who went to satisfy their eyes, and could not see him enough. I think they looked at him as the representative of the American continent. He was there in his Adamitic capacity, as if he alone of all men did not disappoint the eye and ear, but was a fit figure in the landscape. I remember his appearance at Bunker Hill.[3] There was the monument, and here was Webster. He knew well that a little more or less of rhetoric signified nothing; he was only to say plain and equal things;—grand things, if he had them,—and, if he had them not, only to abstain from saying unfit things;—and the whole occasion was answered by his presence. It was a place for behavior, much more than for speech; and Webster walked through his part with entire success.

His wonderful organization, the perfection of his elocution,—and all that thereto belongs,—voice, accent, intonation, attitude, manner, we shall not soon find again. Then he was so thoroughly simple and wise in his rhetoric,—he saw through his matter,—hugged his fact so close,—went to the principal or essential, and never indulged in a weak flourish, though he knew perfectly well how to make such exordiums, episodes, and perorations, as might give perspective to his harangue, without in the least embarrassing his march, or confounding his transitions. In his statement, things lay in daylight;—we saw them in order as they were. Though he knew very well how to present his own personal claims, yet in his argument he was intellectual, and stated his fact pure of all personality, so that his splendid wrath, when his eyes became lamps, was the wrath of the fact and cause he stood for. His power, like that of all great masters, was not in excellent parts, but was total. He had a great and everywhere equal propriety. He worked with that closeness of adhesion to the matter in hand, which a joiner or a chemist uses. And the same quiet and sure feeling of right to his place that an oak or a mountain have to theirs.

After all his talents have been described, there remains that perfect propriety which animated all the details of the action or speech with the character of the whole, so that his beauties of detail are endless. He seemed born for the bar, born for the senate, and took very naturally a leading part in large private and in public affairs; for his head distributed things in their right places, and what he saw so well, he compelled other people to see also. Ah! great is the privilege of eloquence. What gratitude does every human being feel to him who speaks well for the right,—who translates truth into language entirely plain and clear!

The history of this country has given a disastrous importance to the defects of this great man's mind. Whether evil influences and the corruption of politics, or whether original infirmity, it was the misfortune of this country that with this large understanding, he had not what is better than intellect, and the essential source of its health. It is the office of the moral nature to give sanity and right direction to the mind, to give centrality and unity.

HEALTH

Now it is a law of our nature that great thoughts come from the heart. It was for this reason I may here say as I have said elsewhere that the moral is the occult fountain of genius,—the sterility of thought, the want of generalization in his speeches, and the curious fact, that, with a general ability that impresses all the world, there is not a single general remark, not an observation on life and manners, not a single valuable aphorism that can pass into literature from his writings.

Four years ago tonight, on one of those critical moments in history when great issues are determined,—when the powers of right and wrong are mustered for conflict, and it lies with one man to give a casting vote,—Mr. Webster most unexpectedly threw his whole weight on the side of slavery, and caused by his personal and official authority the passage of the Fugitive Slave Bill.

It is remarked of the Americans, that they value dexterity too much and honor too little. That the Americans praise a man by saying that he is smart than by saying that he is right.

Now whether this defect be national or not, it is the defect and calamity of Mr. Webster and it is so far true of his countrymen that namely, they appeal to physical and mental ability, when his character is assailed. And his speeches on the 7th March, and at Albany, Buffalo, Syracuse, and Boston, are cited in justification.[4] And Mr. Webster's literary editor believes that it was his own wish to rest his fame on the Speech of 7 March. Now, though I have my own opinions on this 7th March discourse, and those others, and think them very transparent, and very open to criticisms, yet the *secondary* merits of a speech (i.e. its logic, its illustration, its points,) are not here in question. The primary quality of a speech is its *subject*. Nobody doubts that Daniel Webster could make a good speech. Nobody doubts that there were good and plausible things to be said on the part of the south. But this is not a question of ingenuity, not a question of syllogisms, but of sides. How came he there? There are always texts and thoughts and arguments; but it is the genius and temper of the man which decides whether he will stand for Right or for Might.

Who doubts the power of any clever and fluent man to defend either of our parties, or any cause in our courts? There was the same law in England for Jeffreys and Talbot and Yorke to read slavery out of, and for Lord Mansfield to read freedom.[5] And in this country one sees that there is always margin enough in the statute for a liberal judge to read one way, and a servile judge another. But the question which History will ask is broader.

In the final hour, when he was forced by the peremptory necessity of the closing armies to take a side, did he take the side of great principles, the side of humanity and justice, or the side of abuse and oppression and chaos? Mr. Webster decided for slavery; and *that*, when the aspect of the institution was no longer doubtful, no longer feeble and apologetic, and proposing soon to end itself, but when it was strong and aggressive and threatening an illimitable increase, then he listened to state reasons and hopes and left with much complacency, we are told, the testament of his speech to the astonished State of Massachusetts. *Vera pro gratis.*[6] A ghastly result of all those years of experience in affairs, this, that there was nothing better for the foremost man, the most American man in America, to tell his countrymen, than, that slavery was now at that strength, that they must beat down their conscience and become kidnappers for it. This was like the doleful speech falsely ascribed to the patriot Brutus, "Virtue, I have followed thee through life, and I find thee but a shadow."[7]

Here was a question of an immoral law, a question agitated for ages, and settled always in the same way by every great jurist, that an immoral law cannot be valid. Cicero, Grotius, Coke, Blackstone, Burlamaqui, Vattel, Burke, Jefferson do all affirm this, and I cite them not that they can give plainness to what is so clear, but because though lawyers and practical statesmen, they could not hide from themselves this truth. Here was the question: Are you for man, and for the good of man; or are you for the hurt and harm of man? It was a question, whether man shall be treated as leather? Whether the negroes shall be, as the Indians were in Spanish America, a species of money? Whether this institution, which is a kind of mill or factory for converting men into monkeys, shall be upheld and enlarged? And Mr. Webster and the country went for quadruped law. Immense mischief was done. People were all expecting a totally different course from Mr. Webster. If any man had in that hour possessed the weight with the country which he had acquired, he would have brought the whole country to its senses. But not a moment's pause was allowed. Angry parties went from bad to worse, and the decision of Webster was accompanied with every thing offensive to freedom and good morals.

There was something like an attempt to debauch the moral sentiment of the clergy and of the youth. The immense power of rectitude is apt to be forgotten in politics. But they who brought this great wrong on the country, did not forget it. They wished to avail themselves of the names of men of known probity and honor to endorse the statute. The ancient maxim is still true, that never was any injustice effected except by the help of justice. Burke said, "he would pardon something to the spirit of liberty"—but the opposition was sharply called *treason*, by Webster and prosecuted so. He told the people at Boston, "they must conquer their prejudices," that "agitation of the subject of Slavery must be suppressed." He did, as immoral men usually do, make very low bows to the Christian Church, and went through all the Sunday decorums; but when allusion was made to the sanctions of morality, he very frankly said, at Albany, "Some higher law, something existing somewhere between here and the third heaven,—I do not know where,"—and, if the reporters say true, this wretched atheism found some laughter in the company.

I said I had never in my life suffered before from the slave institution. It was like slavery in Africa or in Japan for me. There was a fugitive law, but it had become, or was fast becoming, a dead letter; and, by the genius and laws of Massachusetts inoperative. The new Bill made it operative; required me to hunt slaves; and it found citizens in Massachusetts willing to act as judges and captors. Moreover, it disclosed the secret of the new times; that slavery was no longer mendicant, but was become aggressive and dangerous.

The way in which the country was dragged to consent to this, and the disastrous defection on the miserable cry of *Union*, of the men of letters, of the colleges, of educated men, nay of some preachers of religion shows that our prosperity had hurt us; and we can not be shocked by crime. It showed that the old religion and the sense of right had faded and gone out; that, whilst we reckoned ourselves a highly cultivated nation, our bellies had run away with our brains, and the principles of culture and progress did not exist. For I suppose that liberty is a very accurate index in men and nations of general progress.

⌈The theory of personal liberty must always appeal to the most refined communities and to the men of the rarest perception and of delicate moral sense. For these are rights which rest on the finest sense of justice, and with every degree of civility,—it will be more truly felt and defined. A barbarous tribe of good stock will by means of their best heads secure substantial liberty. But when there is any weakness in race, as is in the black race, and it becomes in any degree matter of concession and protection from their stronger neighbors, the incompatibility and offensiveness of the wrong will, of course, be most evident to the most cultivated.⌋

For it is, is it not? the very nature of courtesy, of politeness, of religion, of love, to prefer another, to postpone oneself, to protect another from oneself? That is the distinction of the gentleman, to defend the weak, and redress the injured, as it is of the savage and the brute to usurp and use others.

In Massachusetts, as we all know, there has always existed a predominant conservative spirit. We have more money and value of every kind than other people, and wish to keep them. The plea on which freedom was resisted was Union. I went to certain serious men who had a little more reason than the rest, and inquired why they took this part. They told me candidly that they had no confidence in their strength to resist the democratic party in this country; that they saw plainly that all was going to the utmost verge of licence; each was vying with his neighbor to lead the party by proposing the worst measure, and they threw themselves on the extreme right as a drag on the wheel; that they knew Cuba would be had, and Mexico would be had, and they stood stiffly on conservatism, and as near to monarchy as they could, only to moderate the velocity with which the car was running down the precipice: in short, their theory was despair; the whig wisdom was only reprieve, a waiting to be the last devoured. They sided with Carolina or with Arkansas, only to make a show of whig strength, wherewith to resist a little longer this general ruin.

Gentlemen, I have a respect for conservatism. I know how deeply it is founded in our nature, and how idle are all attempts to shake ourselves free of it. We are all conservatives; all half whig, half democrat, in our essences; and might as well try to jump off our planet or jump out of our skins, as to escape from our whiggery. There are two forces in nature by whose antagonism we exist: the power of Fate, of Fortune, the laws of the world, the order of things, or, however else we choose to phrase it,—the material necessities, on the one hand; and Will, or Duty, or Freedom, on the other. *May* and *must:* the sense of right and duty, on one hand; and the material necessities, on the other. *May* and *must.* In vulgar politics, the Whig goes for what has been, for the old necessities, the *musts;* the reformer goes for the better, for the ideal good, for the *mays.*

But each of these parties must of necessity take in, in some manner, the principle of the other. Each wishes to cover the whole ground, to hold fast, and to advance: only, one lays the emphasis on keeping; and the other, on advancing. I, too, think the *musts* are a safe company to follow, and even agreeable. But if we are whigs, let us be whigs of nature and science, and go for *all* the necessities. Let us know that over and above all the *musts* of poverty and appetite, is the instinct of man to rise, and the instinct to love and help his brother.

Now, Gentlemen, I think we have in this hour instruction again in the simplest lesson. Events roll, millions of men are engaged, and the result is some of those first commandments which we heard in the nursery. We never get beyond our first lesson; for really the world exists, as I understand it, to teach the science of liberty which begins with liberty from fear. The events of this month are teaching one thing plain and clear, the worthlessness of good tools to bad workmen, that papers are of no use, resolutions of public meetings, platforms of conventions, no nor laws nor Constitutions any more. These are all declaratory of the will of the moment and are passed with more levity and on grounds much less honorable than ordinary business transactions in the street. You relied on the Constitution. It has not the word slave in it and very good argument has shown that it would not warrant the crimes that are done under it. That with provisions so vague, for an object *not named*, and which would not be suffered to claim a barrel of sugar or a bushel of corn, the robbing of a man and all his posterity,—is effected. You relied on the Supreme Court. The law was right; excellent law for the lambs. But what if, unhappily, the judges were chosen from the wolves? and give to all the law a wolfish interpretation?

What is the use of admirable law forms and political forms if a hurricane of party feeling and a combination of monied interests can beat them to the ground? What is the use of courts, if judges only quote authorities, and no judge exerts original jurisdiction, or recurs to first principles? What is the use of guaranties provided by the jealousy of ages for the protection of liberty,—if these are made of no effect, when a bad act of Congress finds a willing commissioner? You relied on the Missouri Compromise: that is ridden over. You relied on state sovereignty in the free states to protect their citizens. They are driven with contempt out of the courts, and out of the territory of the slave states, if they are so happy as to get out with their lives.[8] And now, you relied on these dismal guaranties infamously made in 1850, and before the body of Webster is yet crumbled,[9] it is found that they have crumbled: this eternal monument at once of his fame and of the common Union, is rotten in four years. They are no guaranty to the free states. They are a guaranty to the slave states; that as they have hitherto met with no repulse, they shall meet with none. I fear there is no reliance to be had on any kind of form or covenant, no, not on sacred forms,— none on churches, none on bibles. For one would have said that a Christian would not keep slaves, but the Christians keep slaves. Of course, they will not dare read the bible. Won't they? They quote the bible and Christ and Paul to maintain slavery.[10] If slavery is a good, then is lying, theft, arson, incest, homicide, each and all goods and to be maintained by union societies. These things show that no forms, neither Constitutions nor laws nor covenants nor churches nor bibles, are of any use in themselves; the devil nestles comfortably into them all. There is no help but in the head and heart and hamstrings of a man. Covenants are of no use without honest men to keep them. Laws are of no use, but with loyal citizens to obey them. To interpret Christ, it needs Christ in the heart. The teachings of the spirit can be apprehended only by the same spirit that gave them forth. To make good the cause of Freedom you must draw off from all these foolish trusts on others. You must be citadels and warriors, yourselves Declarations of Independence, the charter, the battle, and the victory. Cromwell said, "We can only resist the superior training of the king's soldiers, by having godly men."[11] And no man has a right to hope that the laws of New York will defend him from the contamination of slaves another day, until he has made up his mind that he will not owe his protection to the laws of New York, but to his own sense and spirit. Then he protects New York. He only who is able to stand alone, is qualified for society. And that I understand to be the end for which a soul exists in this world, to be himself the counterbalance of all falsehood and all wrong. "The army of unright is encamped from pole to pole, but the road of victory is known to the just." Everything may be taken away, he may be poor, he may be homeless, yet he will know out of his arms to make a pillow and out of his breast a bolster. Why have the minority no influence? because they have not a real minority of one.

ENDS
POWER

I conceive that thus to detach a man, and make him feel that he is to owe all to himself, is the way to make him strong and rich. And here the optimist must find if anywhere the benefit of slavery. We have many teachers. We are in this world for nothing else than Culture: to be instructed in nature, in realities; in the laws of moral and intelligent nature; and surely our education is not conducted by toys and luxuries,—but by austere and rugged masters,—by poverty, solitude, passions, war, slavery,—to know that paradise is under the shadow of swords;[12] that divine sentiments, which are always soliciting us, are breathed into us from on high and are a counterbalance to an universe of suffering and crime,—that self-reliance, the height and perfection of man, is reliance on God. The insight of the religious sentiment will disclose to him unexpected aids in the nature of things. The Persian Saadi said "Beware of hurting the orphan. When the orphan sets a crying the throne of the Almighty is rocked from side to side."[13]

FAITH

Whenever a man has come to this mind, that there is no church for him but his humble morning prayer; no constitution, but his talent of dealing well and justly with his neighbor; no liberty, but his invincible will to do right, then certain aids and allies will promptly appear. For the Eternal constitution of the universe is on his side. It is of no use to vote down gravitation or morals. What is useful will last; whilst that which is hurtful to the world will sink beneath all the opposing forces which it must exasperate. The terror which the Marseillaise thunders against oppression, thunders to-day,—

Tout est soldat pour vous combattre.

"*Everything that can walk turns soldier to fight you down.*" The end for which man was made, is not stealing, nor crime in any form. And a man cannot steal, without incurring all the penalties of the thief; no, though all the legislatures vote that it is virtuous, and though there be a general conspiracy among scholars and official persons to hold him up, and to say, *Nothing is good but stealing*. A man who commits a crime defeats the end of his existence. He was created for benefit, and he exists for harm. And as well-doing makes power and wisdom, ill-doing takes them away. A man who steals another

84

man's labor, (as a planter does,) steals away his own faculties; his integrity, his humanity is flowing away from him.

The habit of oppression cuts out the moral eyes, and though the intellect goes on simulating the moral as before, its sanity is invaded, and gradually destroyed. It takes away the presentiments.

I suppose, in general, this is allowed; that, if you have a nice question of right and wrong, you would not go with it to Louis Napoleon;[14] or to a political hack; or to a slave-driver. The habit of mind of traders in power would not be esteemed favorable to delicate moral perception. It is not true that there is any exception to that in American slavery, or that the system here has called out a spirit of generosity and self-sacrifice. No excess of good nature and of tenderness of moral constitution in individuals has been able to give a new character to the system, to tear down the whipping house. The plea that the negro is an inferior race sounds very oddly in my ear from a slave-holder. "The masters of slaves seem generally anxious to prove that they are not of a race superior in any noble quality to the meanest of their bondmen." And indeed when I hear the southerner point to the anatomy of the negro, and talk of chimpanzee,—I recall Montesquieu's remark, "It will not do to say, that negroes are men, lest it should turn out that whites were not."

I know that when seen near, and in detail, slavery is disheartening. But nature is not so helpless but it can rid itself at last of every wrong. An Eastern poet, in describing the world God made pure in the beginning, said, "that God had made justice so dear to the heart of nature, that, if any injustice lurked anywhere under the sky, the blue vault would shrivel to a snakeskin and cast it out by spasms."[15] But the spasms of nature are centuries and ages and will tax the faith of short-lived men. Slowly, slowly the avenger comes, but comes surely. The proverbs of the nations affirm these delays, but affirm the arrival. They say, "God may consent, but not forever." The delay of the Divine Justice,—this was the meaning and soul of the Greek Tragedy,—this was the soul of their religion. "There has come, too, one to whom lurking warfare is dear,— Retribution,—with a soul full of wiles, a violator of hospitality, guileful without the guilt of guile, limping, late in her arrival."[16]

"This happiness at its close begets itself an offspring, and does not die childless, and instead of good fortune, there sprouts forth for posterity ever-ravening calamity."[17]

> For evil word, shall evil word be said,
> For murderstroke, a murderstroke be paid,
> Who smites must smart.[18]

These delays,—you see them now in the temper of the times. The national spirit in this country is so drowsy, preoccupied with interest, deaf to principle. The Anglo-Saxon race is proud and strong but selfish. They believe only in Anglo-Saxons. Greece found it deaf, Poland found it so, Italy found it so, Hungary found it so. England goes for trade, not for liberty; goes against Greece, against Hungary; against Schleswig-Holstein:[19] against the French Republic whilst it was yet a republic. To faint hearts the times offer no invitation. And the like torpor exists here throughout the active classes on the subject of domestic slavery and its appalling aggressions.

Yes, that is the stern edict of Providence, that liberty shall be no hasty fruit, but that event on event, population on population, age on age, shall cast itself into the opposite scale, and not until liberty has slowly accumulated weight enough to countervail and preponderate against all this, can the sufficient recoil come. All the great cities, all the refined circles, all the statesmen,—Guizot, Palmerston, Webster, Calhoun, are sure to be found banded against liberty; they are all sure to be found befriending liberty with their words; and crushing it with their votes.

Liberty is never cheap. It is made difficult because freedom is the accomplishment and perfectness of a man. He is a finished man, earning and bestowing good, equal to the world, at home in nature and dignifying that; the sun does not see anything nobler and has nothing to teach him. Therefore mountains of difficulty must be surmounted, stern trials met, wiles of seduction, dangers, healed by a quarantine of calamities to measure his strength by before he dare say, I am free.

Whilst the inconsistency of slavery with the principles on which

the world is built guarantees its downfall, I own that the patience
it requires is almost too sublime for mortals and seems to demand
of us more than mere hoping. And when one sees how fast the rot
spreads,—it is growing serious,—I think we demand of superior
men that they shall be superior in this, that the mind and the virtue
give their verdict in their day and accelerate so far the progress of
civilization. Possession is sure to throw its stupid strength for existing power; and appetite and ambition will go for *that*. Let the aid
of virtue and intelligence and education be cast where they rightfully
belong. They are organically ours. Let them be loyal to their own.
English Earl Grey said, on a memorable occasion, "he should stand
by his order."[20] And I wish to see the instructed or illuminated class
know their own flag, and not stand for the kingdom of darkness.
We should not forgive the clergy of a country, for taking on every
issue the immoral side. Nor the Bench, if it throw itself on the side
of the culprit. Nor the Government, if it sustain the mob against
the laws. It is an immense support and ally to a brave man standing
single or with few for the right, to know, when, outvoted and
discountenanced and ostracised in that hour and place, yet better
men in other parts of the country appreciate the service, and will
rightly report him to his own age and to posterity. And without
this assurance he will sooner sink; "if they do not care to be defended," he may well say, "I too will decline the controversy, from
which I only reap invectives and hatred."

Yet the lovers of liberty may tax with reason the coldness and
indifferentism of the scholars and literary men. They are lovers of
liberty in Greece, and in Rome, and in the English Commonwealth,
but they are very lukewarm lovers of the specific liberty of America
in 1854. The universities are not now as in Hobbes's time, the core
of rebellion; no, but the seat of whiggery. They have forgotten their
allegiance to the muse and grown worldly and political. I remember
I listened, on one of those occasions when the university chooses
one of her distinguished sons returning from the political arena
believing that senators and statesmen are glad to throw off the
harness and to dip again in the Castalian pools.[21] But if audiences
forget themselves statesmen do not. The low bows to all the crock-

ery gods of the day were duly made. Only in one part of the discourse the orator allowed to transpire rather against his will a little sober sense.[22] It was this. I am as you see a man virtuously inclined and only corrupted by my profession of politics. I should prefer the right side. You gentlemen of these literary and scientific schools have the power to make your verdict clear and prevailing. Had you done so, you would have found me its glad organ and champion. Abstractly, I should have preferred that side. But you have not done it. You have not spoken out. You have failed to arm me. I can only deal with masses as I find them. Abstractions are not for me. I go then for such parties and opinions as have provided me with a working apparatus. I give you my word, not without regret, that I was first for you, and though I am now to deny and condemn you, you see it is not my will, but the party necessity. Having made this manifesto, and professed his adoration for liberty in the time of grandfathers, he proceeded with his work of denouncing freedom and freemen at the present day, much in the tone and spirit with which Lord Bacon prosecuted his benefactor Essex.[23] He denounced every name and aspect under which liberty and progress dared show itself in this age and country, but with a lingering conscience which qualified each sentence with a recommendation to mercy, death with a recommendation to mercy.

But I put to every noble and generous spirit in the land; to every poetic; to every heroic; to every religious heart; that not so is our learning, our education, our poetry, our worship to be declared, not by heads reverted to the dying Demosthenes, Luther, or Wallace, or to George Fox,[24] or to George Washington, but to the dangers and dragons that beset the United States at this time. It is not possible to extricate oneself from the questions in which your age is involved. I hate that we should be content with standing on the defensive. Liberty is aggressive. Liberty is the Crusade of all brave and conscientious men. It is the epic poetry, the new religion, the chivalry of all gentlemen. This is the oppressed Lady whom true knights on their oath and honor must rescue and save.

Now at last we are disenchanted and shall have no more false hopes. I respect the Anti-Slavery Society. It is the Cassandra that has foretold all that has befallen,[25] fact for fact, years ago,—foretold it all, and no man laid it to heart. It seemed, as the Turks say, "Fate makes that a man should not believe his own eyes." But the Fugitive Law did much to unglue the eyes of men, and now the Nebraska Bill leaves us staring. The Anti-Slavery Society will add many members this year. The Whig party will join it. The Democrats will join it. The population of the Free States will join it. I doubt not, at last, the Slave States will join it. But be that sooner or later,—and whoever comes or stays away,—I hope we have come to an end of our unbelief, have come to a belief that there is a Divine Providence in the world which will not save us but through our own co-operation.

LECTURE ON SLAVERY

25 January 1855

MEANS/ENDS?

Gentlemen,[1]

I approach the grave and bitter subject of American slavery with diffidence and pain. It has many men of ability and devotion who have consecrated their lives to it. I have not found in myself the right qualifications to serve this any more than other political questions, by my speech, and have therefore usually left it in their honored hands. I have not either the taste or the talent that is needed for the disposition of political questions, and I leave them to those who have. Still there is somewhat exceptional in this question, which seems to require of every citizen at one time or other, to show his hand, and to cast his suffrage in such manner as he uses. And, whilst I confide that heaven too has a hand in these events, and will surely give the last shape to these ends which we hew very roughly, yet I remember that our will and obedience is one of its means.

The subject seems exhausted. An honest man is soon weary of crying 'Thief!' Who can long continue to feel an interest in condemning homicide, or counterfeiting, or wife-beating? 'Tis said, endless negation is a flat affair.

One must write with a red hot iron to make any impression. I thought therefore the policy of those societies which have opened

91

HEALTH

HEALTH — PRINCIPLE

courses of instruction on the aspects of slavery, wise, when they invited southern planters, the patrons and fathers of the system, to come hither and speak for it. Nay, I think it would not have been ill-advised had they asked only such, and put the whole duty of expressing it on the slave-holders. I am sure it would have surprised northern men to see how little was to say on its behalf. But a difficulty arose in inducing them to come. The inviting committee were hospitable and urgent; but, most unfortunately, all the persons invited, with one or two brave exceptions, were absolutely pre-engaged. No solicitations were of any avail. It was left to us to open the subject, each as he could. And it is for us to treat it not as a thing that stands by itself;—that quickly tires and cloys,—but as it stands in our system;—how it can consist with the advantages and superiorities we fondly ascribe to ourselves. A high state of general health cannot coexist with a mortal disease in any part. If any one member suffers, all the members suffer. Then, again, we must find relief from the uniform gloom of the theme, in large considerations of history, whereinto slavery and war enter as necessary shadows in the vast picture of Providence.

We have to consider that, however strongly the tides of public sentiment have set or are setting towards freedom, the code of slavery in this country is at this hour more malignant than ever before. The recent action of Congress has brought it home to New England, and made it impossible to avoid complicity.

The crying facts are these, that, in a Republic professing to base its laws on liberty, and on the doctrines of Christianity, slavery is suffered to subsist: and, when the poor people who are the victims of this crime, disliking the stripping and peeling process, run away into states where this practice is not permitted,—a law has been passed requiring us who sit here to seize these poor people, tell them they have not been plundered enough, and must go back to be stripped and peeled again, and as long as they live.

But this was not yet the present grief. It was shocking to hear of the sufferings of these men: But the district was three hundred, five hundred, and a thousand miles off, and, however leagued with ours, was yet independent. And, for the national law which enacted this complicity, and threw us into conspiracy with the thief, it was an old dead law, which had been made in an hour of weakness and fear, and which we had guarded ourselves from executing,—now revived and made stringent. But there was no fear that it would be valid.

But the destitution was here. We found well-born, well-bred, well-grown men among ourselves, not outcasts, not foreigners, not beggars, not convicts, but baptised, vaccinated, schooled, high-placed, official men, who abetted this law. 'O by all means, catch the slave, and drag him back.' And when we went to the courts, the interpreters of God's right between man and man said, 'catch the slave, and force him back.'

Now this was disheartening. Slavery is an evil, as cholera or typhus is, that will be purged out by the health of the system. Being unnatural and violent, I know that it will yield at last, and go with cannibalism, tattooing, inquisition, duelling, burking; and as we cannot refuse to ride in the same planet with the New Zealander, so we must be content to go with the southern planter, and say, you are you, and I am I, and God send you an early conversion.

But to find it here in our sunlight, here in the heart of Puritan traditions in an intellectual country, in the land of schools, of sabbaths and sermons, under the shadow of the White Hills, of Katahdin, and Hoosac;[2] under the eye of the most ingenious, industrious, and self-helping men in the world,—staggers our faith in progress.

It is an accident of a larger calamity. It rests on skepticism, which is not local, but universal. The tone of society and of the press on slavery is only an index of the moral pulse. And I call slavery and the tolerance it finds, worst in this,—the stupendous frivolity it betrays in the heart and head of a society without faith, without aims, dying of inanition. An impoverishing skepticism scatters poverty, disease, and cunning through our opinions, then through practice. The Dark Ages did not know that they were dark; and what if it should turn out, that our material civilization has no sun, but only ghastly gas-lights?

I find this skepticism widely spread. Young men want object,

POWER OF ACTION

want foundation. They would gladly have somewhat to do, adequate to the powers they feel, somewhat that calls them with trumpet note to be heroes, some foeman worthy of their steel, some love that would make them greater than they are; which not finding, they take up some second-best ground, finding no first-best—they slip into some niche or crevice of the state, some counting-room or rail-road, or whatever creditable employment,—not the least of whose uses is the covert it affords. They are not supported by any sense of greatness, and this reputable office screens them from criticism.

We are led to cast shrewd glances into our society. Among intellectual men, you will find a waiting for, an impatient quest for more satisfying knowledge. It is believed that ordinarily the mind grows with the body, that the moment of thought comes with the power of action, and, that, in nations, it is in the time of great external power, that their best minds have appeared. But, in America, a great imaginative soul, a broad cosmopolitan mind, has not accompanied the immense industrial energy. Among men of thought and education, the unbelief is found as it is in the laymen. A dreary superficiality,—critics instead of thinkers, punsters instead of poets. They think the age of poetry is past. They think the Imagination belongs to the savage era. Yes and serious men are found who think our Christianity and religion itself effete;—forms and sentiments that belonged to the infancy of mankind. I say intellectual men; but are there such—if we see to what uses the Intellect is applied? I think the atheism as much shown in the absence of intellectual action, as in the absence of profound morals.

Go into the festooned and tempered brilliancy of the drawing rooms, and see the fortunate youth of both sexes, the flower of our society, for whom every favor, every accomplishment, every facility has been secured. Will you find genius and courage expanding those fair and manly forms? Or is their beauty only a mask for an aged cunning? Have they already grown worldly-wise? No illusions for them. A few cherished their early dream, and resisted to contumacy the soft appliances of fashion. But they tired of resistance and ridicule: they fell into file, and great is the congratulation of the refined companions that these self-willed protestants had settled down into sensible opinions and practices. Time was when a heroic soul conversing with eternity disdained the trifles of hard or easy lot, enamoured of honor and right.

The same career invites us. The method of nature is ever the same. God instructs men through the Imagination. But the opera-glasses of our young men do not reach to ideas and realities.

The ebb of thought drains the law, the religion, the education of the land. We send our boys to the universities. But do those institutions inspire the hope and gratitude, which, at great moments, have filled them with enthusiastic crowds? men eager to impart the light which has kindled them, and to set the whole land on flame? The boy looks at the professor and the textbook, with frightful penetration, and says, 'Has not the professor read his own books? I do not see that he is better or stronger for it all.' He looks into the stable at the horses, and, after a few trials, concludes that the horses can teach him the most. They give him health, courage, and address, with no false pretences. The horse is what he stands for: perhaps he will break the rider's neck, but he never prated of ethics or of humanity, whilst the presidents and professors of the colleges were in this very rabble that voted down the moral sentiments of mankind.

Look at our politics. The great parties coeval with the origin of the government,—do they inspire us with any exalted hope? Does the Democracy stand really for the good of the many? of the poor? for the elevation of entire humanity? Have they ever addressed themselves to the enterprize of relieving this country of the pest of slavery?

The Party of Property, of education, has resisted every progressive step. Did Free Trade come from them? Have they urged the abolition of Capital Punishment? Have they urged any of the prophetic action of the time? No. They would nail the stars to the sky. With their eyes over their shoulders, they adore their ancestors, the framers of the Constitution. *Nolumus mutari.*[3] We do not wish to touch the Constitution. They wish their age should be absolutely like the last. There is no confession of destitution like this fierce conservatism. Can any thing proclaim so loudly the absence of all aim or principle? What means this desperate grasp on the past, if not that they find no principle, no hope, no future in their own mind? Some foundation we must have, and, if we can see nothing, we cling desperately to those whom we believe can see.

Our politics have run very low, and men of character will not willingly touch them. This is fast becoming, if it has not already become, discreditable work. Those who have gone to Congress were honest well-meaning men. I heard congratulations from good men, their friends, in relation to certain recent members, that "these were honest and thoroughly trustworthy, obstinately honest." Yet they voted on the late criminal measures with the basest of the populace. They ate dirt, and saw not the sneer of the bullies who duped them with an alleged state-necessity: and all because they had no burning splendor of law in their own minds. Well, what refuge for them? They had honor enough left to feel degraded: they could have a place in which they could not preserve appearances. They become apathized and indifferentists. We leave them in their retreats. They represented the property of their constituency. Our merchants do not believe in anything but their trade. They loll in republican chairs, they eat and drink in republican Astor, Tremont, and Girard Houses.[4] They roll in easy and swift trains, telegraphing their wishes before them. And the power of money is so obtrusive as to exclude the view of the larger powers that control it.

I am sorry to say, that, even our political reforms show the same desperation. What shall we think of the new movement? We are clear that the old parties could not lead us. They were plainly bankrupt, their machineries and politicians discredited. We will have none of them. Yes, but shall we therefore abdicate our common sense? I employed false guides and they misled me; shall I therefore put my head in a bag?

The late revolution in Massachusetts no man will wonder at who sees how far our politics had departed from the path of simple right. The reigning parties had forfeited the awe and reverence which always attaches to a wise and honest government. And as they inspired no respect, they were turned out by an immense frolic.

But to persist in a joke;—I don't like joking with edge-tools, and there is no knife so sharp as legislation.

An Indian Rajah, Yokasindra, had a poor porter in his gate who resembled him in person. He put his royal robes on him, and seated him on his throne: then he put on his own head the porter's cap, and stood in the gate, and laughed to see his ministers deceived, bowing down before the porter. But Datto the porter said, "Who is that fellow there on the threshold, laughing in my face? Off with his head." They obeyed him, and decapitated the Rajah, and Datto the porter reigned in his stead.

What happens after periods of extraordinary prosperity, happened now. They could not see beyond their eye-lids, they dwell in the senses;—cause being out of sight is out of mind:—They see meat and wine, steam and machinery, and the career of wealth. I should find the same ebb of thought from all the wells alike. I should find it in science. I should find it in the philosophy of France, of England, and everywhere alike, a want of faith in laws, a worship of success. Everywhere dreary superficiality, ignorance and disbelief in principles, a civilization magnifying trifles.

I saw a man in a calico-printing-mill, who fancied there was no reason why this pattern should please, and that pattern should not. They were all jumbles of color, of which one had the luck to take, and the other had the luck not to take, and that was all. I asked him, if he had that blue jelly he called his eye, by chance?

But geometry survives, though we have forgotten it. Everything rests on foundations, alike the globe of the world, the human mind, and the calico print. The calico print pleases, because the arrangement of colors and forms agrees with the imperative requirements of the human eye. Is the reputation of the Parthenon, of the Elgin marbles, the Apollo, and the Torso, a caprice?[5] Greek architecture was made by men of correcter eyes than others, who obeyed the necessities of their work, namely, the use of the building, the necessary support, the best aspect, entrance, light, etc., and, having satisfied these conditions, pared away all that could be spared for strength,—and behold beauty.

Is the arch of the rainbow, the beauty of stars and sunshine, the joy of love, a caprice and an opinion? Or does any man suppose the reputation of Jesus accidental: the saint whom in different forms and opinions, but with unanimity of veneration as to character, the whole race of man worships? Or is the reputation of Socrates, of the Stoics, of Alfred,[6] of Luther, of Washington whimsical and unfounded?

There are periods of occulation when the light of mind seems to be partially withdrawn from nations as well as from individuals. This devastation reached its crisis in the acquiescence in slavery in this country,—in the political servitude of Europe, during the same age. And there are moments of greatest darkness, and of total eclipse. In the French Revolution, there was a day when the Parisians took a strumpet from the street, seated her in a chariot, and led her in procession, saying, "This is the Goddess of Reason." And, in 1850, the American Congress passed a statute which ordained that justice and mercy should be subject to fine and imprisonment, and that there existed no higher law in the universe than the Constitution and this paper statute which uprooted the foundations of rectitude and denied the existence of God.

Thus in society, in education, in political parties, in trade, and in labor, in expenditure, or the direction of surplus capital, you may see the credence of men; how deeply they live, how much water the ship draws. In all these, it is the thought of men, what they think, which is the helm that turns them all about. When thus explored, instead of rich belief, of minds great and wise sounding the secrets of nature, announcing the laws of science, and glowing with zeal to act and serve, and life too short to read the revelations inscribed on earth and heaven, I fear you will find non-credence, which produces nothing, but leaves sterility and littleness.

This skepticism assails a vital part when it climbs into the Courts, which are the brain of the state. The idea of abstract right exists in the human mind, and lays itself out in the equilibrium of nature, in the equalities and periods of our system, in the level of seas, in the action and reaction of forces, that nothing is allowed to exceed or absorb the rest; if it do, it is disease, and is quickly destroyed.

Among men, this limitation of my liberty by yours,—allowing

the largest liberty to each compatible with the liberty of all,—protection in seeking my benefit, as long as it does not interfere with your benefit,—is justice,—which satisfies everybody.

It was an early discovery of the human mind—this benificent rule. This law is: Render to each his own. As thou doest, shall it be done to thee. As thou sowest, thou shall reap. Smite and thou shalt smart; serve, and thou shalt be served. If you love and serve men, you cannot by any dodge or stratagem escape the remuneration. Secret retributions are always restoring the level, when disturbed, of the Divine justice. It is impossible to tilt the beam. All the tyrants and proprietors and monopolists of the world in vain set their shoulders to heave the bar:—settles forevermore the ponderous equator to its line, and man and mote and star and sun must range with it, or be pulverized by the recoil. Any attempt to violate it, is punished, and recoils on you. If you treat a man nobly, though he be of a mean habit, he will make an exception in your behalf, and will aim to do you justice. You cannot use a man as an instrument, without being used by him as an instrument. If you take advantage and steal from him, he watches his opportunity to make accounts square with you. If he is not strong enough to resist, then he will be cunning and cheat you. Lord Coke said, "Any departure from the established principles of law, although at the time wearing the specious appearance of advantage, never fails to bring along with it such train of unforeseen inconveniences, as to demonstrate their excellence, and the necessity of return to them."

Nature is not so helpless but it can rid itself at last of every crime. An Eastern poet, in describing the Golden Age, said, that God had made justice so dear to the heart of Nature, that, if any injustice lurked anywhere under the sky, the blue vault would shrivel to a snake-skin and cast it out by spasms.[7]

The fathers, in July 1787, consented to adopt population as the basis of representation, and to count only three-fifths of the slaves, and to concede the reclamation of fugitive slaves;—for the consideration, that there should be no slavery in the Northwest Territory. They agreed to this false basis of representation and to this criminal complicity of restoring fugitives: and the splendor of the bribe, namely, the magnificent prosperity of America from 1787, is their excuse for the crime. It was a fatal blunder. They should have refused it at the risk of making no Union. Many ways could have been taken. If the southern section had made a separate alliance with England, or gone back into colonies, the slaves would have been emancipated with the West Indians, and then the colonies could have been annexed to us. The bribe, if they foresaw the prosperity we have seen, was one to dazzle common men, and I do not wonder that common men excuse and applaud it. But always so much crime brings so much ruin. A little crime, a minor penalty; a great crime, a great disaster.

If the south country thinks itself enriched by slavery, read the census, read the valuation tables, or weigh the men. I think it impoverished. Young men are born in that country, I suppose, of as much ability as elsewhere, and yet some blight is on their education: in the present generation is there one living son to make good the reputation of the Past? If the north think it a benefit, I find the north saddled with a load which has all the effect of a partnership in a crime, on a virtuous and prosperous youth. It stops his mouth, ties his hands, forces him to submit to every sort of humiliation, and now it is a fountain of poison which is felt in every transaction and every conversation in this country.

Well, certain men were glad perceivers of this Right, with more clearness and steadiness than others, and labored to establish the application of it to human affairs. They were Lawgivers or Judges. And all men hailed the Laws of Menu, the Laws of Lycurgus, laws of Moses, laws of Confucius, laws of Jesus, the laws of Alfred, and of men of less fame, who in their place, believing in an ideal right, strove to make it practical,—the Code of Justinian, the famous jurists, Grotius, Vattel, Daguesseau,[8] Blackstone, and Mansfield. These were original judges, perceivers that this is no child's play, no egotistic opinion, but stands on the original law of the world. And the reputation of all the judges on earth stands on the real perception of these few natural or God-anointed judges. All these men held that law was not an opinion, not an egotism of any king or the will of any mob, but a transcript of natural right. The judge was there as its organ and expounder, and his first duty was to read the law in accordance with equity. And, if it jarred with equity, to disown the law. All the great lawgivers and jurists of the world have agreed in this, that an immoral law is void. So held Cicero, Selden, Hooker;[9] and Coke, Hobart, Holt, and Mansfield, chief justices of England. Even the Canon law says, "Neither allegiance nor oath can bind to obey that which is unlawful." Grotius, Vattel, Daguesseau, and Blackstone teach the same. Of course they do. What else could they? You cannot enact a falsehood to be true, nor a wrong act to be right.

And I name their names, not of course to add authority to a self-evident proposition, but only to show that black-letter lawyers supposed to be more than others tied to precedent and statute, saw the exquisite absurdity of enacting a crime.

And yet in America justice was poisoned at its fountain. In our northern states, no judge appeared of sufficient character and intellect to ask not whether it was constitutional, but whether it was right.

This outrage of giving back a stolen and plundered man to his thieves was ordained and under circumstances the most painful. There was enough law of the State of Massachusetts to resist the dishonor and the crime, but no judge had the heart to invoke, no governor was found to execute it. The judges feared collision of the State and the Federal Courts. The Governor[10] was a most estimable man—we all knew his sterling virtues, but he fell in an era when governors do not govern, when judges do not judge, when Presidents do not preside, and when representatives do not represent.

The judges were skeptics too and shared the sickness of the time. The open secret of the world was hid from their eyes, the art of subliming a private soul with inspirations from the great and public and divine soul from which we live. A man is a little thing whilst he works by and for himself. A judge who gives voice as a judge should, to the rules of love and justice, is godlike; his word is current in all countries. But a man sitting on the Bench servile to precedent, or a windy politician, or a dangler trying to give authority to the notions of his superiors or of his set, pipes and squeaks

POWER FROM THE LAWS OF NATURE

and cheeps ridiculously. Judges are rare, and must be born such. King James said, "O, ay, I can mak him a lord, but I canna mak him a gentleman." And governors and presidents can give a commission to sit on the Bench, but only wisdom can make a judge.

When the city is on fire, you will make but a feeble spray with your engine whilst you draw from your buckets. But once get your pipe screwed on to a hose which is dipped in the river, or in the harbor, and you can pump as long as the Atlantic Ocean holds out.

This was the hiding of the light. But the light shone, if it was intercepted from us. Truth exists, though all men should deny it. There is a sound healthy universe whatever fires or plagues or desolation transpire in diseased corners. The sky has not lost its azure because your eyes are inflamed. Seas and waters, lime and oxygen, magnesia and iron, salts and metals, are not wasted, their virtues are safe, if an individual or a species sicken. And there's a healthy interior universe as well, and men are great and powerful as they conform to, or become recipient of, the great equal general laws.

Now what is the effect of this evil government? To discredit government. When the public fails in its duty, private men take its place. When the British ministry is weak, the Times' editor governs the realm. When the American government and courts are false to their trust, men disobey the government, put it in the wrong; the government is forced into all manner of false and ridiculous attitudes. Men hear reason and truth from private men who have brave hearts and great minds. This is the compensation of bad governments,—the field it affords for illustrious men. And we have a great debt to the brave and faithful men who in the very hour and place of the evil act, made their protest for themselves and their countrymen by word and deed. They are justified, and the law is condemned.

It is not to societies that the secrets of nature are revealed, but to private persons, to each man in his organization, in his thoughts. A serious man who has used his opportunities will early discover that he only works and thinks securely when he is acting on his own experience. All forcible men will agree that books and learned societies could not supply what their own good sense taught them.

It is common to say that the invention of gunpowder has equalized the strong and the weak. Never believe it. It has not made any deep difference, and Lord Wellington's weighing the soldiers proves it.[11] Audacity and good sense have their old superiority, whatever weapons they wield. My political economy is very short, a man's capital must be in him.

'Tis a maxim in our politics that a man cannot be formidable in Congress, unless he is strong at home. I am glad to hear that confession, but I say more,—that he must have his own support. 'Tis only what strength he carries with him everywhere, that can serve him anywhere. Paper money is good only as far as it represents real labor. A member who "walks into the chamber attended only by his own insignificance, cannot get any strength by the distant shouts of electors." All the British batteries can not give comfort to the coward. If he knows there is weakness in his heart, tear off his epaulettes, break his sword, boot him out of the camp.

But whilst I insist on the doctrine of the independence and the inspiration of the individual, I do not cripple but exalt the social action. Patriotism, public opinion, have a real meaning, though there is so much counterfeit rag money abroad under it, that the name is apt to disgust. A wise man delights in the powers of many people. Charles Fourier noting that each man had a different talent, computed that you must collect 1800 or 2000 souls to make one complete man.[12] We shall need to call them all out.

Certainly the social state, patriotism, law, government, all did cover ideas, though the words have wandered from the things. The King or head of the state was godlike in the eyes of the people, whilst he was the foremost man of all the tribe, exponent of the laws, the genius, and the future of the tribe. It was so once in this country when Washington, Adams, Jefferson, really embodied the ideas of Americans. But now we put obscure persons into the chairs, without character or representative force of any kind, and get a figure awful to office hunters.

And as the state is a reality, so it is certain that societies of men, a race, a people, have a public function, a part to play in the history of humanity. Thus, the theory of our government is Liberty. The thought and experience of Europe had got thus far, a century ago, to believe, that, as soon as favorable circumstances permitted, the experiment of self-government should be made. America afforded the circumstances, and the new order began. All the mind in America was possessed by that idea. The Declaration of Independence, the Constitution of the States, the Parties; the newspapers, the songs, star-spangled banner, land of the brave and home of the free, the very manners of the Americans, all showed them as the receivers and propagandists of this lesson to the world. For this cause were they born and for this cause came they into the world. Liberty; to each man the largest liberty compatible with the liberty of every other man. It was not a sect, it was not a private opinion, but a gradual and irresistible growth of the human mind. That is the meaning of our national pride. It is a noble office. For liberty is a very serious thing. It is the severest test by which a government can be tried. All history goes to show, that it is the measure of all national success. Religion, arts, science, material production are as is the degree of liberty. Montesquieu said, "Countries are not cultivated in proportion to their population, but in proportion to their freedom."

Most unhappily, this universally accepted duty and feeling has been antagonized by the calamity of southern slavery. And that institution in its perpetual encroachment has had through the stronger personality, shall I say, of the southern people, and through their systematic devotion to politics, the art so to league itself with the government, as to check and pervert the natural sentiment of the people by their respect for law and statute.

And this country exhibits an abject regard to the forms, whilst we are swindled out of the liberty.

Lord Nelson was a man of sterling English sense,[13] and knowing himself to mean rightly, and being a rough plain man being much annoyed by the pedantic rules of the service, he went back to first principles, and once for all made up his mind. "To obey orders,"

LIBERTY

he said, "is thought to be all perfection but the great order of all is to serve your country, and down with the French; and, whenever any statute militates with that, I go back," he said, "to the great order of all, and of which the little orders spring." And he was careful to explain to his officers, that, in case of no signals, or, in case of not understanding signals, no captain could go wrong who brought his ship close alongside an enemy's ship.

So every wise American will say, 'in the collision of statutes, or in the doubtful interpretation, liberty is the great order which all lesser orders are to promote.' That is the right meaning of the statute, which extirpates crime, and obtains to every man the largest liberty compatible with the liberty of every other man. No citizen will go wrong who on every question leans to the side of general liberty. And whilst thus the society is no fiction, but has real rank, (he who represents the ideas of the society being the head,) it has a real function. That of our race is to liberty. So it has public actions which it performs with electric energy.

Men inspire each other. The affections are Muses. Hope is a muse, Love is, Despair is not, and selfishness drives away the angels. It is so delicious to act with great masses to great aims. For instance the summary or gradual abolition of slavery. Why in the name of common sense and the peace of mankind is not this made the subject of instant negotiation and settlement? Why do not the men of administrative ability in whose brain the prosperity of Philadelphia is rooted;—the multitude of able men who lead each enterprize in the City of New York; in Boston, in Baltimore; why not the strong courageous leaders of the south; join their heads and hearts to form some basis of negotiation to settle this dangerous dispute on some ground of fair compensation, on one side, and of satisfaction, on the other, to the conscience of the Free States. Is it impossible to speak of it with reason and good nature? Why? Because it is property? Why, then it has a price. Because it is political? Well then, it ultimately concerns us, threatens us, and there will never be a better time than the present time. It is really the great task fit for this country to accomplish, to buy that property of the planters, as the British nation bought the West Indian slaves. I say *buy*,—never conceding the right of the planter to own, but that we may acknowledge the calamity of his position, and bear a countryman's share in relieving him, and because it is the only practicable course, and is innocent.

Well, here is a right social or public function which one man cannot do, which all men must do. We shall one day bring the states shoulder to shoulder, and the citizens man to man, to exterminate slavery. It is said, it will cost two thousand millions of dollars. Was there ever any contribution levied that was so enthusiastically paid as this will be? The United States shall give every inch of the public lands. The states shall give their surplus revenues, their unsold lands. The citizen his private contribution. We will have a chimney-tax. We will give up our coaches, and wine, and watches. The churches will melt their plate. The Father of his country shall wait well-pleased a little longer for his monument:[14] Franklin for his; the Pilgrim Fathers for theirs. We will call on those rich benefactors who found Asylums, Hospitals, Athenaeums, Lowell Institutes, Peabody Institutes, Bates and Astor City Libraries.[15] On wealthy bachelors and wealthy maidens to make the State their heir as they were wont in Rome. The merchant will give his best voyage. The mechanic will give his fabric. The needlewomen will give. Children will have cent societies. If really the matter could come to negotiation and a price were named, I do not think any price founded on an estimate that figures could tell would be quite unmanageable. Every man in the land would give a week's work to dig away this accursed mountain of sorrow once and forever out of the world.

Assault on
Charles Sumner

26 May 1856

Mr. Chairman,

I sympathize heartily with the spirit of the Resolutions.[1] The events of the last few years and months and days have taught us the lesson of centuries. I do not see how a barbarous community and a civilized community can constitute one state. I think we must get rid of slavery, or we must get rid of freedom. Life has no parity of value in the free-state and in the slave-state. In one, it is adorned with education, with skilful labor, with arts, with long prospective interests, with sacred family ties, with honor and justice. In the other, life is a fever; man is an animal, given to pleasure, frivolous, irritable, spending his days on hunting and practising with deadly weapons to defend himself against his slaves, and against his companions brought up in the same idle and dangerous way. Such people live for the moment, they have properly no future, and readily risk on every passion a life which is of small value to themselves or to others. Many years ago, when Mr. Webster was challenged in Washington to a duel by one of these madcaps, his friends came forward with prompt good sense, and said, such a thing was not to be thought of; Mr. Webster's life was the property of his friends and of the whole country, and was not to be risked on the turn of a vagabond's ball.[2] Life and life are incommensurate.

The whole State of South Carolina does not now offer any one or any number of persons who are to be weighed for a moment in the scale with such a person as the meanest of them all has now struck down.[3] The very conditions of the game must always be,—the worst life staked against the best. It is only the best whom they desire to kill. It is only when they cannot answer your reasons, that they wish to knock you down. If therefore Massachusetts could send to the Senate a better man than Mr. Sumner, his death would be only so much the more quick and certain. Now as men's bodily strength, or skill with knives and guns is not usually in proportion to their knowledge and mother wit, but oftener in the inverse ratio, it will only do to send foolish persons to Washington, if you wish them to be safe.

The outrage at Washington is the more shocking from the singularly pure character of its victim. Mr. Sumner's position is exceptional in its honor. He had not taken his degrees in the caucus, and in hack politics. It is notorious, that, in the long time when his election was pending, he refused to take a single step to secure it. He would not so much as go up to the State House to shake hands with this or that person whose goodwill was reckoned important by his friends. He was elected. It was a homage to character and talent. In Congress, he did not rush into a party position. He sat long silent and studious. His friends, I remember, were told, that they would find Sumner a man of the world, like the rest: 'tis quite impossible to be at Washington, and not bend: he will bend as the rest have done. Well, he did not bend. He took his position and kept it. He meekly bore the cold shoulder from some of his New England colleagues, the hatred of his enemies, the pity of the indifferent, cheered by the love and respect of good men with whom he acted, and has stood for the North, a little in advance of all the North, and therefore without adequate support. He has never faltered in his maintenance of justice and freedom. He has gone beyond the large expectations of his friends in his increasing ability and his manlier tone.

I have heard that some of his political friends tax him with indolence or negligence in refusing to make electioneering speeches, or otherwise to bear his part in the labor which party organization requires. I say it to his honor. But more to his honor are the faults which his enemies lay to his charge. I think, sir, if Mr. Sumner had any vices, we should be likely to hear of them. They have fastened their eyes like microscopes, now for five years, on every act, word, manner, and movement to find a flaw, and with what result? His opponents accuse him neither of drunkenness, not debauchery, nor job, nor peculation, nor rapacity, nor personal aims of any kind; no, but with what? Why, beyond this charge which it is impossible was ever sincerely made, that he broke over the proprieties of debate, I find him accused of publishing his opinion of the Nebraska Conspiracy in a letter to the People of the United States with some discourtesy.[4] Then, that he is an abolitionist; as if every sane human being were not an abolitionist, or a believer that all men should be free. And the third crime he stands charged with, is, that his speeches were written before they were spoken; which of course must be true in Sumner's case, as it was true of Webster, of Adams, of Calhoun, of Burke, of Chatham,[5] of Demosthenes, of every first-rate speaker that ever lived. It is the high compliment he pays to the intelligence of the Senate and of the country. When the same reproach was cast on the first orator of ancient times by some caviller of his day, he said, "I should be ashamed to come with one unconsidered word before such an assembly."

Mr. Chairman, when I think of these most small faults as the worst which party hatred could allege, I think I may borrow the language which Bishop Burnet applied to Sir Isaac Newton, and say, that Charles Sumner "has the whitest soul I ever knew."[6]

Well, sir, this noble head, so comely and so wise, must be the target for a pair of bullies to beat with clubs! The murderer's brand shall stamp their foreheads wherever they may wander in the earth.

But I wish, sir, that the high respects of this meeting shall be expressed to Mr. Sumner; that a copy of the Resolutions that have been read may be forwarded to him. I wish that he may know the shudder of terror which ran through all this community on the first tidings of this brutal attack. Let him know, that every man of worth in New England loves his virtues; that every mother thinks of him as the protector of families; that every friend of freedom thinks him *the* friend of freedom. And if our arms at this distance cannot defend him from assassins, we confide the defence of a life so precious, to all honorable men and true patriots, and to the Almighty Maker of men.

KANSAS RELIEF MEETING

10 September 1856

I regret, with all this company, the absence of Mr. Whitman of Kansas, whose narrative was to constitute the interest of this meeting.[1] Mr. Whitman is not here; but knowing, as we all do, why he is not, what duties kept him at home, he is more than present. His vacant chair speaks for him. For quite other reasons, I had been wiser to have stayed at home, unskilled as I am to address a political meeting, but it is impossible for the most recluse to extricate himself from the questions of the times.

There is this peculiarity about the case of Kansas, that all the right is on one side. We hear the screams of hunted wives and children answered by the howl of the butchers. The testimony of the telegraphs from St. Louis and the border confirm the worst details. The printed letters of the border ruffians avow the facts. When pressed to look at the cause of the mischief in the Kansas laws, the President falters and declines the discussion; but his supporters in the Senate, Mr. Cass, Mr. Geyer, Mr. Hunter, speak out, and declare the intolerable atrocity of the code.[2] It is a maxim that all party spirit produces the incapacity to receive natural impressions from facts; and our recent political history has abundantly borne out the maxim. But these details that have come from Kansas are so horrible, that the hostile press have but one word in reply, namely, that it is all exaggeration, 'tis an Abolition lie. Do the Committee of Investigation say that the outrages have been over-stated? Does their dismal catalogue of private tragedies show it? Do the private letters? Is it an exaggeration, that Mr. Hopps of Som-erville, Mr. Hoyt of Deerfield, Mr. Jennison of Groton, Mr. Phillips of Berkshire, have been murdered? That Mr. Robinson of Fitchburg has been imprisoned? Rev. Mr. Nute of Springfield seized, and up to this time we have no tidings of his fate?[3]

In these calamities under which they suffer, and the worse which threaten them, the people of Kansas ask for bread, clothes, arms, and men, to save them alive, and enable them to stand against these enemies of the human race. They have a right to be helped for they have helped themselves.

This aid must be sent, and this is not to be doled out as an ordinary charity; but bestowed up to the magnitude of the want, and, as has been elsewhere said, "on the scale of a national action." I think we are to give largely, lavishly, to these men. And we must prepare to do it. We must learn to do with less, live in a smaller tenement, sell our apple-trees, our acres, our pleasant houses. I know people who are making haste to reduce their expenses, and pay their debts, not with a view to new accumulations, but in preparation to save and earn for the benefit of the Kansas emigrants.

We must have aid from individuals;—we must also have aid from the State. I know that the last Legislature refused that aid. I know that lawyers hesitate on technical grounds, and wonder what method of relief the Legislature will apply. But I submit that, in a case like this, where citizens of Massachusetts, legal voters here, have emigrated to national territory under the sanction of every law, and are then set on by highwaymen, driven from their new homes, pillaged, and numbers of them killed and scalped, and the whole world knows that this is no accidental brawl, but a systematic war to the knife, and in loud defiance of all laws and liberties, I submit that the Governor and Legislature should neither slumber nor sleep till they have found out how to send effectual aid and comfort to these poor farmers, or else should resign their seats to those who can. But first let them hang the halls of the State House with black crape, and order funeral service to be said there for the citizens whom they were unable to defend.[4]

We stick at the technical difficulties. I think there never was a people so choked and stultified by forms. We adore the forms of law, instead of making them vehicles of wisdom and justice. I like the primary assembly. I own I have little esteem for governments. I esteem them only good in the moment when they are established. I set the private man first. He only who is able to stand alone is qualified to be a citizen. Next to the private man, I value the primary assembly, met to watch the government and to correct it. That is the theory of the American State, that it exists to execute the will of the citizens, is always responsible to them, and is always to be changed when it does not. First, the private citizen, then the primary assembly, and the government last.[5]

In this country for the last few years the government has been the chief obstruction to the common weal. Who doubts that Kansas would have been very well settled, if the United States had let it alone? The government armed and led the ruffians against the poor farmers. I do not know any story so gloomy as the politics of this country for the last twenty years, centralizing ever more manifestly round one spring, and that a vast crime, and ever more plainly, until it is notorious that all promotion, power and policy are dictated from one source—illustrating the fatal effects of a false position to demoralize legislation and put the best people always at a disadvantage;—one crime always present,—always to be varnished over, to find fine names for, and we free-statesmen, as accomplices to the guilt, ever in the power of the grand offender.

Language has lost its meaning in the universal cant. *Representative Government* is really misrepresentative; *Union* is a conspiracy against the Northern States which the Northern States are to have the privilege of paying for; the *adding of Cuba and Central America* to the slave marts is *enlarging the area of Freedom. Manifest Destiny, Democracy,*

Freedom, fine names for an ugly thing. They call it otto of rose and lavender,—I call it bilge water. It is called Chivalry and Freedom; I call it the taking all the earnings of a poor man and the earnings of his little girl and boy, and the earnings of all that shall come from him, his children's children forever.

But this is Union, and this is Democracy; and our poor people, led by the nose by these fine words, dance and sing, ring bells and fire cannon, with every new link of the chain which is forged for their limbs by the plotters in the Capitol.

What are the results of law and union? There is no Union. Can any citizen of Massachusetts travel in honor through Kentucky and Alabama and speak his mind? Or can any citizen of the Southern country who happens to think kidnapping a bad thing, say so? Let Mr. Underwood of Virginia answer.[6] Is it to be supposed that there are no men in Carolina who dissent from the popular sentiment now reigning there? It must happen, in the variety of human opinions, that there are dissenters. They are silent as the grave. Are there no women in that country, women, who always carry the conscience of a people? Yet we have not heard one discordant whisper.

In the free States, we have a snivelling support to slavery. The judges give cowardly interpretations to the law, in direct opposition to the known foundation of all law, that *every immoral statute is void.* And here of Kansas, the President says: "Let the complainants go to the courts;" though he knows that when the poor plundered farmer comes to the court, he finds the ringleader who has robbed him, dismounting from his own horse, unbuckling his knife to sit as his judge.[7]

The President told the Kansas Committee that the whole difficulty grew from "the factious spirit of the Kansas people, respecting institutions which they need not have concerned themselves about." A very remarkable speech from a Democratic President to his fellow citizens, that they are not to concern themselves with institutions which they alone are to create and determine. The President is a lawyer, and should know the statutes of the land. But I borrow the language of an eminent man, used long since, with far less occasion; "If that be law, let the ploughshare be run under the foundations of the Capitol; and if that be Government, extirpation is the only cure."[8]

I am glad to see that the terror at disunion and anarchy is disappearing. Massachusetts, in its heroic day, had no government—was an anarchy. Every man stood on his own feet, was his own governor; and there was no breach of peace from Cape Cod to Mount Hoosac. California, a few years ago, by the testimony of all people at that time in the country, had the best government that ever existed. Pans of gold lay drying outside of every man's tent, in perfect security. The land was measured into little strips of a few feet wide, all side by side. A bit of ground that your hand could cover was worth one or two hundred dollars, on the edge of your strip; and there was no dispute. Every man throughout the country was armed with knife and revolver, and it was known that instant justice would be administered to each offence, and perfect peace reigned. For, the Saxon man, when he is well awake, is not a pirate, but a citizen, all made of hooks and eyes, and links himself naturally to his brothers, as bees hook themselves to one another, and to their queen, in a loyal swarm.

But the hour is coming when the strongest will not be strong enough. A harder task will the new revolution of the nineteenth century be, than was the revolution of the eighteenth century. I think the American Revolution bought its glory cheap. If the problem was new, it was simple. If there were few people they were united, and the enemy, 3,000 miles off. But now, vast property, gigantic interests, family connections, webs of party, cover the land with a network that immensely multiplies the dangers of war.

Fellow Citizens, in these times full of the fate of the Republic, I think the towns should hold town meetings, and resolve themselves into Committees of Safety, go into permanent sessions, adjourning from week to week, from month to month.[9] I wish we could send the Sergeant-at-Arms to stop every American who is about to leave the country. Send home every one who is abroad, lest they should find no country to return to. Come home and stay at home, while there is a country to save. When it is lost it will be time enough then for any who are luckless enough to remain alive to gather up their clothes and depart to some land where freedom exists.

SPEECH AT A MEETING TO AID
JOHN BROWN'S FAMILY

18 November 1859

Mr. Chairman and Fellow Citizens:[1] I share the sympathy and the sorrow which has brought us together. Gentlemen who have preceded me have well said that no wall of separation could here exist. This commanding event which has brought us together,—the sequel of which has brought us together—eclipses all others which have occurred for a long time in our history, and I am very glad to see that this sudden interest in the hero of Harper's Ferry, has provoked an extreme curiosity in all parts of the republic, in regard to the details of his history. Every anecdote is eagerly sought, and I do not wonder that gentlemen find traits of relation readily between him and themselves. One finds a relation in the church, another in the profession, another in the place of his birth. He was happily a representative of the American public. Captain John Brown is a farmer, the fifth in descent from Peter Brown, who came to Plymouth in the Mayflower, in 1620.[2] All the six have been farmers. His grandfather, of Simsbury, in Connecticut, was a captain in the Revolution. His father, largely interested as a raiser of stock, became a contractor to supply the army with beef, in the war of 1812, and our Captain John Brown, then a boy with his father, was present and witnessed the surrender of General Hull.[3] He cherishes a great respect for his father as a man of strong character, and his respect is probably just. For himself, he is so transparent that all men see him through. He is a man to make friends wherever on earth courage and integrity are esteemed [applause];—the rarest of heroes, a pure idealist, with no by-ends of his own. Many of you have seen him, and every one who has heard him speak has been impressed alike by his simple artless goodness, joined with his sublime courage. He joins that perfect puritan faith which brought his fifth ancestor to Plymouth Rock, with his grandfather's ardor in the Revolution. He believes in two articles—two instruments, shall I say—The Golden Rule, and the Declaration of Independence [applause]; and he used this expression in conversation here. "Better that a whole generation of men, women and children should pass away by a violent death, than that one word of either should be violated in this country." There is a Unionist—there is a strict constructionist for you. [Applause and laughter.] He believes in the union of the United States, he believes in the union of America, and he conceives that the only obstruction to the union is slavery, and for that reason as a patriot, he works for its abolition. The Governor of Virginia has pronounced his eulogy in a manner that discredits the moderation of our timid parties.[4] His own speeches to the Court have interested the nation in him. What magnanimity, and what innocent pleading, as of childhood. You remember his words—"If I had interfered in behalf of the rich, the powerful, the intelligent, the so-called great, or any of their friends, parents, wives or children, it would all have been right. No man in this court would have thought it a crime. But I believe that to have interfered as I have done, for the despised poor, I have done no wrong, but right."

It is easy to see what a favorite he will be with history, which plays mad pranks with temporary reputations. Nothing can resist the sympathy which all elevated minds must feel with Brown, and through them the whole civilized world; and, if he must suffer, he must drag official gentlemen into an immortality most undesirable, and of which they have already some disagreeable forebodings. [Applause.] Indeed, it is the *reductio ad absurdum* of slavery, when the Governor of Virginia is forced to hang a man whom he declares to be a man of the most integrity, truthfulness, and courage he has ever met. Is that the kind of man the gallows is built for? It were bold to affirm that there is within that broad Commonwealth, at this moment, another citizen as worthy to live, and as deserving of all public and private honor, as this poor prisoner.

But we are here to think of relief for the family of John Brown. To my eyes that family looks very large and very needy of relief. It comprises his brave fellow sufferers in the Charlestown Jail; the fugitives still hunted in the mountains of Virginia and Pennsylvania; the sympathizers with him in all the States; and, I may say, almost every man who loves the Golden Rule and the Declaration of Independence, like him, and who sees what a tiger's thirst threatens him in the malignity of public sentiment in the slave States. It seems to me that a common feeling joins the people of Massachusetts with him. I said John Brown was an idealist. He believed in his ideas to that extent, that he existed to put them all into action. He did not believe in moral suasion;—he believed in putting the thing through. [Applause.] He saw how deceptive the forms are. We fancy, in Massachusetts, that we are free; yet it seems the Government is quite unreliable. Great wealth,—great population,—men of talent in the executive, on the Bench,—all the forms right,—and yet, life and freedom are not safe. Why? Because the judges rely on the forms, and do not, like John Brown, use their eyes to see the fact behind the forms.

They assume that the United States can protect its witness or its prisoner. And, in Massachusetts, that is true; but the moment he is carried out of the bounds of Massachusetts, the United States, it is notorious, afford no protection at all; the Government, the Judges, are an envenomed party, and give such protection as they give in Utah to honest citizens; or in Kansas: such protection as they gave to their own Commodore Paulding, when he was simple enough to mistake the formal instructions of his Government for their real meaning.[5] [Applause.] The judges fear collision between their two allegiances. But there are worse evils than collision; namely, the doing substantial injustice. A good man will see that the use of a judge is to secure good government, and where the citizen's weal is imperilled by abuse of the Federal power, to use that arm which can secure it, viz.: the local government. Had that been done, on certain calamitous occasions, we should not have seen the honor of Massachusetts trailed in the dust, stained to all ages, once and again by the ill-timed formalism of a venerable Bench. If judges cannot find law enough to maintain the sovereignty of the State, and to protect the life and freedom of every inhabitant not a criminal, it is fine to compliment them as learned and venerable,—what avails their learning or veneration? At a pinch they are of no more use than idiots.[6] After the mischance, they wring their hands, but they had better never have been born. A Vermont Judge, Hutchinson,[7] who has a Declaration of Independence in his heart, a Wisconsin Judge, who knows that laws are for the protection of citizens against kidnappers, is worth a court house full of lawyers so idolatrous of forms as to let go the substance. Is any man in Massachusetts so simple as to believe that when a United States Court in Virginia, now, in its present reign of terror, sends to Connecticut, or New York, or Massachusetts for a witness, it wants him for a witness? No; it wants him for a party; it wants him for meat to slaughter and eat. And your *habeas corpus* is, in any way in which it has been, or, I fear, is likely to be used, a nuisance, and not a protection; for it takes away his right reliance on himself, and the natural assistance of his friends and fellow-citizens, by offering him a form which is a piece of paper.[8] But I am detaining the meeting on matters which others understand better. I hope, then, that in administering relief to John Brown's family, we shall remember all those whom his fate concerns, all who are in sympathy with him, and not forget to aid him in the best way, by securing freedom and independence in Massachusetts.

John Brown

6 January 1860

Mr. Chairman: I have been struck with one fact, that the best orators who have added their praise to his fame—and I need not go out of this house to find the purest eloquence in the country—have one rival who comes off a little better, and that is John Brown. Every thing that is said of him leaves people a little dissatisfied; but as soon as they read his own speeches and letters they are heartily contented—such is the singleness of purpose which justifies him to the head and the heart of all. Taught by this experience, I mean, in the few remarks I have to make, to cling to his history, or let him speak for himself.

John Brown, the founder of liberty in Kansas, was born in Torrington, Litchfield County, Conn., in 1800. When he was five years old his father emigrated to Ohio, and the boy was there set to keep sheep, and to look after cattle, and dress skins; he went bareheaded and barefooted, and clothed in buckskin.[1] He said that he loved rough play, could never have rough play enough; could not see a seedy hat without wishing to pull it off. But for this it needed that the playmates should be equal; not one in fine clothes and the other in buckskin; not one his own master, hale and hearty, and the other watched and whipped. But it chanced that in Pennsylvania, where he was sent by his father to collect cattle, he fell in with a boy whom he heartily liked, and whom he looked upon as his superior. This boy was a slave; he saw him beaten with an iron shovel, and otherwise maltreated; he saw that this boy had nothing better to look forward to in life, whilst he himself was petted and made much of; for he was much considered in the family where he then stayed, from the circumstance that this boy of twelve years had conducted alone a drove of cattle a hundred miles. But the colored boy had no friend, and no future. This worked such indignation in him that he swore an oath of resistance to Slavery as long as he lived. And thus his enterprise to go into Virginia and run off five hundred or a thousand slaves, was not a piece of spite or revenge, a plot of two years or of twenty years, but the keeping of an oath made to heaven and earth forty-seven years before.[2] Forty-seven years at least, though I incline to accept his own account of the matter, at Charlestown, which makes the date a little older, when he said, "This was all settled millions of years before the world was made."

He grew up a religious and manly person in severe poverty; a fair specimen of the best stock of New England; having that force of thought and that sense of right which are the warp and woof of greatness. Our farmers were Orthodox Calvinists, mighty in the Scriptures; had learned that life was a preparation, a "probation," to use their word, for a higher world, and was to be spent in loving and serving mankind.

Thus was formed a romantic character absolutely without any vulgar trait; living to ideal ends, without any mixture of self-indulgence or compromise, such as lowers the value of benevolent and thoughtful men we know; abstemious, refusing luxuries, not sourly and reproachfully, but simply as unfit for his habit; quiet and gentle as a child in the house. And, as happens usually to men of romantic character, his fortunes were romantic. Walter Scott would have delighted to draw his picture and trace his adventurous career. A shepherd and herdsman, he learned the manners of animals, and knew the secret signals by which animals communicate. He made his hard bed on the mountains with them; he learned to drive his flock through thickets all but impassable; he had all the skill of a shepherd by choice of breed, and by wise husbandry to obtain the best wool, and that for a course of years. And the anecdotes preserved show a far-seeing skill and conduct which, in spite of adverse accidents, should secure, one year with another, an honest reward, first to the farmer, and afterwards to the dealer. If he kept sheep, it was with a royal mind; and if he traded in wool, he was a merchant prince, not in the amount of wealth, but in the protection of the interests confided to him.

I am not a little surprised at the easy effrontery with which political gentlemen, in and out of Congress, take it upon them to say that there are not a thousand men in the North who sympathize with John Brown. It would be far safer and nearer the truth to say that all people, in proportion to their sensibility and self-respect, sympathize with him. For it is impossible to see courage, and disinterestedness, and the love that casts out fear, without sympathy.

All women are drawn to him by their predominance of sentiment. All gentlemen, of course, are on his side. I do not mean by "gentlemen," people of scented hair and perfumed handkerchiefs, but men of gentle blood and generosity, "fulfilled with all nobleness," who, like the Cid,[4] give the outcast leper a share of their bed; like the dying Sidney, pass the cup of cold water to the wounded soldier who needs it more. For what is the oath of gentle blood and knighthood? What but to protect the weak and lowly against the strong oppressor?

Nothing is more absurd than to complain of this sympathy, or to complain of a party of men united in opposition to Slavery. As well complain of gravity, or the ebb of the tide. Who makes the Abolitionist? The Slaveholder. The sentiment of mercy is the natural recoil which the laws of the universe provide to protect mankind from destruction by savage passions. And our blind statesmen go up and down, with committees of vigilance and safety, hunting for the origin of this new heresy. They will need a very vigilant committee indeed to find its birthplace, and a very strong force to root it out. For the arch-Abolitionist, older than Brown, and older than the Shenandoah Mountains, is Love, whose other name is Justice, which was before Alfred, before Lycurgus, before Slavery, and will be after it.[5]

ATTEMPTED SPEECH

24 January 1861

The President then announced Ralph Waldo Emerson, of Concord, who was received with three vigorous cheers by the audience, followed by three cheers for the Union from the mob, and a succession of disturbing groans and outcries.[1] Toward the close of Mr. Phillips's speech, several policemen had entered the gallery, and their glazed caps were conspicuous among the rioters. Rev. Mr. Waterston, in the midst of the tumult, rose and asked—"Will not the police do their duty?"[2] The appeal had no effect, however, and Mr. Emerson was obliged to wait some time before his voice could be heard. At length, when comparative silence was obtained, he said:—

Mr. President,—It is little I have to say; but to fill up the interval between the gentleman who is about to follow me, and the organ of thought and opinion who has just spoken, I will say, that I am very happy to see this Society, through its organs here, asserting those principles which belong to this soil, which belong to every person who now hears me [hisses]; and I am glad that a Boston boy, educated here in our schools, here in our colleges, all his life spent among you, has learned to find in your hearts an answer to every burning word he speaks. Why, ladies and gentlemen, I feel that really the Boston boys are all right. I am a little proud of this village. Let me say to those young foreigners, to those young strangers, that I was born on the spot where the post-office now stands; that all my education has been in her town schools here, here in her college, and all the best of my life spent here.[3] That is true, too, of the gentleman who presides here, and of Mr. Phillips, who has just addressed us.[4] I think the same record cannot be shown by the young people who have endeavored to interrupt this meeting.

But I have to say, that one thing seems only too plain in the new history of the country, as well as in the old. They say that the Asiatic cholera takes the vital principle out of the air by decomposing the air. I think it is the same with the moral pestilence under which the country has suffered so long; it actually decomposes mankind. This institution of slavery is based on a crime of that fatal character that it decomposes men. The barbarism which has lately appeared wherever that question has been touched, and in the action of the States where it prevails, seems to stupify the moral sense. The moral injury of slavery is infinitely greater than its pecuniary and political injury. I really do not think the pecuniary mischief of slavery, which is always shown by statists, worthy to be named in comparison with this power to subvert the reason of men, so that those who speak for it, who defend it, who act in its behalf, seem to have lost the moral sense. Here are young men from the Southern country, whom we have always supposed were in the minority, who had not spoken, but who would yet save their country—they also have been educated here in our institutions, have been educated in Europe, and when they have gone back, they have suffered from this ophthalmia, this blindness, which hides from them the great facts of right and wrong. They do not perceive the political, economical and moral mischief done by the institution. I chanced, within a few days, to be reading the travels in Alabama of the English naturalist, Gosse, who has set all our boys making aquariums,[5] and he recites precisely those facts which are denied by our Southern friends—the burning of books and the like, the utter suppression of all freedom of thought and conversation among friends. [Noise in the gallery, which obliged the speaker to pause.]

I was going to say, that I hope that, in the great action now pending, all the forbearance, all the discretion possible, and yet all the firmness, shall be used by the representatives of the North, and by the people at home. Gentlemen, friends, no man of patriotism, no man of natural sentiment, can undervalue the sacred Union which we possess; but if it is sundered, it will be because it had already ceased to have a vital tension. The action of to-day is only the ultimatum of what had already occurred. The bonds had ceased to exist, because of this vital defect of slavery at the South actually separating them in sympathy, in thought, in character, from the people of the North; and then, if the separation had gone thus far, what is the use of a pretended tie! As to concessions, we have none to make. The monstrous concession made at the formation of the Constitution is all that can ever be asked; it has blocked the civilization and humanity of the times up to this day. I cannot help thinking just now, in connection with some facts that were mentioned, of a story of Mr. Wilson. You all know Prof. Wilson, the author of the *"Noctes"*—the wit of Edinboro' and London.[6] When some gentlemen, strangers at the lake—[Noise in the gallery, hisses, groans, calls of "put him out," "dry up," "unbutton your coat," etc.]

Mr. Emerson. I know you will hear my story: it is very good. One of Prof. Wilson's family had been insulted in a boat upon the lake. The fact was brought to his knowledge, and he immediately prepared to horse-whip the offenders. They learned to whose family the offended person belonged, and got a mutual friend to go with them to the Professor's house, to propitiate him. He introduced them, and said, "These are the gentlemen who have, by some mistake, interfered with your friend." Prof. Wilson heard their apology coldly, and allowed them to depart. When they had gone, his friend said, "Why, Professor, you should have more magnanimity than to receive their apology with such coolness." "Magnanimity!" said he; "was ever magnanimity more enormous than mine! There they sat, and I did not pitch them out of the window!" [Laughter.] It seems to me that is really a fair illustration of the immense concessions that have already been made, and we do not need any more.

But I will not detain the company longer.

"THE PRESIDENT'S PROCLAMATION"

12 October 1862

In so many arid forms which states incrust themselves with,—once in a century, if so often, a poetic act and record occur.[1] These are the jets of thought into affairs, when roused by danger or inspired by genius, the political leaders of the day break the else insurmountable routine of class and local legislation, and take a step forward in the direction of catholic and universal interests. Every step in the history of political liberty is a sally of the human mind into the untried future, and has the interest of genius and is fruitful in heroic anecdotes. Liberty is a slow fruit. It comes, like religion, for short periods and in rare conditions, as if awaiting a culture of the race which shall make it organic and permanent. Such moments of expansion in modern history were, the Confession of Augsburg; the plantation of America; the English Commonwealth of 1648; the Declaration of American Independence in 1776; the British emancipation of slaves in the West Indies; the passage of the Reform Bill; the repeal of the Corn Laws; the magnetic ocean Telegraph; though yet imperfect, the passage of the Homestead Bill in the last Congress; and now, eminently, President Lincoln's Proclamation on the twenty-second of September.[2] These are acts of great scope, working on a long future, and on permanent interests, and honoring alike those who initiate and those who receive them. These measures provoke no noisy joy, but are received into a sympathy so deep as to apprise us that mankind are greater and better than we know. At such times, it appears as if a new public were created to greet the new event. It is as when an orator, having ended the compliments and pleasantries with which he conciliated attention, and having run over the superficial fitness and commodities of the measure he urges, suddenly lending himself to some happy inspiration, announces with vibrating voice the grand human principles involved,—the bravoes and wits who greeted him loudly thus far, are surprised and overawed. A new audience is found in the heart of the assembly, an audience hitherto passive and unconcerned, now at last so searched and kindled, that they come forward, every one a representative of mankind, standing for all nationalities.

The extreme moderation with which the President advanced to his design; his long-avowed expectant policy, as if he chose to be strictly the executive of the best public sentiment of the country, waiting only till it should be unmistakeably pronounced; so fair a mind, that none ever listened so patiently to such extreme varieties of opinion; so reticent, that his decision has taken all parties by surprise, whilst yet it is the just sequel of his prior acts; the firm tone in which he announces it, without inflation, or surplusage; all these have bespoken such favor to the act, that great as the popularity of the President has been, we are beginning to think that we have underestimated the capacity and virtue which the Divine Providence has made an instrument of benefit so vast.

He has been permitted to do more for America than any other American man. He is well entitled to the most indulgent construction. Forget all that we thought shortcomings, every mistake, every delay. In the extreme embarrassments of his part, call these endurance, wisdom, magnanimity, illuminated, as they now are, by this dazzling success. When we consider the immense opposition that has been neutralized or converted by the progress of the war, (for it is not long since the President anticipated the resignation of a large number of officers in the army, and the secession of three states, on the promulgation of this policy); when we see how the great stake which foreign nations hold in our affairs has recently brought every European power as a client into this court, and it became every day more apparent what gigantic and what remote interests were to be affected by the decision of the President,—one can hardly say the deliberation was too long. Against all timorous counsels, he had the courage to seize the moment; and such was his position, and such the felicity attending the action, that he has replaced government in the good graces of mankind. "Better is virtue in the sovereign, than plenty in the season," say the Chinese.

'Tis wonderful what power is, and how ill it is used, and how its ill use makes life mean, and the sunshine dark. Life in America had lost much of its attraction in the later years. The virtues of a good magistrate undo a world of mischief, and, because nature works with rectitude, seem vastly more potent than the acts of bad governors, which are ever tempered by the good nature in the people, and the incessant resistance which fraud and violence encounter. The acts of good governors work at a geometrical ratio, as one midsummer day seems to repair the damage of a year of war. A day which most of us dared not hope to see; an event worth the dreadful war, worth its costs and uncertainties, seems now to be close before us. October, November, December will have passed over beating hearts and plotting brains: then the hour will strike, and all men of African descent who have faculty enough to find their way to our lines, are assured of the protection of American Law.

It is by no means necessary that this measure should be suddenly marked by any signal results on the negroes or on the rebel masters. The force of the act is that it commits the country to this justice; that it compels the innumerable officers, civil, military, naval, of the Republic, to range themselves on the line of this equity. It draws the fashion to this side. It is not a measure that admits of being taken back. Done, it cannot be undone by a new administration. For slavery overpowers the disgust of the moral sentiment only through immemorial usage. It cannot be introduced as an improvement of the nineteenth century. This act makes that the lives of our heroes have not been sacrificed in vain. It makes a victory of our defeats. Our hurts are healed; the health of the nation is repaired. With a victory like this, we can stand many disasters. It does not promise the redemption of the black race: that lies not with us: but it relieves it of our opposition. The President by this act has paroled all the slaves in America; they will no more fight against us; and it relieves our race once for all of its crime and false position. The first condition of success is secured in putting ourselves right. We have recovered ourselves from our false position and planted ourselves on a law of nature. "If that fail, the pillared firmament is rottenness, and earth's base built on stubble."[3]

The government has assured itself of the best constituency in the world; every spark of intellect, every virtuous feeling, every religious heart, every man of honor, every poet, every philosopher, the generosity of the cities, the health of the country, the strong arms of the mechanics, the endurance of farmers, the passionate conscience of women, the sympathy of distant nations,—all rally to its support.

Of course, we are assuming the firmness of the policy thus declared. It must not be a paper proclamation. We confide that Mr. Lincoln is in earnest, and, as he has been slow in making up his mind, has resisted the importunacy of parties and of events to the latest moment, he will be as absolute in his adhesion. Not only will he repeat and follow up his stroke, but the nation will add its irresistible strength. If the ruler has duties, so has the citizen. In times like these, when the nation is imperilled, what man can, without shame, receive good news from day to day, without giving good news of himself? What right has any one to read in the journals tidings of victories, if he has not bought them by his own valor, treasure, personal sacrifice, or by service as good in his own department? With this blot removed from our national honor, this heavy load lifted off the national heart, we shall not fear henceforward to show our faces among mankind. We shall cease to be hypocrites and pretenders, but what we have styled our free institutions will be such. In the light of this event the public distress begins to be removed. What if the brokers' quotations show our stocks discredited and the gold dollar costs one hundred and twenty-seven cents. These tables are fallacious. Every acre in the free states gained substantial value on the twenty-second of September. The cause of disunion and war has been reached, and begun to be removed. Every man's house lot and garden are relieved of the malaria which the purest winds and the strongest sunshine could not penetrate and purge. The territory of the Union shines today with a lustre, which every European emigrant can discern from far; a sign of inmost security and permanence.

Is it feared that taxes will check immigration? That depends on what the taxes are spent for. If they go to fill up this yawning Dismal Swamp which engulfed armies and populations, and created plague, and neutralized hitherto all the vast capabilities of this continent,—then this taxation, which makes the land wholesome and habitable, and will draw all men unto it,—is the best investment in which property-holder ever lodged his earnings.

Whilst we have pointed out the opportuneness of the Proclamation, it remains to be said that the President had no choice. He might look wistfully for what variety of courses lay open to him. Every line but one was closed up with fire. This one too bristled with danger, but through it was the sole safety. The measure he has adopted was imperative. It is wonderful to see the unseasonable senility of what is called the Peace party, through all its masks blinding their eyes to the main feature of the war, namely, its inevitableness. The war existed long before the cannonade of Sumter and could not be postponed. It might have begun otherwise or elsewhere, but war was in the minds and bones of the combatants, it was written on the iron leaf, and you might as easily dodge gravitation. If we had consented to a peaceable secession of the rebels, the divided sentiment of the border states made peaceable secession impossible, the insatiable temper of the South made it impossible, and the slaves on the border, wherever the border might be, were an incessant fuel to rekindle the fire. Give the Confederacy New Orleans, Charleston, and Richmond, and they would have demanded St. Louis and Baltimore. Give them these, and they would have insisted on Washington. Give them Washington, and they would have assumed the Army and Navy, and through these Philadelphia, New York, and Boston. It looks as if the battlefield would have been at least as large in that event as it is now. The war was formidable, but could not be avoided. The war was and is an immense mischief, but brought with it the immense benefit of drawing a line, and rallying the Free States to fix it impassably; preventing the whole force of Southern connection and influence throughout the North from distracting every city with endless confusion, detaching that force and reducing it to handfuls, and, in the progress of hostilities, dis-infecting us of our habitual proclivity through the affection of trade, and the traditions of the Democratic Party, to follow Southern leading.

These necessities which have dictated the conduct of the Federal government are overlooked especially by our foreign critics. The popular statement of the opponents of the war abroad is, the impossibility of our success. 'If you could add,' say they, 'to your strength the whole army of England, of France, and of Austria, you could not coerce eight millions of people to come under this government against their will.' This is an odd thing for an Englishman, a Frenchman, or an Austrian to say, who remembers the Europe of the last seventy years,—the condition of Italy, until 1859; of Poland, since 1793; of France, of French Algiers; of British Ireland, and British India. But, granting the truth, rightly read, of the historical aphorism, that "the people always conquer," it is to be noted, that, in the Southern States, the tenure of land, and the local laws, with slavery, give the social system not a democratic, but an aristocratic complexion; and these states have shown every year a more hostile and aggressive temper, until the instinct of self-preservation forced us into the war. And the aim of the war on our part is indicated by the aim of the President's Proclamation, namely to break up the false combination of Southern society, to destroy the piratic feature in it which makes it our enemy only as it is the enemy of the human race, and so allow its reconstruction on a just and healthful basis. Then new affinities will act, the old repulsions will cease, and, the cause of war being removed, nature and trade may be trusted to establish a lasting peace.

We think we cannot overstate the wisdom and benefit of this act of the government. The malignant cry of the secession press within the Free States, and the recent action of the Confederate Congress[4] are decisive as to its efficiency and correctness of aim. Not less so is the silent joy which has greeted it in all generous hearts. And the new hope it has breathed into the world. It was well to delay the steamers at the wharves, until this edict could be put on board. It will be an insurance to the ship as it goes plunging through the sea with glad tidings to all people. Happy are the young who find the pestilence cleansed out of the earth, leaving open to them an honest career. Happy the old, who see Nature purified before they depart. Do not let the dying die: hold them back to this world, until you have charged their ear and heart with this message to other spiritual societies, announcing the melioration of our planet.

> "Incertainties now crown themselves assured,
> And Peace proclaims olives of endless age."[5]

Meantime, that ill-fated much-injured race which the Proclamation respects will lose somewhat of the dejection sculptured for ages in their bronzed countenance, uttered in the wailing of their plaintive music,—a race naturally benevolent, joyous, docile, industrious, and whose very miseries sprung from their great talent for usefulness, which, in a more moral age will not only defend their independence, but will give them a rank among nations.

"Fortune of the Republic"

1 December 1863

It is a rule that holds in economy, as well as in hydraulics, that you must have a source higher than your tap.[1] The mills, the shops, the theatre, the caucus, the college, and the church, have all found out this secret. The sailors sail by chronometers that do not lose two or three seconds in a year, ever since Newton explained to Parliament that the way to improve navigation, was, to get good watches, and they must offer public premiums for a better time-keeper than any in use. The manufacturers rely on turbines of hydraulic perfection. The carpet-mill, on mordants and dyes, which exhaust the skill of chemists. The calico print, on designers of genius, who draw the wages of artists, not of artisans. Wedgwood in England bravely took the sculptor Flaxman to counsel,[2] who said, send to Italy, search the museums for the forms of old Etruscan vases, urns, waterpots, domestic and sacrificial vessels of all kinds. They built great works, and called their manufacturing village, *Etruria*. Flaxman, with his Greek taste, selected and combined the loveliest forms which were executed in English clay; sent boxes of these as gifts, to every court of Europe, and formed the taste of the world. It was a *renaissance* at the breakfast table and china-closet. The brave manufacturers made their fortune. The jewellers were not slow to imitate the revived models in silver and gold. The theatre avails itself of the best talent of poet, of painter, and of amateur of taste, to make the ensemble of dramatic effect. The marine insurance office has its mathematical counsellor to settle averages. The Life Assurance, its Table of Annuities. The wine-merchant has his analyst and taster,—the more exquisite the better. He has also, I fear, his debts to the chemist, as well as to the vineyard.

Our modern wealth stands on a few staples, and the interest nations took in our war was exasperated by the importance of the cotton-trade. And what is cotton? One plant out of some 200,000 plants known to the botanist,—vastly the largest part of which are reckoned weeds. And what is a weed? A plant whose virtues have not yet been discovered. And every one of the 200,000, probably yet to be of utility in the arts. As Bacchus of the vine, Ceres of the wheat,—as Arkwright and Whitney were the demigods of cotton, so prolific Time will yet bring an inventor to every plant.[3] There is not a property in nature, but a mind is born to seek and find it.

Our sleepy civilization, when Roger Bacon and Monk Schwartz had invented gunpowder,[4]—built its whole art of war,—all fortification by land and sea, all drill and military education,—on that one compound; all is an extension of a gunbarrel;—and is very scornful about bows and arrows, and reckons Greeks and Romans and middle ages little better than Indians and bow and arrow times. As if of the earth, water, gases, lightning, and caloric, had not a million energies,—the discovery of any one of which could change the art of war again, and put an end to war, by the exterminating forces man can apply.

Now if this is true in all the useful, and in the fine arts, that the direction must be drawn from a superior source, or there will be no good work,—does it hold less in our social and civil life? In our popular politics, you may note that each aspirant who rises above the crowd, however at first making his obedient apprenticeship in party tactics, if he have sagacity, soon learns, that it is by no means by obeying the vulgar weathercock of his party, the resentments, the fears and whims of it, that real power is gained, but that he must often face and resist the party, and abide by his resistance, and put them in fear: that the only title to their permanent respect and to a larger following, is, to see for himself what is the real public interest, and stand for that;—that is a principle,—and all the cheering and hissing of the crowd must by and by accommodate itself to that. Our times easily afford you very good examples.

The law of water and all fluids is true of wit. Prince Metternich said, "Revolutions begin in the best heads, and run steadily down to the populace." It is a very old observation, and not truer because Metternich said it, and not less true.

Never country had such a fortune,—as men call fortune,—as this,—in its geography, its history, in the present attitude of its affairs, and in its majestic possibility. At every moment some one country more than any other represents the sentiment and the future of mankind. At the present time, none will doubt that America occupies this place in the opinion of nations. Not only it is the illustration of the theories of political economists, it is the topic to which all foreign journalists return as soon as they have told their local politics. Not only Buonaparte affirmed in 1816,[5] that, in twenty-five years, the United States would dictate the politics of Europe,—a prophecy a little premature, but fast being confirmed, but it is proved by the fact of the vast emigration into this country from all the nations of western and central Europe: and, when the adventurers have planted themselves, and looked about, they send back all the money they can spare to bring their friends. Meantime they find this country just passing through a great crisis in its history, as necessary as lactation, or dentition, or puberty, to the human individual. We are in these days settling for ourselves and our descendants questions, which, as they shall be determined in one way or another, will make the peace and prosperity, or the calamity of the next ages.

The questions of Education, of Society, of Labor, the direction of talent, of character, the nature and habits of the American, may well occupy us: and more, the question of Religion. "The superior man thinks of virtue; the small man thinks of comfort." "There are times," said Niebuhr, "when something better than comfort can be obtained."[6] It is an old oracle, that nations die by suicide, and the sign of it is the decay of thought.

The difficulty with the young men is, not their opinion and its consequences, not that they are copperheads, but that they lack idealism. A man for success must not be *pure* idealist;—then he will practically fail: but he must have ideas, must obey ideas, or he might as well be the horse he rides on. A man does not want to be sun-dazzled, sun-blind, but every man must have glimmer enough to keep him from knocking his head against the walls. And it is in the interest of civilization, and good society, and friendship, that I dread to hear of well-born, gifted, and amiable men, that they have this indifference, this despair, disposing them in the present attitude of the war to short and hasty peace, on any terms.

It is the young men of the land, who must save it: it is they to whom this wonderful hour, after so many weary ages, dawns, the Second Declaration of Independence, the proclaiming of liberty, land, justice, and a career for all men; and honest dealings with other nations. Philip de Comines says, in writing of the wars of Charles of Burgundy with Louis XI, of France, "Our Lord does not wish that one kingdom should play the devil with another."[7] Nations were made to help each other as much as families were; and all advancement is by ideas, and not by brute force, or mechanic force.

I call this spirit a remainder of Europe, imported into this soil. To say the truth, England is never out of mind. Nobody says it, but all think and feel it. England is the model in which they find their wishes expressed, not, of course, middle-class England, but rich, powerful and titled England.

Now, English nationality is babyish, like the self-esteem of villages, like the nationality of Carolina, or of Cheraw, or of Hull, or the conceit and insolence of the shabby little kings on the Gambia River, who strut up to the traveller, "What do they say of me in America?" The English have a certain childishness,—it is at once their virtue and their fault, and every traveller, I am sure, can find in his personal experience comic examples of it. They are insular, and narrow. They have no higher worship than Fate. Excellent sailors, farmers, ironsmiths, weavers, potters, they retain their Scandinavian strength and skill; but their morals do not reach beyond their frontier. The old passion for plunder. England watches like her old war-wolf for plunder.

Never a lofty sentiment, never a duty to civilization, never a generosity, a moral self-restraint is suffered to stand in the way of a commercial advantage. In sight of a commodity, her religion, her morals are forgotten. Even her ablest living writer, a man who has earned his position by the sharpest insights, is politically a fatalist.[8] In his youth he announced himself as a "theoretical sansculotte fast threatening to become a practical one." Now he is practically in the English system, a Venetian aristocracy, with only a private stipulation in favor of men of genius. In the "History of Frederick the Great," the reader is treated as if he were a Prussian adjutant, solely occupied with the army and the campaign. He is ever in the dreary circle of camp and courts. But of the people you have no glimpse. No hint of their domestic life. Were there no families, no farms, no thoughtful citizens, no beautiful and generous women, no genial youth with beating hearts then alive in all the broad territories of that kingdom? We are, to be sure, well accustomed to this pedantic way of writing history. We should not bring this criticism on another writer. But from Carlyle, who has taught us to make it, we had a right to expect an account of a nation, and not of a campaign.

But if the leaders of thought take this false direction, what can you expect from those who do not think, but are absorbed in maintaining their class privileges, their luxury, or their trade? As compared with France, in the distinction given to intellect in the state, and in society, England is Chinese in her servility to wealth, and to old wealth. Hence the discovery of 1848,—that Paris was the capital of Europe; Paris, and not London.[9] All men waited for Paris. If Paris revolted, so would Vienna and Berlin, and in the same way. In the revolt of the German cities, in that year,[10] they imitated the forms and methods of the insurrectionists in the French capital. They had the creed that the idea of human freedom was present in Paris, the liberty of London was selfish and mixed, a liberty quite too much drenched in respect for privileges, cast-iron artistocracy and church hierarchy. The socialism of France indicates the more searching character of their aims, full of crude thoughts

141

and wishes, but sincere, and aiming to lift the condition of mankind; to be a new experiment for a higher civilization. The continent waited for the action of Paris. London waited too, showing that Paris was the capital not of Europe only, but of London also. And London waits still. By the accident of a strong Emperor, and by the energy of the French nation when firmly led, the whole policy of England in the last ten years has waited on France like a spaniel. Silently, Waterloo[11] is avenged by the falling of the court of London into the second place, and expecting the initiative in every question from the French. It was not that France was wise, but that England was weak.

There have been revolutions which were not in the interest of feudalism and barbarism, but in that of society. A series of wars in Europe are read with passionate interest, and never lose their pathos by time. 1. The planting of Christianity. 2. The driving of the Moors from Spain, France, and Germany. 3. The rise of towns. 4. The Reformation of Luther. 5. The decay of the temporal power of the Pope; the breaking of the power of the Jesuits; the breaking of the power of the Inquisition.[12] 6. The establishment of free institutions in England, France, America. 7. The revolutions effected in all the arts of life by science. 8. The destruction of slavery. And these are distinguished not by the numbers of the combatants, or the numbers of the slain, but by the motive. No interest now attaches to the wars of York and Lancaster,[13] to the wars of England and Scotland, to the wars of German, French, and Spanish emperors, which were only dynastic wars, but to those in which a principle was involved.

When the cannon is aimed by ideas, then gods join in the combat, then poets are born. More gunpowder is burned in this state on the 4th July, in squibs and fireworks, than in battles that have decided the fate of nations. When men die for what they live for, and the mainspring that works daily urges them to hazard all, then the cannon articulates its explosions with the voice of a man. Then the rifle seconds the cannon, and the fowling-piece the rifle, and the women make cartridges, and all shoot at one mark, and the better code of laws at last records the victory. Now the chiefest of these,—

culmination of these triumphs of humanity, and which did virtually include the extinction of slavery,—is, the planting of America.

If the general history of Europe is dreary with war and oppression, neither can we pretend that our own record is quite clean. In America, we have had great faults also. Here there has been torpor of the nobler faculties; here have prevailed vulgar estimates of success. Our foreign policy has not been republican, not in the interests of freedom or humanity. We had no character. In the European crisis, once and again we should have great weight, if we had character. But Austria, Prussia, France, and Russia, looked at America, and said,—"'Tis worse than we." For this reason, there is very little in our history that rises above commonplace, and we are forced to go back to the Revolution in 1775, to find any ground of praise. In the Greek Revolution, Clay and Webster persuaded Congress into some cold declaration of sympathy.[14] Once we tendered Lafayette a national ship, gave him an ovation, and a tract of land.[15] We attempted some testimony of national sympathy to Kossuth and Hungary.[16] We sent corn and money to the Irish Famine.[17] These were spasmodic demonstrations. They were ridiculed as sentimentalism. They were sentimentalism, for it was putting us into a theatrical attitude. We belied our sympathy with Hungary, by greeting her oppressor: our sympathy with French liberty, by striking hands with her usurper: our sympathy with Ireland, by the dimensions of the Know-Nothing party.[18]

Now let me show you some of the points that make the fortune or felicity of this nation.

Our estimate of America variable. Yesterday insignificant; today, all-commanding. America was opened after the feudal mischief was spent, and so the people made a good start. We begun well. No inquisition here; no kings, no nobles, no dominant church. In every other country, the accusation of heresy brings want and danger to a man's door. Here it has lost its terrors. Saadi says, "the subjects are always of their master's opinion in religion." We have eight or ten religions in every large town, and the most that comes of it is a degree or two on the thermometer of fashion. A pew in a particular church gives an easier entrance to the subscription ball. We have repealed the old abuses. We have ample domain,—and thence facility of living. Greater freedom of circumstance is here. English and Europeans are girt with an iron belt of condition.

The legislature heard and heeded the voice of the professor of Natural History[19] when he told them that he trusted to live to see the day when as many scholars would come to his museum from Europe as now go hence to theirs; and that he wished them to put Natural Science on an equal footing with the support of public worship. And if one sees the tendency of our steps, the gifts to learning by private benefactors; the enlarging appropriations of town meetings and of states to the schools; the gift of scholarships and fellowships; recent foundation of agricultural schools,—of military, of naval, of gymnasiums, of the Nautical Almanac, and astronomic observatories; it looks as if vast extension was given to this popular culture, and, as the appetite grows by feeding, the next generation will vote for their children,—not a dame-school, nor a Latin school, but a university, complete training in all the arts of peace and war, letters, science; all the useful and all the fine arts. And thus the voters in the Republic will at last be educated to that public duty. In America, the government is acquainted with the opinions of all classes, knows the leading men in the middle class, knows the leaders of the humblest class. The President comes near enough to these: if he does not, the caucus does,—the primary ward—and town-meeting, and, what is important does reach him. Not such,—far enough from such—is England, France, and Austria: and, indeed, not such was America under previous administrations.

The politics of Europe are feudal. The six demands of chartism,[20] are: 1. Universal suffrage; 2. Vote by ballot; 3. Paid legislation; 4. Annual Parliament; 5. Equality of Electoral District; 6. No property qualification. In England, they are still postponed. They have all been granted here to begin with.

We are coming,—thanks to the war,—to a nationality. Put down your foot, and say to England, we know your merits. In past time, we have paid them the homage of ignoring your faults. We see them still. But it is time that you should hear the truth,—that you have failed in one of the great hours that put nations to the test. When the occasion of magnanimity arrived, you had none: you forgot your loud professions, you rubbed your hands with indecent joy, and saw only in our extreme danger the chance of humbling a rival and getting away his commerce. When it comes to divide an estate, the politest men will sometimes quarrel. Justice is above your aim. Stand aside. We have seen through you. We shall not again give you any advantage of honor. We shall be compelled to look at the stern facts. And we cannot count you great. Your inches are conspicuous, and we cannot count your inches against our miles and leagues and parallels of latitude. We are forced to analyse your greatness. We who saw you in a halo of honor which our affection made, now we must measure your means; your true dimensions; your population; we must compare the future of this country with that, in a time when every prosperity of ours knocks away the stones from your foundation.

My own interest in the country is not precisely the same as that of my neighbors. I do not compute the annual production, the imports, or the valuation. My interest is perhaps professional. I wish that war, as peace, shall bring out the heart and genius of the men. In every company, in every town, I seek knowledge and character, and so in every circumstance.

These native masters, and only these should have the discretion in every department. Therefore I read with great pleasure that Mr. Jenckes of Rhode Island has submitted to Congress a bill prescribing an examination for every officer who may be appointed to a civil office under Government, and for every promotion, with certain exceptions.[21] Of course all incompetent persons would at once cease to apply, whilst fit persons who will not now submit to the degradation of lobbying, begging, and bribing, would offer themselves, when the knowledge and skill were to be tested. Honest members of Congress who have appointments in their gift to the Naval School, or to West Point, have already set excellent example of advertising a fair competition by examination free to all candidates in their district. In the English government Lord Macaulay introduced the like innovation to the East-India service.[22] If this become

American law, we shall not send ignorant drunkards, who happen to be political favorites, to represent the Republic in foreign nations, whose languages they do not know, and will not learn, and so become ridiculous there.

Our forefathers scraped the rough surface of the earth for clams and acorns, or venison brought down with a flint arrowhead, and a little corn ground between two stones. Every invention carries us forward a century; steam and the telegraph have blotted out the word *distance* from the Dictionary. Hoe's press, and McCormick's Reaper, and the sewing machine and the photograph, the use of ether, (American inventions) have left behind them the witchcraft of Merlin and Cornelius Agrippa.[23]

See how this civil freedom moderates the ferocity incident elsewhere to political changes. We in the midst of a great revolution still enacting the sentiment of the Puritans, and the dreams of young people of thirty years ago,—we passing out of old remainders of barbarism into pure Christianity and humanity,—into freedom of thought, of religion, of speech, of the press, of trade, of suffrage, or political right, and working through this tremendous ordeal which elsewhere went by beheadings and reign of terror, passing through this like a sleep, calmly reading the newspaper, and drinking our tea the while. This serenity of the northern states 'tis like a brick house moved from its foundations, and passing through our streets, whilst all the family are pursuing their domestic work as usual within doors.

Nature says to the American, 'I understand mensuration and numbers. I compute the ellipse of the moon; the ebb and flow of waters; the curve and the errors of planets; the balance of attraction and recoil. I have measured out to you by weight and tally the power you need. I give you the land and sea, the forest and the mine, the elemental forces, nervous energy. When I add difficulty, I add brain. See to it that you hold and administer the continent for mankind. One thing you have rightly done. You have offered a patch of land in the wilderness to every son of Adam who will till it. Other things you have begun to do,—to strike off the chains which snuffling hypocrites have bound on the weaker race. You are to imperil your lives and fortunes for a principle.'

Chartism in England asks that intellect and not property, or, at least, intellect as well as property, be represented in Parliament. Humanity asks that government shall not be ashamed to be tender and parternal; but that democratic institutions shall be more thoughtful for the interests of women,—for the training of chldren, for care of sick and unable persons and serious care of criminals, than was ever any the best government of the old world. Mathematicians say, that, "in the end, the cards beat all the players, were they never so skilful." And we say, that revolutions beat all the insurgents, be they never so determined and politic; that the great interests of mankind, being at every moment, through ages, in favor of justice, and the largest liberty,—will always, from time to time, gain on the adversary, and, at last, win the day. The same felicity comes out of our reverses. Now as we have owed commanding advantages to our geography, and to the planting of the country by exiles from Europe, who wished to avoid the evils of the old world; and these exiles were the idealists of Europe, aiming at freedom in religion and state.

It will hereafter be found that what immense benefit accrued to this country, and to the society of nations from the American Revolution of 1775, no less benefit accrued from the present calamities. Crises and war help us. War shatters porcelain dolls,—breaks up in a nation Chinese conservatism. War always ennobles an age. What munificence has it not disclosed! How easily a sentiment has unclasped the grip of avarice in the rich, and made those who were not rich prodigally generous, through the painfullest economy! We used to think that the feeling of patriotism did not exist in this country, or had a feeble pulse. The country was too large. We could not be very hot about the enormous reaches of a continent. It was as if one were to praise the Atlantic as a better ocean than the Pacific or Indian or take a pride in our globe as a more desireable globe to live on than Saturn or Mars. But the moment an enemy appeared, we woke out of sleep. No country! We had nothing else but a country. Business was thrust aside. Every house hung out the flag. Every street was full of patriotic songs. Almost every able bodied man put on uniform. As the smoke of the combat begins to lift, the people see their debt successively to passages that gave most alarm when they befel.

To enumerate some of these shortly:

1. To South Carolina for taking the initiative, as relieving us from the far greater danger, which, in the last years of the peace, overhung us,—that the South in possession of the government should have forced through Congress an act securing to the planter the right of transit with his slaves, which, it is easy to see, in the old state of parties, would have made slavery familiar in Massachusetts and Illinois, and, with the army and navy in possession of the South, could only have been resisted by a religious war in the North.

2. That an eminent benefactor of the Union in this war has been the Vice President of the Confederacy proclaiming the theory and policy of his government,—a manifesto hitherto unrebuked, never disowned,—that "Slavery was the cornerstone of their State." No public act has served us so much at home and abroad, except Emancipation.

3. A felicity of the Republic has been, what gave great apprehension in the beginning, the extreme caution, not to say timidity and tardiness, of President Lincoln, which has served us as a more determined leader might not.

4. We owe very much to the sympathizers with the rebellion in the North, to Governor Seymour, Vallandigham, the Woods, and Pierce,[24] whose mobs, councils, platforms, and the casual disclosure of the correspondence of some of these persons have repelled honest men, and driven them to the support of the country, as entreaties from the Republicans could never have drawn them.

5. Lastly, we owe main thanks to the firmness of the tone of the Rebels, and the rancor of their hatred, now in the extreme of their fortunes.

'Tis vain to say that the war was avoidable by us, or, that both are in the wrong. The difference between the parties is eternal,—

it is the difference of moral and immoral motive. Your action is to build, and their action is to destroy: yours to protect and establish the rights of men, and theirs to crush them, in favor of a few owners. Machiavel himself said, " 'Tis not the violence which repairs, but the violence which destroys, that is to blame."[25]

It is difficult to exasperate the Northern people. In this climate, the genius of the people is mild, the mind active, and perpetually diverted to trade, manufactures, and railroads, public works, politics, and general knowledge, which hinder men from brooding on any bad blood. We are therefore placable, and, through the whole war, there has been danger that on the first hint of peace from the South, our people would forget and forgive all, and rush inconsiderately into the arms of their returning prodigals, and, in the gladness of the hour, would accept any terms,—the Union as it was,—losing by this social weakness half the fruit of their valor and their sacrifice of life and treasure. If we had conquered in the early part of the War, there was the greatest danger of a reckless generosity on our part. But, better than we could think, our defeats have been our protection from this fatal imprudence. And now, when the rebels seem to be pushed almost to their boundaries, and ready to be driven overboard into the gulf, they exhibit the same effrontery in their demands as at their best fortunes,—the vanquished claiming the terms of victory. This audacity comes timely in to disgust us, and teach "What one is why may not millions be?"

American past is diffusion. We have a longer scale, and can reach the highest and the lowest degrees. And it is possible that here we shall have the happiness of lifting the low. Every body hates vulgarity. But he that goes to the outcast to save him is defended by his motive from the pollution of that society. The steps already taken to teach the freedman his letters, and the decencies of life, are not worth much if they stop there. They teach the teacher,— open his eyes to new methods. They give him manliness and breadth he had not; and accustom him to a courage and poise: he learns to encounter the vulgarities of common society in town and country. And there is no society, there is hardly the individual,— that has not his vulgar side for as people are not altogether wise, but wise locally or topically, so they are locally or in some points graceful and cultivated, and in others strangely obtuse and mean.

Two facts appear:

1. That, in the activity of the people, up to this time, is a certain fatalism: That they have obeyed the materialities the continent offered them, and, being the contemporary of pine, chestnut, oak, granite, ice, waterfall, of wheat, cotton, copper, iron, and coal, they have wrought in them, and have done the best with these means. What could be done with leather, or with calico, a pine log, that they have not done? This productivity, the admirable tools, finer and coarser, embracing all the armoury of modern Mechanics,— steam, railway, telegraph, up to Representative Government and Common School,—all these, they have conquered for the use of posterity. In short they have been in system and detail, the river-hand, and the sea-hand. On the coast, they have followed the sea; in the west, followed the river. We have worked and have eaten. We have got our wages. This was the poor man's paradise;—it has fed him fat. The poor man is getting rich: he is getting nervous, too. His prosperity has fairly alarmed him. What! nothing but putting money in our pockets, and having everything we want! There must come some end to this, or it would go to madness. Meat and drink and pampering, at last, pulls the man down. It runs to softening of the brain, corruption of principles, and to hypocrisy and canting. Already the verdict of mankind is that the race is morally injured, that they have not kept the promise of their founders and early constitutions. They are in search of nothing grand or heroic. They have known no trait of enlarged policy. A liberal measure has no chance; a just measure, very little chance, if there is no powerful party to extort it.

Crisis and war is often useful, even though the insurgents for liberty may be foiled. It traces the lines, it shows what justice they seek, and they see it clearer by the light of the passions and the battle fires. It spots the bad church, or bad priesthood, or bad king, or bad law, and the tradition of these is well kept, and secures a new attempt by larger numbers, in the next age.

2. Let the passion for America cast out the passion for Europe.

Here let there be what the earth waits for,—exalted manhood, the new man, whom plainly this country must furnish. Freer swing his arms, further pierce his eyes, more forward and forthright his whole build and carriage, goeth, than the Englishman's, who, we see, is much imprisoned in his backbone. What a change! We are all of English race. But climate and country have told on us so that John Bull does not know us. It is the Jonathanizing of John. They have grown cosmopolitan. Once the most English of English men, hating foreigners, they have grown familiar with the foreigner, and learned to use him according to his gift.

England has long been the cashier of the world. The progress of trade threatens to supplant London by New York, and that England must cross to India if she keeps it and to China, by the Pacific Railroad; and the London merchant must lose his privilege of buying and selling Exchange on London, and buy Exchange on New York. This hastens, and is only checked by the War, and, though no man in England suffers such a word to pass his lips, it passes through his nose in this translation. How dreadful it is to see the Americans slaughter each other! Let us recognize the Southern independence and we will have a strict alliance with the South, check the Yankee prosperity, or share it. The one foreign interest of England is to assure herself in all times of the alliance of America, as bound by blood, language, religion, trade, and equal civilization. In all the dangers which are likely to threaten her from France, Austria, or Russia, America was sure to sympathize, and what protection would be so noble to bestow and to receive. Then the more ambitious a state is, the more vulnerable. England, France, have ships, towns, colonies, treasure, and can very ill afford to give every Yankee Skipper a chance to hack at these.

In speaking of England, I lay out of question the truly cultivated class. They exist in England, as in France, in Italy, in Germany, in America. The inspirations of God, like birds, never stop at frontiers or languages, but come to every nation. This class like Christians, or poets, or chemists, exist for each other, across all possible nationalities, strangers to their own people,—brothers to you. I lay them out of question. They are sane men, as far removed

151

as we, from the arrogance and mendacity of the English press, and the shoptone of the cities. They wish to be exactly informed and to speak and act not for us or against us, but for the public good and the truth.

Neither do I think that we are to lay up malice against England, or to make Punch's pictures or the opinions of the House of Lords a *casus belli*. Shall we go to war with England on account of Punch's pictures, or the opinions of a drunken Lord Soft?[26] Having penetrated the people, and known their unworthiness, we can well cease to respect their opinion, even their contempt, and not go to war, at our disadvantage, for the avoiding of this. Who are they that they should despise us? these who cringe before Napoleon and Gortchakoff.[27] We remember the wise saying of General Scott, "Resentment is a bad basis for a campaign."[28] When I think who these are that insult us, and pierce to the motive, I am not sure of the wisdom of Burke's saying, "Contempt is not a thing to be despised."

I believe this cannot be accomplished by dunces or idlers, but requires docility, sympathy, and religious receiving from higher principles; for liberty like religion, is a short and hasty fruit, and, like all power, subsists only by new rallyings on the source of inspiration. Power *can* be generous. The very grandeur of the means which offer themselves to you should suggest grandeur in the direction of your expenditure. If your mechanic arts are unsurpassed in usefulness, if you have taught the river to make shoes and nails and carpets, and the bolt of heaven to write your letters like a gillot pen,[29]—let these wonders work for honest humanity, for the poor, for justice, genius, and the public good. I wish you to see that this country, the last found, is the great charity of God to the human race.

The times are dark, but heroic. The war uplifts us into generous sentiments. We do not often have a moment of grandeur in these hurried slipshod lives. The people have met the dreadful issues so frankly. The youth have shown themselves heroes. The women have shown a tender patriotism, and an inexhaustible charity. And in each new threat of faction the ballot of the people has been beyond expectation right and decisive. We will not again disparage

America, now that we have seen what men it will bear. The slavery is broken, and, if we use our advantage, irretrievably. For such a gain,—to end once for all that pest of all free institutions,—one generation might well be sacrificed,—perhaps it will be,—that this continent be purged, and a new era of equal rights dawn on the universe. Who would not, if it could be made certain, that the new morning of universal liberty should rise on our race, by the perishing of one generation,—who would not consent to die?

The revolution is the work of no man, but the eternal effervescence of nature. It never did not work. And not a republican, not a statesman, not an idealist, not an abolitionist, can say without effrontery, I did it. Go push the globe, or scotch the globe, to accelerate or to retard it in its orbit. It is elemental. It is the old gravitation. Beware of the firing and the recoil. Who knows or has computed the periods? A little earlier, and you would have been sacrificed in vain. A little later, and you are unnecessary. "If I had attempted in 1806, what I performed in 1807," said Napoleon, "I had been lost."[30] Fremont was superseded in 1861, for what his superseders are achieving in 1863.[31]

Mazzini and Kossuth,—'tis fine for them to sit in committee in London, and hope to direct revolution in Italy, Hungary, or Poland.[32] Committees don't manage revolutions. A revolution is a volcano, and from under everybody's feet flings its sheet of fire into the sky.

The end of all political struggle, is, to establish morality as the basis of all legislation. 'Tis not free institutions, 'tis not a republic, 'tis not a democracy, that is the end,—no, but only the means: morality is the object of government. We want a state of things in which crime will not pay. A state of things which allows every man the largest liberty compatible with the liberty of every other man.

The guiding star to the arrangement and use of facts, is in your leading thought. You will have come to the perception that justice satisfies everybody, and justice alone. You will stand there for vast interests, North and South, East and West will be present to your mind, and your vote will be as if they voted. And you well know that your vote secures the foundations of the state, goodwill, liberty, and security of traffic and of production, and mutual increase of goodwill in the great interests, for no monopoly has been foisted in, no weak party or nationality has been sacrificed, no coward compromise has been conceded to a strong partner. Every one of these is the seed of vice, war, and national disorganization. In seeing this guidance of events, in seeing this felicity without example, that has rested on the Union thus far,—I find new confidence for the future. I could heartily wish that our will and endeavor were more active parties to the work. But I see in all directions the light breaking; that trade and government will not alone be the favored aims of mankind, but every useful, every elegant art, every exercise of imagination, the height of Reason, the noblest affection, the purest religion will find their house in our institutions, and write our laws for the benefit of men.

Textual Commentary

Joel Myerson

This book contains eighteen works by Ralph Waldo Emerson on the subject of slavery written between 1838 and 1863. Fourteen of these are public speeches and four are published letters. Of the fourteen speeches, one is previously unpublished, four are available only in contemporary newspaper accounts and have never been collected in any edition of Emerson's writings, and nine were published posthumously in either the 1884 or 1904 editions of *Miscellanies* in a form much revised for later readers.

We publish here for the first time Emerson's 1855 lecture on slavery. We have also edited five other public speeches from manuscript and present in notes a relevant manuscript that forms the background to Emerson's letter to President Van Buren on the Cherokees.

We present each text in a form as close as possible to what Emerson originally wrote or delivered. In some cases, Emerson's manuscript no longer exists, while in other cases we have been able to use the manuscript in establishing our text. Emerson's titles are shown in quotation marks; we assigned the remaining titles. Each text presents its own editorial problems, which we discuss in detail in the comments devoted to each work.

Emerson's letters are reprinted from their first appearance in print, since no manuscripts have been located for any of them. Emerson definitely intended for his letters to Martin Van Buren and to the Kidnapping Committee to be published, and he may have known that his letters to William Rotch and to Mary Merrick Brooks would be used in a public forum. At any rate, because they were published, they represent public statements by Emerson on antislavery that were read by his contemporaries and thus deserve to be included here.

"An Address . . . on . . . the Emancipation of the Negroes in the British West Indies" was published the year Emerson delivered it, in 1844. No manuscript has been located. Because Emerson undoubtedly saw the text through publication, we have reprinted the 1844 text rather than the posthumously edited text in *Miscellanies*.

No manuscripts exist for seven other speeches; accounts of these texts come from contemporary newspapers or books. (Readers should be aware that newspaper accounts of Emerson's lectures are based on stenographic reports, not Emerson's manuscript, and should thus be used with care.) For these speeches, we have reprinted either the only account or the most complete account. In the latter instance, we have noted significant differences among the accounts. Some of these speeches were published in *Miscellanies*, and we have noted significant differences in that edition as well.

The two addresses on the Fugitive Slave Law were first published in *Miscellanies*. We have edited them from the surviving manuscripts. We have also noted significant differences between the manuscripts and the printed texts.

The lecture on slavery of 1855 is previously unpublished, and we have edited it from the surviving manuscript.

Emerson's speech on the assault on Charles Sumner was reported in contemporary newspapers and published in *Miscellanies*. We have edited it from the surviving manuscript. There are no significant differences between the manuscript and the printed texts.

"The President's Proclamation" was published the year Emerson delivered it, in 1862. The manuscript exists and served as the printer's copy. For this address, we have chosen the manuscript as our base text and emended it from the published text, which Emerson definitely saw through publication.

"Fortune of the Republic" was delivered in 1863. In 1878, after Emerson's creative powers had severely diminished, James Elliot Cabot and Emerson's daughter Ellen assembled a new lecture from the original manuscript and from other lectures and published it with the same title. This text was reprinted in *Miscellanies*. We have edited the surviving manuscript of the earlier form of the lecture.

The manuscripts of Emerson's lectures and addresses must be approached with care. Rarely does the surviving manuscript represent what the audience actually heard. Emerson often revised the wording and organization of a talk when he presented it before different audiences. Even when he gave a talk only once, Emerson may have removed parts of it for use in later speeches; Cabot and Ellen may have also removed parts of it for use in various published works they compiled. In this volume we publish the final layer of the extant manuscript and report significant variations from contemporary accounts or posthumously published texts. We also list any changes we have made in Emerson's wording. We have silently changed Emerson's punctuation only when the manuscript punctuation would result in a loss of clarity of expression. We have also silently imposed some regularity on Emerson's capitalization, paragraphing, spelling, and hyphenation practices, and we have spelled out abbreviations, such as ampersands. Because only one of the manuscripts ("The President's Proclamation") was prepared with an eye toward publication, Emerson's practices in them are erratic. In the case of "The President's Proclamation," Emerson clearly expected a uniform house styling to be imposed on his punctuation by the *Atlantic Monthly*, and he made no attempt to retain his own usage; we have restored Emerson's punctuation from the manuscript. (For a detailed discussion of how another Emerson text was treated by the *Atlantic*, see Joel Myerson, "Emerson's 'Thoreau': A New Edition from Manuscript," *Studies in the American Renaissance 1979*, ed. Myerson [Boston: Twayne, 1979], pp. 17–92.)

Emerson's texts in the *Miscellanies* volumes of the Riverside Edition (1884), Little Classic Edition (1884), and Centenary Edition

(1904) (all published by Houghton Mifflin of Boston) are textually unsound. Cabot often added material from other speeches that he thought better expressed ideas in the speech being edited, inserted his own transitional material, and substituted his own wording for Emerson's when he thought it more appropriate. (For a full discussion of Cabot's editorial work, see Nancy Craig Simmons, "Arranging the Sibylline Leaves: James Elliot Cabot's Work as Emerson's Literary Executor," *Studies in the American Renaissance 1983*, ed. Joel Myerson [Charlottesville: University Press of Virginia, 1983], pp. 335–389.) Edward Waldo Emerson did much the same when he prepared the 1904 edition of *Miscellanies*. House styling of spelling, punctuation, hyphenization, paragraphing, and capitalization was imposed on Emerson's texts in all three editions. Significant differences remain between the texts we have printed and these three posthumous editions, which we discuss below.

In the comments that follow we give more detailed information about the location of manuscripts, published accounts of speeches, first book and magazine appearances, first collected appearances in editions of Emerson's works, and variations between manuscripts and published texts. For extant manuscripts, we list alterations in the manuscript and emendations we have made and we discuss particularly difficult textual issues in Textual Notes. Each entry in the textual apparatus begins with the page and line number(s) at which the entry may be found. The reading to the left of the bracket is that of our version. The reading to the right of the bracket in the Alterations in the Manuscript and Emendations sections is that of the manuscript; in the Textual Notes, it is an explanation of the textual crux. In describing manuscript readings, we have employed standard editorial symbols: angle brackets (< >) indicate deletions in the manuscript, and up- and down-arrows (↑ ↓) represent insertions in the manuscript. Thus, '<boy> girl' means that Emerson wrote 'boy', canceled it, and wrote 'girl' immediately after it on the same line; '<boy>girl' means that Emerson wrote 'boy' and canceled it by writing 'girl' directly over it; and '<boy> ↑girl↓' means that Emerson wrote 'boy', canceled it, and inserted 'girl'.

We use the following abbreviations throughout the Textual Commentary:

L for *The Letters of Ralph Waldo Emerson*, ed. Ralph L. Rusk and Eleanor M. Tilton, 8 vols. to date (New York: Columbia University Press, 1939; 1990–).

JMN for *The Journals and Miscellaneous Notebooks of Ralph Waldo Emerson*, ed. William H. Gilman et al., 16 vols. (Cambridge, Mass.: Harvard University Press, 1960–1982).

LETTER TO MARTIN VAN BUREN

No manuscript has been located. The letter was first published as "Communication," in the *Daily National Intelligencer* (Washington), 14 May 1838, p. 2. We have reprinted this text. The letter was subsequently reprinted in the *Yeoman's Gazette*, 19 May 1838 (where it is introduced as "a copy of a letter" obtained "from our esteemed fellow citizen, Rev. R. Waldo Emerson"); *Christian Register*, 2 June 1838, p. 1; *Old Colony Memorial*, 2 June 1838; and as "Words Fitly Spoken," *Liberator*, 22 June 1838, p. 98. There is only one change between these printed versions and the first one: in the first paragraph, the phrase 'through the medium of the press' has been deleted, as if to obscure the fact that the letter had been published before. It was subsequently published in the Centenary Edition of *Miscellanies* (1904), pp. 89–96. One change in the *Miscellanies* text is of interest: in the seventh paragraph, the phrase 'Our wise men shake their heads dubiously' is deleted, lessening the impact of Emerson's statement.

A draft of this letter appears in Emerson's journal (*JMN*, 12:26–29). Another relevant document of interest is the following unpublished manuscript fragment on Indians at the Houghton Library of Harvard University (bMS Am 1280.197 [9]). Bracketed numbers indicate manuscript page numbers.

[1] I call on you to make this movement in behalf of civilization
The one thing that means & makes union, is justice: if there

are two men that mean justly <th> between them union
begins & will spread and they two are stronger than ten
thousand men meaning injustice though they call it by all the
names of patriotism

[2] [first six lines at the top right]
↑ Hiawatha
Wyoming
beautiful names
flints arrowheads
oldestman
Mr Agassiz ↓

Buck
treat him as wolf he is wolf

his traits power, valor, self command,
his passions are noble & not base,
revenge, but it was never forbidden him
but when he in turn is visited by the
avenger of blood, he submits

his knowledge <i>as a naturalist
    But
his traditional skill
to make a tent or a sledge or a bow or a boat
wise as a hound
looks at the bottom of the tree
looks at the north or the west of a rock
can call a muskrat to him & he will come
a moose
Redjacket & Mr Parker
    But how have we treated him
He held all the land & now has not where to spr[e]ad
a blanket

[3] Always time to do right

Alas for them, their day is oer,
Their fires are out by hill & shore,
<Their pleasant springs are dry
<The white man's axe is in their woods
The white man's sail is on their floods>>
No more for them the wild deer bounds
The plough is on their hunting grounds
<Their pleasant springs are dry
Their children, look, by power opprest
Beyond the mountains of the west
Their children go to die>
The pale mans ax rings in their woods
The pale mans sail is on their floods
Their pleasant springs are dry.
Their children,—look,—by power opprest,
Beyond the mountains of the west
Their children go to die.

[4] Sketch of speech for the Indians

The council fires are never extinguished on their thousand hills the war knife is never buried on their boundless plains.

I live in the hope that out of the very evils now reaching their crisis a new happier era is to be inaugurated I trust the legalised crime is to be ended that the strewing sugar on a bottled spider the attempt to cover over with sacred associations & religious & loyal names the hideous oppression & injustice <&>to call the essence of the devils by the name of God as we have allowed our politicians to do,

"AN ADDRESS . . . ON . . . THE EMANCIPATION
OF THE NEGROES IN THE BRITISH WEST INDIES"
No manuscript has been located. The address was first published as *An Address Delivered in the Court-House in Concord, Massachusetts,*

on 1st August, 1844, on the Anniversary of the Emancipation of the Negroes in the British West Indies (Boston: James Munroe, 1844). We have reprinted this text. Accounts of Emerson's delivery of the address were published as "Celebration of the 1st August—West India Emancipation at Concord, Mass. 1844," in the *New-York Daily Tribune*, 5 August 1844, p. 2, and as "Ralph W. Emerson's Oration," in the *Liberator*, 16 August 1844, p. 129. Emerson substantially revised and expanded the address between delivery and publication in early September (see Len Gougeon, *Virtue's Hero: Emerson, Antislavery, and Reform* [Athens: University of Georgia Press, 1990], pp. 88–90). Two reprintings appeared in England: *The Emancipation of the Negroes in the British West Indies* (London: John Chapman, 1844), for which Emerson had supplied proofs from the American edition as setting copy (see *L*, 8:611), and an unauthorized version in *Orations, Lectures, and Addresses* (London: George Slater, 1849). The Chapman edition contains numerous variations in spelling (mostly in '-or'/'-our' words), capitalization, and punctuation from the American edition. There are also about three dozen differences in wording between the two editions; there is no evidence that Emerson is responsible for any of them. Because Emerson had no part in writing these British texts, we did not consider them an accurate source. The address was subsequently reprinted, without any differences in wording from the first printing, in the Riverside Edition of *Miscellanies* (1884), pp. 131–175, and in the Little Classic Edition of *Miscellanies* (1884), pp. 109–143.

EMENDATIONS

10.25	Sharp] Sharpe
10.31	Sharp] Sharpe
10.34	Sharp] Sharpe
10.35	Sharp] Sharpe
10.36	Sharp] Sharpe
13.9	Sharp] Sharpe
27.7	Sharp] Sharpe
30.14	Phillippo] Philippo

Textual Commentary

ANNIVERSARY OF WEST INDIAN EMANCIPATION

No manuscript has been located for Emerson's remarks at the meeting on the anniversary of West Indian emancipation held on 1 August 1845 in Waltham. The most thorough account of the address was published as "Speech of Ralph Waldo Emerson at the Celebration in Waltham, Mass. Aug. 1, 1845," in the *New-York Daily Tribune*, 7 August 1845, p. 2; reprinted as "Celebration of the First of August in Massachusetts," *National Anti-Slavery Standard*, 14 August 1845, p. 1, and as "Speech of Ralph Waldo Emerson," in the *Liberator*, 15 August 1845, p. 130. A shorter account, which includes a paragraph not present in the *Tribune* report, appeared as "Speech of Ralph Waldo Emerson," in the *Liberator*, 8 August 1845, pp. 126–127. We have reprinted the *Tribune* text and added the first paragraph from the *Liberator* account.

EMENDATIONS

36.25   if He has] if He have

LETTER TO WILLIAM ROTCH

No manuscript has been located. The letter was first published as "To the Public," in the *Liberator*, 16 January 1846, p. 10. We have reprinted this text.

ANTISLAVERY SPEECH AT DEDHAM

No manuscript has been located for Emerson's speech at the Massachusetts Anti-Slavery Society Meeting held on 4 July 1846. The only printed account of the speech we have found was published in "Speeches at Dedham," in the *National Anti-Slavery Standard*, 16 July 1846, pp. 5–6. We have reprinted this text.

LETTER TO THE KIDNAPPING COMMITTEE

No manuscript has been located. The letter was first published in *Address of the Committee Appointed by a Public Meeting, Held at Faneuil*

Hall, September 24, 1846, for the Purpose of Considering the Recent Case of Kidnapping from Our Soil, and of Taking Measures to Prevent the Recurrence of Similar Outrages (Boston: White and Potter, 1846), p. 31. We have reprinted this text.

ANTISLAVERY REMARKS AT WORCESTER

No manuscript has been located for Emerson's speech at the Massachusetts Anti-Slavery Society meeting held on 3 August 1849. The only printed account of the speech we have found was published as "Remarks of Ralph Waldo Emerson," in the *Liberator*, 17 August 1849, p. 131. We have reprinted this text.

Some or all of the speech may have been delivered extempore. The *Liberator*'s account of the ceremonies indicates that Emerson was "very hoarse" on this occasion, but "on being called on, [he] said he felt it his duty to make some sort of response to the call."

LETTER TO MARY MERRICK BROOKS

No manuscript has been located. The letter was first published in "Middlesex Co. A. S. Society," in the *Liberator*, 18 April 1851, p. 64. We have reprinted this text.

Rusk and Tilton both tentatively assign Mary Merrick Brooks as the unidentified addressee of this letter; Tilton also names Henry Thoreau's sister, Sophia, as a possible alternative recipient (see *L*, 4:245, 8:273). However, we feel confident that Brooks is the person to whom Emerson addressed the letter.

"ADDRESS TO THE CITIZENS OF CONCORD"
ON THE FUGITIVE SLAVE LAW

Emerson first delivered his address to the citizens of Concord on the Fugitive Slave Law in his hometown on 3 May 1851. He delivered it on several occasions that spring as a campaign stump speech, in an unsuccessful attempt to get John Gorham Palfrey elected to Congress from Middlesex County on the Free Soil ticket.

The manuscript of the address is at the Houghton Library of Harvard University (bMS Am 1280.201 [22]) and is the basis for our text.

Two other manuscript texts exist at Harvard. The first, fifty-eight pages long and titled "Rough draft of Address at Concord 3d May 1851" (bMS Am 1280.201 [20]), is clearly a series of notes toward the finished address. It is marked by an extended attack (at the beginning, rather than the end, as in the final version) on Daniel Webster, much of which was omitted from the final version, as was this representative example (bracketed numbers indicate manuscript page numbers):

[5] Mr Webster has deliberately taken out his name from all the files of honour in which he had enrolled it, from all association with liberal virtuous & philanthropic men, & read his recantation on his knees at Richmond & Charleston. He has gone over in an hour to the party of force, & stands now on the precise ground of the Metternichs, the Castlereaghs, the Polignacs, without the example of hereditary bias, & of an [6] an ancient name & title which they had. He has undone all that he has spent his years in doing.

[7] . . . It is the need of Mr Webster's position that he should have [8] an opinion; that he should be a step in advance of everybody else, & make the strongest statement in America; that is vital to him; he cannot maintain himself otherwise.

He may bluster it:—it is his tactics. We shall make no more mistakes. He has taught us the ghastly meaning of liberty in his mouth It is kidnapping, & hunting to death men & women; it is making treason & matter of fine & imprisonment & armed intervention, of pity & of humanity.

[9] <I am sorry to say it, but> ↑ It has happened ↓ New Hampshire has always been distinguished for the servility of its eminent men. Mr Webster had resisted for a long time the habit of his compatriots—I mean no irony by the word,— and, by adopting the spirited tone of Boston, had recommended himself, as much as by his great talents, to the people

of Massachusetts: but blood is thicker than water; the deep servility of New Hampshire politics, which have [10] marked all prominent statesmen from that district, with the great exception of Mr Hale, has appeared late in life, with all the more strength that it had been resisted so long, & he has renounced what must have cost him some perplexity, all the great passages on which his fame is built.

[11] . . . In the last ↑ week's ↓ newspaper, is his letter to the feasters on Washington's Birth Day at N.Y. containing I know not what apostrophes to "Liberty! Liberty!" <Pho!> ↑ We have ceased to wonder at effrontery, but ↓ Let him for decency's sake drop the use of that word. The <sound> ↑ word ↓ *liberty* in the mouth of Mr Webster, sounds like the word *love* in the mouth of a courtezan.

The second manuscript (bMS Am 1280.201 [21]) bears the same title as the third, final version and is nearly as long (133 pages as opposed to 140). It is very similar to the final version in outline and content. Again, sharp comments on Webster were omitted from the final version, as this comparison between the two shows:

[Final version]: . . . they have torn down his picture from the wall, they have thrust his speeches into the chimney. (65.27–28)

[Second version]: . . . that they have taken his picture from the wall & thrown the pieces in the gutter; that they have taken his book of speeches from the shelf, & thrust it into the <watercloset> ↑ stove ↓. (pp. 93–94)

It also contains evaluations of the roles played by some of Emerson's contemporaries in the passage of or movement against the Fugitive Slave Law, all of which, except those on Webster, are omitted in the final version.

We have been unable to locate any published accounts of this address that include its text. Surprisingly, the *Liberator* mentions it in only a single paragraph as "a fine intellectual and moral treat" (9 May 1851, p. 75). The *Liberator* also mentions a reciting of the address in Cambridge, where Emerson was booed and hissed by unruly Harvard students ("Mr. Emerson's Lecture," 23 May 1851, p. 3). Edwin P. Whipple was present at the occasion and gives his account in "Some Recollections of Ralph Waldo Emerson," *Harper's New Monthly Magazine* 65 (September 1882): 583–584.

The address was first published in the Centenary Edition of *Miscellanies* (1904), pp. 177–214. There are approximately forty differences in wording between our text and the one in *Miscellanies*, some due to misreadings of Emerson's handwriting (for example, *vile* for *rice*, *must* for *most*, and *flock* for *stock*). There are also significant differences in three passages, all appearing in the last quarter of the address.

First, our version does not contain the following passage, added by Edward Waldo Emerson, between 'use.' and '[paragraph] The destiny' (67.16–17 in this book):

> In Mr. Webster's imagination the American Union was a huge Prince Rupert's drop, which, if so much as the smallest end be shivered off, the whole will snap into atoms. Now the fact is quite different from this. The people are loyal, law-loving, law-abiding. They prefer order, and have no taste for misrule and uproar. (p. 205)

This appears in the final manuscript as part of a two-leaf gathering with Edward's notation at the top of the first page that the printer is to skip to the bottom of the second leaf and begin with this passage. These lines do appear in the second manuscript (pp. 115–116), but they are clearly inserted by Edward in the final manuscript and are therefore not incorporated into our text.

Second, two paragraphs in our text, from 'Nothing' to 'Whose deed is that?' (68.5–29), are not in the *Miscellanies* text. These lines are also present in the second manuscript. They appear in the final manuscript on a two-leaf gathering and the first leaf of the following two-leaf gathering, marked with a note by Edward for the printer to skip over them. We have ignored Edward's comment and restored Emerson's original reading.

Third, the most egregious example of editorial interference occurs with these lines in our text:

> It is said, it will cost a thousand millions of dollars to buy the slaves,—which sounds like a fabulous price. But if a price were named in good faith,—with the other elements of a practicable treaty in readiness, and with the convictions of mankind on this mischief once well awake and conspiring, I do not think any amount that figures could tell, founded on an estimate, would be quite unmanageable. Every man in the world might give a week's work to sweep this mountain of calamities out of the earth. (69.21–30)

This concluding part of the paragraph is replaced in *Miscellanies* with a separate paragraph:

> We shall one day bring the States shoulder to shoulder and the citizens man to man to exterminate slavery. Why in the name of common sense and the peace of mankind is not this made the subject of instant negotiation and settlement? Why not end this dangerous dispute on some ground of fair compensation on one side, and satisfaction on the other to the conscience of the free states? It is really the great task fit for this country to accomplish, to buy that property of the planters, as the British nation bought the West Indian slaves. I say buy,—never conceding the right of the planter to own, but that we may acknowledge the calamity of his position, and bear a countryman's share in relieving him; and because it is the only practicable course, and is innocent. It is a right social or public function, which one man cannot do, which all men must do. 'T is said it will cost two thousand millions of dollars. Was there ever any contribution that was so enthusiastically paid as this will be. We will have a chimney-tax. We will give up our coaches, and wine, and watches. The churches will melt their plate. The father of his country shall wait, well pleased, a little longer for his monument; Franklin for his, the Pilgrim Fathers for theirs, and the patient Columbus for his.

The mechanics will give, the needle-women will give; the children will have cent-societies. Every man in the land will give a week's work to dig away this accursed mountain of sorrow once and forever out of the world. (pp. 208–209)

The source for this text may be found in Edward's notes to *Miscellanies*, where he states that his "appeal" was "so much better in an anti-slavery address in New York, in 1855, than in the Concord speech four years earlier, that I have substituted the later version here" (p. 586n). This, and Edward's source, is clear from his instructions in the manuscript: "Introduce here . . . the extract from Mr. Cabot's *Memoir* & begin again at the bottom of p. 128 of this lecture." The text is that printed in James Elliot Cabot, *A Memoir of Ralph Waldo Emerson*, 2 vols. (Boston: Houghton, Mifflin, 1887), 2:592.12–593.13. Cabot is unclear about his source, though he mentions that the 1855 lecture was reported in the *Boston Traveller* of 26 January (2:759). However, the report of the lecture in the *Boston Daily Evening Traveller* of 26 January differs significantly from Cabot's text (pp. 1–2), some parts of which seem derived from the report of the lecture as delivered in New York on 6 February and published in the *National Anti-Slavery Standard* of 17 February (p. 1). The section from Cabot used in *Miscellanies* can also be found in the last two paragraphs of the manuscript of the 1855 address (printed here on pp. 105–106). Cabot may have drawn his text from a combination of the newspaper reports and the manuscript of the 1855 address. At any rate, the text for this section in *Miscellanies* is clearly not the one Emerson intended, and we have thus rejected it.

A complete textual apparatus will be published in *The Later Lectures of Ralph Waldo Emerson*, ed. Ronald A. Bosco and Joel Myerson, to be published by the University of Georgia Press.

THE FUGITIVE SLAVE LAW

Emerson delivered his second address on the Fugitive Slave Law in New York on 7 March 1854. The manuscript of the address is at the Houghton Library of Harvard University (bMS Am 1280.202 [7]) and is the basis for our text.

The manuscript, a working copy of the address, includes revisions and additions and is not a clear, clean version. A number of additions were made on separate sheets of paper and marked for insertion.

Accounts of the address were published as "Last of the Anti-Slavery Lectures," in the *New-York Daily Tribune*, 8 March 1854, p. 5, and as "The Seventh of March. A Lecture by Ralph Waldo Emerson," in the *New York Herald*, 8 March 1854, p. 1. A report of the address, "compiled" from these two papers and described as "not perfect" but showing "the spirit and the substance of what the speaker uttered," was published as "Ralph Waldo Emerson's Lecture," in the *National Anti-Slavery Standard*, 18 March 1854, p. 169. A letter from "Delta," dated 8 March and published in the *Boston Evening Transcript*, 11 March 1854, p. 1 (reprinted as "Ralph Waldo Emerson at the New York Tabernacle," *Liberator*, 17 March 1854, p. 44), summarizes the address. The newspaper accounts do not report some portions of the address present in the manuscript.

The newspaper accounts suggest that on at least one point Emerson extemporized. In the fourth paragraph, after commenting, "I have lived all my life without suffering any known inconvenience from American slavery," Emerson notes: "I never saw it." The *Tribune* report adds "except a glimpse of it I caught in my youth in Florida and Carolina, but to little purpose then," as does the *Herald*, which substitutes "saw" for "caught."

The address was published in the Riverside Edition of *Miscellanies* (1884), pp. 205–230, and in the Little Classic Edition of *Miscellanies* (1884), pp. 169–188. This text contains heavy editing of the manuscript and no authority can be found for the many changes. The *Miscellanies* text deletes nearly 250 individual words from the manuscript (plus another 450 words omitted when seven large passages were deleted), changes the wording in approximately 140 instances, adds nearly 150 words not present in the manuscript, and shifts the location of one long passage ('I conceive . . . side."', 84.1–16).

In short, there are roughly a thousand variations between the manuscript and the *Miscellanies* text.

A complete textual apparatus will be published in *The Later Lectures of Ralph Waldo Emerson*, ed. Ronald A. Bosco and Joel Myerson, to be published by the University of Georgia Press.

LECTURE ON SLAVERY

Emerson first delivered his lecture on slavery before the Massachusetts Anti-Slavery Society at the Tremont Temple in Boston on 25 January 1855. He repeated it in New York on 6 February, in Philadelphia on 8 February, in Rochester on 21 February, and in Syracuse on 25 February. The manuscript of the lecture is at the Houghton Library of Harvard University (bMS Am 1280.202 [10]) and is the basis for our text.

A second, fragmentary manuscript exists at Harvard (bMS Am 1280.202 [9]). Untitled, this 52-page manuscript contains notes toward the address, including drafts of passages, references to materials to be used from Emerson's reading and journals, and lists of topics to be covered. Over a quarter of Emerson's "WO Liberty" notebook deals with topics to be covered in this address and contains drafts of passages in it (see *JMN*, 14:373–430).

The completed manuscript is 119 pages long and generally quite clean, though it contains revisions and additions. Wrapped around the manuscript is a leaf headed 'Boston, January 25' and 'New York 6 February 1855.' The manuscript was probably composed in two parts, since a separate pagination sequence occurs toward the end. The leaves containing the concluding paragraph (see below) are missing.

An account of the lecture was published as "Anti-Slavery Lectures" in the *Boston Daily Evening Traveller*, 26 January 1855, pp. 1–2, and a three-paragraph summary appeared as "Mr. Emerson's Lecture" in the *Boston Daily Journal*, 26 January, p. 1. In New York, an account of the lecture as delivered there was published as "Lectures on Slavery" in the *New-York Daily Tribune*, 7 February, p. 6

(reprinted as "Ralph Waldo Emerson's Lecture," *National Anti-Slavery Standard*, 17 February, p. 1). A four-paragraph summary (which includes two paragraphs describing the audience's reaction to a man who cried, "three cheers for [pro-abolitionist New York] Governor Seward's election") appeared as "Anti-Slavery Lecture at the Tabernacle," *New York Herald*, 7 February 1855, p. 296. We have been unable to locate any notices in the Philadelphia papers. A long untitled paragraph summarizing the lecture was published in the *Rochester Daily Union*, 22 February, p. 3. Two paragraphs from near the end of the lecture were published as "Buying the Slaves," in the *Syracuse Daily Standard*, 24 February, p. 2.

The Boston and New York newspaper accounts were clearly prepared by someone in the audience, not from Emerson's manuscript; they summarize rather than attempt to transcribe every word or sentence. There are a number of differences between the newspaper accounts and the lecture and among the newspaper accounts themselves. This may be due to the varying accuracy of the different recorders and to Emerson's delivering a different version of the lecture in New York.

Both newspapers omit the first paragraph in the manuscript, although the *Traveller* does start with "I am oppressed at opening this topic with the difficulties of the subject." Both accounts open with this section, not present in the manuscript:

> Gentlemen and ladies:—We sit here, the third generation in the humiliation of our forefathers, when they made the evil contract with the slave-holders, at the formation of the Government. We have added to that the new stringency of the fugitive law of 1850. The last year has added the ponderous Nebraska and Kansas legislation; and we have now to consider that however strongly the tides of public sentiment have set or are setting towards freedom, the code of slavery in this country is at this hour unrepealed, and is at this hour more malignant in present and in prospect, than ever before. Recent action has brought it home to New England, and made it impossible for us to avoid.

The *Tribune*'s account differs slightly from the *Traveller*'s, printed above. The New York paper mentions only 'Gentlemen' and talks of the 'strange' Fugitive Slave Law (possibly a mishearing of the unfamiliar 'stringency'). Emerson made two other revisions for his new audience: the 'tides of public sentiment' are now in New York, Massachusetts, and Wisconsin; the 'recent action' is brought home not to 'New England' but to 'the Northern States'.

Also, both report a section between the 'opera-glasses of our young men' (95.6–7) and 'The ebb of thought . . .' (95.8) not in the manuscript:

> The method of nature is not changed. God still instructs through the imagination. A God is still there, sitting in his sphere. The young mortal comes in at the gates of life, and on the instant and incessantly a whole snow storm of illusions. Among other things he fancies himself nobody, and lost in a crowd. There is he with them alone—they pouring their grand persuasions professing to lead him to Olympus—he baffled, misled, distracted by the snowy illusions; and when for an instant the cloud clears off and day appears, there they are still sitting round their thrones.

(This text from the *Traveller* is substantially repeated in the *Tribune*.)

Only the *Tribune* adds a section after the mention of the chief justices of England (pp. 100–101), stating,

> they held that acts of Parliament (which in England are held to be technically omnipotent) might be controlled by common law or natural equity. "No human laws," said Blackstone, speaking of the laws of nature, "are of any validity contrary to this; nay if any law should allow, or enjoin us to a crime,"— (his instance is murder)—"we are bound to transgress that human law, or else we must offend both the natural and divine."

This passage was used in the 1851 address on the Fugitive Slave Law (59.28–31), and Emerson might have added it for New York because he felt it had already been heard or read by his Boston audience.

Many passages present in the manuscript are not reported in the newspaper accounts. The *Traveller* omits 'Thus in society . . . brain of the state.' (98.20–31), 'You cannot use a man . . . square with you.' (99.17–20), and 'When the city . . . holds out.' (102.5–8). The *Tribune* omits 'We have to consider . . . avoid complicity.' (92.20–24) and 'Yes and serious men . . . profound morals.' (94.22–27)—the latter possibly because of its religious content. Both newspapers omit 'This law is: . . . Divine justice.' (99.5–10), 'Any attempt . . . do you justice.' (99.14–17), and 'If he is not strong . . . spasms.' (99.20–30).

Both newspapers add a final paragraph not present in the manuscript. Because the *Traveller* is generally the more accurate and complete of the two, its account is printed here:

> Gentlemen and ladies: I think in bad times we must rely on these simple truths. Men are beginning to suspect that in spite of all chance and change a Divine Providence does rule in the world, and brings victory to the right at the last. And thus by every new creation, to those shameful statutes which blacken the code of this country, the opposition will never end, never relax, whilst the statutes exist. As long as the grass grows, as long as there is Summer or Winter, as long as there are men, so long will the sentiments condemn them. We cannot educate men, or raise them to any mental power, without their discovering the wrong. We do not differ ['suffer' in the *Tribune*] by defeat. There is longevity in the cause of freedom. It can well afford to wait, if God pleases, for ages. It is the order that chemistry, nature, the stars of Heaven, the thoughts of the mind, all are to the emancipation of the slave!

This lecture is not included in any edition of Emerson's writings. Some of the material here was published in "The Sovereignty of Ethics" in the *North American Review* of May 1878, and a large section was printed in James Elliot Cabot, *A Memoir of Ralph Waldo*

Emerson, 2 vols. (Boston: Houghton, Mifflin, 1887), 2:588–593.

A complete textual apparatus will be published in *The Later Lectures of Ralph Waldo Emerson*, ed. Ronald A. Bosco and Joel Myerson, to be published by the University of Georgia Press.

ASSAULT ON CHARLES SUMNER

Emerson delivered his remarks on the assault on Charles Sumner on 26 May 1856 in Concord. The manuscript, titled "Mr Emerson's Remarks," is at the Houghton Library of Harvard University (fMS Am 1301 [110]) and is the basis for our text.

An account of the remarks was published as "Remarks of Mr. R. W. Emerson at a Meeting in Concord on the 26th, to Consider the Outrage upon Mr. Sumner," in the *Boston Evening Telegraph*, 29 May 1856, p. 1. It was reprinted with the same title in the *Boston Evening Transcript*, 31 May 1856, p. 1; *Liberator*, 6 June 1856, p. 91; and *National Anti-Slavery Standard*, 14 June 1856, p. 1. All of these accounts differ in minor ways from the manuscript. Other printings, differing in minor ways from both the manuscript and the contemporary newspaper accounts, were published as "An Unpublished Speech of Mr. Emerson's," *Boston Evening Transcript*, 29 April 1874, p. 6, and in the Riverside Edition of *Miscellanies* (1884), pp. 233–237, and in the Little Classic Edition of *Miscellanies* (1884), pp. 191–194.

ALTERATIONS IN THE MANUSCRIPT

107.8	I do] <They te>I do
108.14	outrage] outrage <that>
109.10–11	charge which it is impossible was ever] charge which <I cannot think> ↑ it is impossible ↓ was ↑ ever ↓
109.20	high compliment] ↑ high ↓ compliment
109.23	his day,] <the>his day,
110.1	man] man ↑ <sorry sorry if> ↓

107.5   Mr.] *Mr. Emerson's Remarks.* [new line] Mr.
108.10   skill with knives] skill [new page] knives

KANSAS RELIEF MEETING

No manuscript has been located for Emerson's speech at the Kansas Relief Meeting held on 10 September 1856 in Cambridge. A three-paragraph summary of the speech appeared under the heading "Kansas Meeting in Cambridge," in the *Boston Daily Evening Traveller*, 11 September 1856, p. 2. A fuller account, described as "Furnished for publication in the Evening Telegraph," was published as "Mr. R. W. Emerson's Remarks at the Kansas Relief Meeting in Cambridge, Wednesday Evening, Sept. 10," in the *Boston Evening Telegraph*, 15 September 1856, p. 1 (reprinted as "Ralph Waldo Emerson's Remarks at the Kansas Relief Meeting in Cambridge," *Liberator*, 19 September 1856, p. 154; as "Mr. R. W. Emerson's Remarks," *National Anti-Slavery Standard*, 20 September 1856, p. 2). We have reprinted the *Evening Telegraph* text. The speech was subsequently reprinted, with minor variations from the *Evening Telegraph* version, in the Riverside Edition of *Miscellanies* (1884), pp. 241–248, and in the Little Classic Edition of *Miscellanies* (1884), pp. 197–203.

SPEECH AT A MEETING TO AID
JOHN BROWN'S FAMILY

No manuscript has been located for Emerson's remarks at a meeting for relief of the family of John Brown, held on 18 November 1859 at the Tremont Temple in Boston. The remarks were published simultaneously as "Meeting to Aid John Brown's Family," in the *Boston Atlas and Daily Bee*, 21 November 1859, p. 1, and as "Meeting in Aid of the Family of John Brown," in the *Boston Daily Courier*, 21 November 1859, p. 1 (reprinted in the *Liberator*, 25 November 1859, pp. 186–187). A somewhat shorter account of the remarks was printed as "Relief for the Family of John Brown," in the *National*

Anti-Slavery Standard, 26 November 1859, p. 2. The texts in the two Boston newspapers are quite similar, but since the *Courier* account of the event is fuller, we have reprinted that text of Emerson's remarks. The *Courier* text was reprinted, with approximately twenty minor differences in wording, as "Speech of Mr. Ralph Waldo Emerson," in *The John Brown Invasion* (Boston: James Campbell, 1860), pp. 103–105, and as "Ralph Waldo Emerson," in James Redpath, *Echoes of Harpers Ferry* (Boston: Thayer and Eldridge, 1860), pp. 67–70. The remarks were subsequently reprinted, without any differences in wording from the book texts, in the Riverside Edition of *Miscellanies* (1884), pp. 251–256, and in the Little Classic Edition of *Miscellanies* (1884), pp. 207–211.

JOHN BROWN

No manuscript has been located for Emerson's speech on John Brown, delivered on 6 January 1860 in Salem. No newspaper accounts have been located. The speech was first published as "Speech by Ralph Waldo Emerson," in James Redpath, *Echoes of Harpers Ferry* (Boston: Thayer and Eldridge, 1860), pp. 119–123, possibly from a copy prepared by F. B. Sanborn (see *L*, 5:188). We have reprinted this text. The speech was subsequently reprinted, with only one difference in wording (*Sorrington* is corrected to *Torrington*), in the Riverside Edition of *Miscellanies* (1884), pp. 259–263, and in the Little Classic Edition of *Miscellanies* (1884), pp. 215–218.

ATTEMPTED SPEECH

No manuscript has been located for Emerson's attempted speech at the meeting of the Massachusetts Anti-Slavery Society on 24 January 1861 at the Tremont Temple in Boston. Brief summary accounts of the event were printed as "Massachusetts Anti-Slavery Society," in the *Boston Daily Evening Traveller*, 24 January 1861, p. 2; "Annual Meeting of the Massachusetts Anti-Slavery Society," in the *Boston Daily Advertiser*, 25 January 1861, pp. 1, 4; and "Anti-Slavery Meeting in Tremont Temple," in the *Boston Daily Courier*, 25 January 1861, p. 2. The fullest account of Emerson's attempted speech appeared as "Annual Meeting of the Massachusetts Anti-Slavery Society," in the *Liberator*, 1 February 1861, pp. 17–19 (reprinted in the *National Anti-Slavery Standard*, 9 February 1861, p. 1). We have reprinted the *Liberator* text.

"THE PRESIDENT'S PROCLAMATION"

Emerson delivered "The President's Proclamation" on 12 October 1862 before the Parker Fraternity in the Music Hall in Boston. We have been unable to locate any published accounts of the lecture. The manuscript, at the Houghton Library of Harvard University (Ms Am 82.4), is the basis for our text.

The manuscript served as the printer's copy for publication of the address as "The President's Proclamation," in the *Atlantic Monthly* 10 (November 1862): 638–642 (reprinted in the *Commonwealth* [Boston], 15 November 1862, p. 1). Emerson undoubtedly read proof for the *Atlantic* printing, and we have adopted the *Atlantic* version of all the differences in wording between the manuscript and the *Atlantic* as part of our text (listed below under Emendations), believing that Emerson most likely made these changes. However, because the *Atlantic* imposed its house style on Emerson in matters of paragraphing, spelling, punctuation, hyphenation, and capitalization, we have followed the manuscript in these instances, silently emending only when Emerson's meaning is unclear. The *Atlantic* text was the basis for reprintings in the Riverside Edition of *Miscellanies* (1884), pp. 293–303, and in the Little Classic Edition of *Miscellanies* (1884), pp. 243–251, both of which have nine minor differences in wording from the *Atlantic* text.

129.6	thought] thought <& action,>
129.7	else] ↑ else ↓

129.12	Liberty is] <Providence means that Liberty is shall be> ↑ Liberty is ↓
129.14–15	Such moments of expansion in modern history were,] ↑ Such moments of ↓ <Such m <in>of cosmical interest> ↑ expansion in modern history ↓ [new page] <Such moments ↑ <of cosmical interest> ↓ in modern history> were,
129.18	slaves] <slavery> ↑ slaves ↓
129.20	the last] ↑ the last ↓
129.21	eminently, President Lincoln's] <lastly> ↑ eminently ↓ , <the> President<'s Emancipation> ↑ Lincoln's ↓
129.22	These are acts] ↑ These are acts ↓ [new page] <These are acts>
129.23	honoring] <they> honor ↑ ing ↓
129.24	initiate] <enact> ↑ initiate ↓
130.1	deep] deep <that>
130.2–3	At such times, it appears] <It appears> <The public> <It appears> ↑ At such times, it appears ↓
130.3	public were] public <had been> ↑ were ↓
130.5–6	having run] < ↑ has ↓ ran over> having run
130.7	suddenly lending] suddenly [new page] <Tis as when <the> ↑ a great ↓ orator in presence of a mass meeting, ha<s>ving passed through compliments & pleasantries at the beginning of his speech, <has> ↑ and ↓ run over the superficial <benefits> ↑ fitness & commodities ↓ of the measure he commends, <and now> ↑ suddenly ↓ lending
130.9	wits] <jokers> ↑ wits ↓
130.9	thus far,] <already> ↑ thus far, ↓
130.13	nationalities.] <the> nationalities.
130.15	his long] <the> ↑ his ↓ long
130.20	whilst] <and> ↑ whilst ↓
130.22	act,] <man,> ↑ act, ↓
130.22	that great] that [new page] <that in our sudden gratitude we are beginning to think high as> great
130.24	virtue] virtue <to>
130.31	success.] ↑ success. ↓ [new page] <<success.> He had the courage to seize the moment against all tim-

orous counsels. & such was his place, & such the felicity attending the action, that he has replaced government in the good graces of mankind. "Better is virtue in the sovereign, than plenty in the season," say the Chinese.>

130.35 promulgation] <event of this> promulgation

131.2–3 apparent what gigantic and what remote interests] apparent <how> ↑ what ↓ gigantic & <how> ↑ what ↓ remote <were the> interests

131.4 long. Against] long, against all timorous [blank page] [new page] <He> ↑ Against all timorous counsels, he ↓

131.5 moment;] moment; <against all timorous counsels,>

131.14 governors,] governors, <all things fly into place & the>

131.17 repair] <replace> repair

131.17–18 war. A day] war [new page] <An hour> ↑ a day ↓

131.18 dared not] <have not> dared not

131.20 October, November, December] ↑ October November December ↓ [blank page] [new page] <October, November, December,>

131.26 rebel masters.] <rebels.> ↑ rebel masters. ↓

131.30 measure] <step> ↑ measure ↓

132.1 disasters. It does] disasters. ↑ It does ↓ [blank page] [new page] It does

132.6 position. The first] position. ↑ The first ↓ [blank page] [new page] <The first>

132.7 recovered] <planted ourselves recovered> recovered

132.9 firmament] <heave>firmament

132.10 assured] <now> assured

132.12–13 the generosity of the cities, the health of the country,] 2 the health of the country, 1 the generosity of the cities,

132.15 nations,—all] nations,—<are> all

132.23 citizen.] citizen. <What right has any>

132.30 lifted off] lifted off <from>

132.32 but what] but <our> what

132.33–34 In the light of this event the public distress begins to be removed. What if the brokers'] [new page]

	↑ <The> <Under every aspect our affairs> In the light of this event the public distress <is> begins to be removed. What if the ↓ <The> brokers'
132.35	discredited and the] discredited<.> ↑ and ↓ The
133.5	today] <now> ↑ today ↓
133.8	Is it feared] <It is> ↑ Is it ↓ feared
133.13	habitable,] habitable, ↑ & ↓
133.17	wistfully for] wistfully <on> ↑ for ↓
133.18	fire. This] fire: <but this one> This
133.36	Philadelphia,] ↑ Philadelphia ↓
134.5	whole force] whole <Southern>force
134.12	foreign] <foreign>foreign
134.14	could add,'] ↑ could ↓ add,'
134.17	will.' This] will.' <It> ↑ This ↓
134.20	of Poland, since] <the> ↑ of ↓ Poland, <of 1793> since
134.35	the wisdom] the <importance of this> wisdom
135.3	joy which has] joy which <it> has
135.4	delay] <stop> ↑ delay ↓
135.5	edict] <message> ↑ edict ↓
135.9	Nature] <the earth> ↑ Nature ↓
135.12	the melioration of our planet.] <a meliorated> ↑ the melioration of <this> <our>our ↓ planet.
135.15	Meantime, that] ↑ <Meantime>Meantime, ↓ That
135.18	naturally] ↑ naturally ↓
135.19	very] ↑ <very>very ↓
135.21	rank] <higher> rank

EMENDATIONS

129.6	jets of thought into affairs,] sudden enlargements of thought
129.22	September.] the last month.
131.4	long. Against] long, against all timorous Against
131.13	acts of bad] act of bad
131.20	will have passed] will pass
131.34	century. This act] century. It
132.1–2	disasters. It] disasters. It does It
132.31	shall cease to] shall not

132.35–36	one hundred and twenty-seven] 123
133.3	garden are] garden is
133.8	immigration?] emigration?
133.18	bristled] was fraught
133.20	imperative.] inevitable.
133.27	If we] If you
133.30	impossible, and] impossible, and and
134.3–4	of drawing] to draw
134.4	rallying] rally
134.7	detaching that force] detaching it
134.11	necessities] actual necessities
134.13	war abroad is,] war, is,
134.16	could not coerce] cannot coerce
134.22–26	conquer," . . . the instinct] conquer," the apology of the American government and people is in the instinct
134.26–27	self-preservation forced us into the war.] self-preservation.
134.28	aim of the President's] President's
135.4	world. It] world. [blank page] [new page] Delay the steamers at the wharves until the message can be put abroad. It will be insurance to them, as they go <bounding over> ↑ plunging thro ↓ the sea with glad tidings for all people. Do not let the <dead> dying die. Hold them back still to this world, until you have charged their ear & heart with this message to other spiritual societies, announcing the melioration of this <world.> ↑ planet. ↓ [new page] [paragraph] "Incertainties now crown themselves assured, [new line] And Peace proclaims olives of endless age." [new page] [paragraph] Since the above pages were written, President Lincoln has proposed to Congress that the government shall cooperate with any State that shall enact a gradual abolishment of slavery. In the recent series of national successes, this Message is the best. It marks the happiest day in the political year. The American Executive ranges itself for the first time on the side of freedom. If Congress has been backward, the President has ad-

vanced. This state-paper is the more interest[new page]ing that it appears to be <an> ↑ the President's ↓ individual act, <of the utmost seriousness &> done under ↑ a ↓ strong sense of duty. He speaks his own thought in his own style. All thanks & honor to the Head of the State! The message has been received throughout the country, with praise, &, we doubt ↑ not, ↓ with more pleasure than has been spoken. If Congress accords with the President, it is not [new page] yet too late to begin the Emancipation, but we think it will always be too late to make it gradual. All experience agrees that it should be immediate. More ↑ & better ↓ than the President has spoken shall perhaps the effect of this message be; but, we are sure, <that> not more or better than he hoped in his heart, when, thoughtful of all the complexities of his position, he penned these cautious words. [blank page] [new page] It

"FORTUNE OF THE REPUBLIC"

Emerson first delivered "Fortune of the Republic" in Boston before the Parker Fraternity on 1 December 1863. He repeated this popular lecture in Feltonville, Massachusetts, on 9 December, in Newburyport on 11 December, in Concord on 16 December, in Brooklyn on 21 December, in Manchester, Massachusetts, on 30 December, in Worcester on 5 January 1864, in Lynn on 6 January, in Cambridgeport on 12 January, in Augusta, Maine, on 14 January, in Bangor on 15 January, in North Bennington, Vermont, on 20 January, in Salem on 27 January, and in Taunton, Massachusetts, on 9 February. The manuscript of the lecture, at the Houghton Library of Harvard University (bMS Am 1280.207 [11]), is the basis for our text.

We have been able to locate only a few published accounts of the lecture, none an attempt at a complete rendering of what Emerson said. The address was well reported in Boston, with a six-paragraph summary appearing as "Fifth Fraternity Lecture," in the

Boston Daily Advertiser, 2 December 1863, p. 1; a seven-paragraph summary as "Ralph Waldo Emerson's Lecture on 'Our Country,'" in the *Boston Daily Evening Traveller*, 2 December, pp. 1–2; and a full-column summary as "The Parker Fraternity Lectures. Ralph Waldo Emerson on 'Our Country,'" in the *Boston Post*, 2 December, p. 2. Other accounts are "The Fortune of the Republic," *Brooklyn Daily Eagle*, 22 December, p. 2 (half-column paragraph); "Mercantile Library Lectures. 'The Fortune of the Republic'—A New Lecture by Ralph Waldo Emerson," *Brooklyn Daily Union*, 22 December, p. 1 (five paragraphs); "Local and Other Items," *Bangor Daily Whig and Courier*, 16 January 1864, p. 3 (four paragraphs); and "Library Association Lecture," *Daily Gazette* (Taunton), 10 February, p. 2 (a little over one column). The accounts generally agree with one another, though they suggest slightly different orderings of the material, and the account in the *Boston Post* mentions a reference to Henry Ward Beecher not present in the manuscript but listed in the notes to the 1904 *Miscellanies* edition discussed below.

In 1878, after Emerson's creative powers had diminished and he had ceased original writing, he was "asked to give a summing-up of the position of the country after the war, and its spiritual needs and prospects for the new generation." James Elliot Cabot describes his subsequent lecture on 25 February at the Old South Church as "a paper of the war-time, with additions from his journals" (*A Memoir of Ralph Waldo Emerson*, 2 vols. [Boston: Houghton, Mifflin, 1887], 2:677; Cabot also prints two paragraphs from the manuscript at 2:608–609). Emerson read it at least once more, at the home of Cyrus Bartol on 30 March. When the *Atlantic Monthly* declined to print it, Cabot and Ellen Emerson reworked the lecture and published it separately as *Fortune of the Republic* (Boston: Houghton, Osgood, 1878; it is incorrectly described on the title page as delivered on 30 March). Ellen's description of the state of her father's manuscript differs markedly from Cabot's. Nancy Craig Simmons, in "Arranging the Sibylline Leaves: James Elliot Cabot's Work as Emerson's Literary Executor" (*Studies in the American Renaissance 1983*, ed. Joel Myerson [Charlottesville: University Press of Virginia, 1983], pp 349–350) quotes Ellen as saying, most of it [was] from the lecture named F. of R. which Mr. C. had already sifted but there was then no order at all. As read at the Old South it had copious additions from Moral Forces and some other lectures, one on N. England particularly. As read at Dr. Bartol's it had been helped by all we could collect from American Nationality. . . . Father never had these things combined, so *he* never had any order for them. I thought and so did Mr. C. that the final arrangement was truer and easier for the mind, but maybe it isn't so. . . .

The corrections are largely Father's . . . where he could understand what he wanted. [When he didn't] Mr. Cabot had to make it and he always does it in the modest manner of scratching out a word or altering a tense, or something that will still leave it Father's words if possible.

This 1878 version of the lecture was subsequently published in the Riverside Edition of *Miscellanies* (1884), pp. 395–425, and in the Little Classic Edition of *Miscellanies* (1884), pp. 331–351, as well as in the Centenary Edition of *Miscellanies* (1904), pp. 511–544, where passages "from the earlier lecture" were printed in notes (pp. 643–648). As Ellen's remarks suggest, the published version of the lecture bears little resemblance to the manuscript.

The 155-page manuscript is generally in good shape, making it likely that Cabot and Ellen made a fair copy of their compiled text and then returned the various manuscripts to their original sources whenever possible. There are numerous comments about the possible order of the pages, paste-overs (probably by Cabot), and penciled revisions and cancellations, only some of which can definitely be attributed to Emerson. The lecture's multiple deliveries and formats are reflected in the multiple pagination sequences present— as many as four on some pages. In keeping with our editorial policies, we have presented the final layer of text but have not included the passages marked "from the earlier lecture" in the 1904 edition. We have omitted them because all the contemporary published accounts of the lecture are closer in readings to the manuscript than to the passages published in 1904 (except the Beecher passage mentioned above) and because most of the 1904 passages are in turn keyed to sections not actually in the manuscript.

ALTERATIONS IN THE MANUSCRIPT

137.4–5	It . . . you] ↑ It . . . hydraulics, that ↓ You
137.5	mills, the] ↑ mills, the ↓
137.6	the college, and the church,] ↑ the college, & the church, ↓
137.7	secret.] secret. [paragraph] <The manufacturers, the navigators>
137.7	chronometers] chro<mo>nometers
137.7–8	that . . . year,] ↑ that do not <vary> lose 2 or 3 seconds in a year, ↓
137.10	premiums for] premiums for <the>
137.12	hydraulic] <hygrometric> ↑ hydraulic ↓
137.12	carpet-mill,] <calico pr> carpet-mill,
137.13	calico print,] calico-<mill> print,
137.16	old] o<f>ld
137.18	built great works,] ↑ built great works, ↓
137.18	village,] <mills> ↑ village ↓ ,
137.19	Flaxman,] Flaxman <combined ↑ copied & ↓ >,
137.19	selected and combined] ↑ selected & combined ↓
137.20	loveliest] lovel<y>iest
137.22	and china-closet.] ↑ & china-closet ↓ .
137.23	made their] <for their share obtained a princely> ↑ made their ↓
137.23	jewellers] <silver & goldsmiths were not slow to> ↑ jewellers ↓
137.24	revived] revived <&>
138.1	talent] <taste &> talent
138.1	painter,] painter, <of>
138.2	dramatic] ↑ dramatic ↓
138.2	marine] ↑ marine ↓
138.3	mathematical] mathematicia<n>l
138.3	counsellor] ↑ counsellor ↓
138.3–4	The . . . Annuities.] ↑ The . . . Annuities. ↓
138.8	took] ↑ took ↓
138.12	the 200,000] the<m> ↑ 200 000, ↓

138.14   demigods] ↑ demi- ↓ gods

138.15   inventor] <experimenter &> inventor

138.16   nature, but] nature, <but>

138.17   Our] <So>Our

138.20   compound;] <chemical> compound;

138.24   change] <not> change

138.27   useful,] <arts in the> useful,

138.29   life?] life? [new page] [paragraph] <The <law of> water & all fluids is true of wit. Metternich said "revolutions begin in the best heads, & run steadily down to the populace." It is a very old observation, & not truer because Metternich said it, & not less true.> [new page] <Resources of Masstts [new line] of United States [new line] Machinery [paragraph] VA 186 Grand recuperative force> [new line] Elizabeth Hoar KL 208 [new page] [paragraph] <The wine merchant has his analyst & taster,—the more exquisite the better>

138.31   obedient] ↑ obedient ↓

138.32   have sagacity,] ha<s>ve sagacity,

138.33   obeying] <fo> obeying

138.33   resentments,] resentments, <&>

138.35   resist the party,] resist <it> ↑ the party, ↓

138.36   and put them in fear:] ↑ & put them in fear: ↓

139.1   to a larger] ↑ to ↓ a larger

139.1   what is the] <a> ↑ what is the ↓

139.2   and stand for] <& stand for> ↑ and stand for ↓

139.3–4   accommodate itself] <come round> ↑ accommodate itself ↓

139.5   Metternich] ↑ Prince ↓ Metternich

139.8–9   true. [paragraph] Never] true. [new page] [paragraph] < ↑ Now I believe ↓ Revolutions cannot be accomplished by dunces or idlers, but require docility sympathy & religious receiving from higher principles.> [new page] [paragraph] <With all the immense sympathy which at first & again has upheld the War, I fear the country does not yet apprehend the salvation that is offered it;—that we may yet be punished to rouse the egotists, the skeptics, the fash-

ionist, <&> the pursuers of ease & pleasure.>
[paragraph] Never

139.10–11 possibility. At] possibility <Yet our young soldiers returning on thirty days furlough from the camps,
wonder at the apathy of the cities, & at the more
than apathy of multitudes of young men seeking
their pleasure in the> [new page] <and even putting
on airs of superiority, & wondering, like so many
Talleyrands, at their too much zeal & excitement.
But we cannot think of what is passing, of what is
still at risk, & on what questions the nation may
presently> [new page] *America.* [paragraph] At

139.11 one] ↑ one ↓

139.16 foreign] ↑ foreign ↓

139.19 Europe,—a] Europe,—<that> a

139.20 it is proved] ↑ it ↑ as ↓ is ↓ <best> proved

139.21 western] <ea>western

139.21–22 when the adventurers] <that> when <they> ↑ the
adventurers ↓

139.24 country] <(& its people)>

139.26 human] ↑ human ↓

139.30–32 The questions . . . Religion.] ↑ The questions of Education, of Society, of Labor, the direction of talent,
of character, the nature & habits of the Amer-
ica<n>n, <are the> may well occupy us<.>: ↑ &
more, the question of Religion. ↓ ↓

139.32 "The superior] <be called to pass, without alarm.>
"The superior

140.4–5 ideas . . . on.] <ideas, or his head, is punk.> ↑ ideas,
or he <has> might as well be the horse he rides
on. ↓

140.5–6 want to be sun-dazzled, sun-blind,] <ask> ↑ want ↓
to be <dazzled with a blaze of sunlight> [new page]
<it will make him sunblind,> ↑ sun-dazzled,—sun-
blind, ↓

140.7 knocking] <breaking>knocking

140.7 walls.] walls ↑ . ↓ <& posts.>

140.9 dread] <hate> ↑ dread ↓

140.10–11 this indifference, . . . terms.] this <low tendency>

↑ indifference ↓ , this despair<.> ↑ , ↓ ↑ ↑ ↑ disposing ↓ <leading> them ↑ <in the present attitude of the war> ↓ to <short & hasty peace, on any terms—> ↓ <Their death is no loss to their country.>

140.14–16   Independence, . . . nations.] Independence, <the decree of Emancipation,> ↑ <the new commanding of> ↓ ↑ the <declaration>proclaiming of ↓ liberty, <to all men> land, <for all> ↑ justice, and ↓ a career for all ↑ men; ↓ <& justice from this land to all other lands people> ↑ and honest dealings with other nations ↓ .

140.19–21   Nations . . . force.] ↑ Nations . . . force ↓

140.30–31   strut . . . America?"] ↑ strut . . . America?" ↓

140.31   at once] <their> at once

140.33   insular,] <narrow &> insular,

140.35   ironsmiths,] iron<mongers>smiths,

140.36   but] but <also>

140.36–141.1   do . . . The] ↑ do . . . The ↓

141.2   like] like <a>

141.4–5   is suffered . . . advantage.] ↑ is suffered . . . advantage ↓ .

141.6   Even her] Even <Carlyle her most> ↑ her ↓

141.6   writer,] writer, <&>

141.7   a fatalist] a<n oriental> fatalist

141.8   In] <If though> <in>In

141.8   announced] <once> announced

141.9   Now he] ↑ Now he ↓

141.10   system, a] system, <of> a

141.11–12   In . . . Great," the] [paragraph] <It is curious that> in the "Life ↑ History ↓ of Frederic the Great," <there is no recognition of the people.> <T>the

141.13   He is] <You are> ↑ He is ↓

141.14   glimpse.] glimpse ↑ . ↓ <of.>

141.16   beautiful] <genial youth> beautiful

141.17–18   alive . . . kingdom?] alive<?> ↑ in all <these> ↑ the ↓ broad territories of that kingdom? ↓

141.18   We] <We should not> We

141.19	bring this criticism on] ↑ bring this criticism ↓ <complain of it> <in>on
141.20	But from] But <in> ↑ from ↓
141.30–31	In . . . French] <They imitated,> in the ↑ revolt of the ↓ German cities, ↑ in that year, they imitated ↓ the forms & methods of ↑ the <popular leaders in the> insurrectionists in ↓ the French
141.32	creed] <instinct> ↑ creed ↓
142.5	Emperor,] <French> <e>Emperor,
142.6	the French] th<at>e ↑ French ↓
142.6	firmly] ↑ firmly ↓
142.7	like a spaniel.] ↑ like a spaniel ↓ .
142.12	There have] <England is gross & Fatal But> there have
142.16	Moors] Moors <or Saracens>
142.17	decay] ——— ↑ decay ↓
142.20–21	The revolutions . . . by] The ——— ↑ revolutions . . . by ↓
142.28	gods] <angels> gods
142.29	in this state] ↑ in this state ↓
142.30	July,] July, <than>
142.31	nations.] nations. <A Waterloo in the air.>
142.32	urges] <works> urges
142.33	its explosions] ↑ its explosions ↓
142.35–36	better code of] ↑ better code of ↓
143.1	triumphs] <humane> triumphs
143.1	which did] which <show> did
143.2	extinction] <last> extinction
143.2	America.] America. ↑ <by the European races> ↓ [new page] [paragraph] <In America great faults also [new line] torpor of the great faculties [new line] vulgar estimates [new line] our action has not been above commonplace>
143.5	torpor] <great> torpor
143.12	history] ↑ our ↓ history
143.14	persuaded] persuaded <the>
143.16–17	ovation, and a tract of land.] ovation, and <200 000 acres of public land.> ↑ a tract of land. ↓
143.18	sent] sent <out>

143.21	putting us into a theatrical] <not our natural> ↑ putting us into a theatrical ↓
143.23	usurper:] <emperor> usurper:
143.24	dimensions of the] ↑ dimensions of the ↓
143.25	points] points <of>
143.27	Yesterday] <to>Yesterday
143.29	the people] ↑ the people ↓
143.30	here;] ↑ <here;>here; ↓
143.30–31	every other] every ↑ other ↓
143.34	every large] <this> ↑ every large ↓
143.35–36	fashion. . . . ball.] fashion. ↑ <a pew in a particular church gives an easier entrie to p[e]asants assembly> a pew in a particular church gives an easier entrance to the subscription ball. ↓
144.2	living.] living. <a homestead for every child of Adam> *See* Textual Notes
144.8	footing with] footing <as they put> ↑ with ↓
144.9–10	steps, . . . private] steps ↑ . ↓ <in this direction> the <direction> ↑ gifts ↓ to learning <of> ↑ by ↓ private
144.10	enlarging] enlarg<ed>ing
144.11–12	gift of scholarships and fellowships] ↑ gift of scholarships & fellowships ↓
144.14	vast] <a> vast
144.16	vote] <require> ↑ vote ↓
144.17	university,] ↑ university, ↓
144.18	science; all] science ↑ all ↓
144.18	and all] & ↑ all ↓
144.19–20	And . . . duty.] ↑ And <as> thus . . . that ↑ public ↓ duty. ↓
144.21	classes,] classes, <with those>
144.28	demands] <points> ↑ demands ↓
144.31	In England, they] ↑ In England, ↓ They
144.34	In past time,] ↑ In past time, ↓
144.35	them] them<, in the past,>
144.35	We] <I>We
145.1	put] <come> put
145.2	none:] <it not> ↑ none ↓ :
145.2	forgot] forgot <all>

145.3	professions,] professions, <and saw only the chance of profiting by>
145.3–4	you . . . in] ↑ you . . . in ↓
145.4–5	humbling . . . commerce.] <profiting by> humbling ↑ a ↓ <the great> rival ↑ . ↓ <of your commerce & power.> ↑ & getting away his commerce. ↓
145.6	will sometimes] ↑ will sometimes ↓
145.7	you. We] you. [new page] <<Besides> Henceforth you have lost the benefit of the old veneration which shut our eyes to the altered facts.> We
145.10	your inches] <them> ↑ your inches ↓
145.11	leagues] <horizons.> ↑ leagues. ↓
145.13	now we] ↑ Now ↓ We
145.15	away] away <a bulwark>
145.16–17	foundation. [paragraph] My] foundation [new page] <There can be no true valor in a bad cause One omen is good, to fight for our country Ye shall not count dead but living those who are slain in the way of God. Be sure you are right, then go ahead.> [line space] "The integrity of moral principles is of more consequence than the interest of nations." [new line] *De Stael* [new page] [paragraph] <There is no time to go into the enumerating all the traits of the good fortune of this country [new line] And yet I <count this calami> our people have come to the conviction that this <w>calamitous war is one> [new page] [paragraph] My
145.20	the heart and genius] ↑ the heart & ↓ genius ↑ <& the heart> ↓
145.23	These native masters, and] ↑ <These ↑ <[uncovered]> ↓ &> ↑ These native masters, & ↓ ↓
145.25	prescribing] prescribing <that>
145.28	Of course all] <This> of course <would strike out> all
145.29	who will] who <now decline> will
145.29–30	degradation] degrad<ing>ation<s>

145.31	knowledge] <right> knowledge
145.34	free] <of> free
145.35	Lord] ↑ <In England> ↓ Lord
145.36	innovation to] innovation <in>to
146.4–5	there. [paragraph] Our] there. [line space] <General Grant, the papers tell us, asks for the passage of a law, that no officer below the rank of colonel, shall be promoted, until he has passed an examination before the regular board.> [new page] <let these wonders work for honest humanity, for the poor, for justice, genius, & the public good. <Civilization and ideas are turning the poor chaotic globe, which>> our
146.5	scraped . . . earth] scraped ↑ the ↑ rough ↓ surface of the <globe> ↑ earth ↓ ↓
146.6	flint arrowhead, and] <stone> ↑ flint ↓ arrowhead, ↑ & ↓
146.7–8	Every . . . century;] <Oh America> [new line] <Let the passion for America cast out the passion for Europe Here let there be what the earth waits for—exalted manhood.> <Here where> ↑ Every . . . century; ↓
146.9	Hoe's] <where the> Hoe's
146.9	McCormick's] <the> McCormicks
146.10–11	machine . . . inventions)] machine ↑ & the . . . inventions) ↓
146.12	Cornelius Agrippa] <Cornelius> ↑ Cornelius ↓ ↑ Agrippa ↓
146.17	Christianity and] Christianity <into>&
146.18	press, of trade,] press, <&> of trade, <&>
146.21	calmly reading the newspaper,] ↑ calmly reading the newspaper, ↓
146.22	This . . . states] ↑ This . . . states ↓
146.27	compute the] compute the <curve of the rainbow>
146.28	the curve and] ↑ the curve and ↓
146.31–32	energy. . . . . brain.] energy <& a good brain>. ↑ When I add difficulty, I add brain. ↓
146.34	patch of land] <lot> ↑ patch of land ↓
147.1	bound] bound ↑ on ↓

147.1	You are] ↑ You are ↓
147.2–3	principle.' [paragraph] Chartism] principle. [new page] [paragraph] <Greater freedom of circumstance here. English & Europeans girded with an iron belt of condition [new line] Z 128> [new line] <cashier of the world> [paragraph] Chartism
147.3	property,] property, <be represented in Parliament,>
147.7–8	women,—for . . . sick] women, <&> ↑—for ↓ the ↑ training ↓ of children, ↑ for care ↓ & <the> of <its> sick
147.8	serious care] ↑ serious care ↓
147.10	beat] beat<s>
147.14	always,] always, <at>
147.15	last,] last, <secure>
147.15–16	The . . . commanding] [paragraph] <In the first place, then, we owe> ↑ The same felicity comes out of our reverses. Now as we have owed ↓ commanding
147.20	state.] state. <Then we owe much>
147.21	what immense] what<ever> immense
147.23–24	calamities. Crises] calamities. [new page] [paragraph] <Now in a plight like this harsh remedies,> crises
147.25	conservatism.] conservatism, <death in life>.
147.26	easily] ↑ easily ↓
147.27	those who] those w<a>ho
147.28	prodigally] <yet> ↑ prodigally ↓
147.32	were to] were to <try to get> up <a sentiment of cosmic>
147.32–33	praise . . . pride] ↑ praise the Atlantic as a better ocean than the Pacific or Indian or take ↓ ↑ a ↓ pride
147.33–34	globe . . . than] globe as <superior &> <better> ↑ a ↓ ↑ more desireable ↓ globe ↑ to live on ↓ than
147.35	We had] <Now> we had <one &>
148.1	country. . . . house] country. <Everything else

was forgotten> ↑ Business was thrust aside ↓ .
<Every body put on uniform> Every <street>
house

148.1	out] out ↑ the ↓
148.2	patriotic] ↑ patriotic ↓
148.2–3	Almost . . . uniform.] ↑ Almost . . . uniform ↓
148.3	As] <So to the> <a>As
148.10	forced] <passed> forced
148.10–11	Congress . . . right] Congress <the right of> ↑ an act securing to ↓ the planter <to a transit> the right
148.16	2. That . . . been] 2. <We are deeply indebted to> ↑ That an eminent benefactor in this war has been ↓
148.17	Confederacy] Confederacy <for> ↑ <has eminently served us by> ↓
148.18	government,—a manifesto] government,— ↑ a manifesto ↓
148.19–21	No . . . Emancipation.] ↑ No . . . Emancipation. ↓
148.23	caution,] caution, <of President Lincoln>
148.28	councils,] councils, <&>
148.29	these persons] the<m>se ↑ persons ↓
148.30	driven them] driven <these>them
148.31	never have drawn] <not> ↑ never ↓ have <hoped to> drawn
148.33	hatred,] ↑ their ↓ hatred,
148.35–36	'Tis . . . wrong.] ↑ Tis vain to say that the war was avoidable by us, or, ↑ that ↓ both are in the wrong. ↓
149.7	perpetually] <the attention> perpetually
149.8–9	diverted . . . general] diverted to <a thousand objects of> trade <of politics> ↑ manufactures, ↓ & <of enterprise in> ↑ <mills, of> railroads, ↓ public works, of politics, & <of> general
149.10	blood.] blood. <But>
149.14	hour,] hour, <the era of good feelings,>
149.18	part.] part,—<averse as we are to war,—eager as we are to get back to our prosperous trade.>

149.19	fatal] <im> fatal
149.20	pushed] pushed <to the>
149.20	their boundaries,] the ↑ ir ↓ boundaries,
149.21–22	effrontery] <audacity in> effrontery
149.22	fortunes,—the] fortunes<,>. <in the beginning of the war,>—the
149.24	"What . . . be?"] ↑ "What . . . be?" ↓
149.25	past] <call>past
149.29	The steps] <And> The steps <that>
149.31–32	They . . . methods.] They <open the eyes of the> ↑ teach the ↓ teacher ↑ ,— ↓ <to> ↑ —open his eyes to ↓ new <& more expansive> methods.
149.32	They give him] They give <the teacher the> ↑ him ↓
149.35–36	society, . . . that] society, <that> ↑ there is hardly the individual,—that ↓
149.36	not his] not <its>his
149.36	altogether] ↑ altogether ↓
150.1	locally or] locally <&>or
150.1	are locally] ↑ are ↓ locally
150.9	a pine log] ↑ a pine log ↓
150.14	have been] have ↑ been ↓
150.14	detail,] detail, <been>
150.15	sea;] sea; <in the east, heard & obeyed the voice of the waterfall;>
150.23	softening] <corruption of> softening
150.24–26	Already . . . constitutions.] ↑ Already the verdict of mankind is that ↓ The race is morally injured. ↑ that they have not kept the promise of their <eas> founders & early constitutions ↓
150.30	Crisis and war is often] <The> crisis, <the> ↑ & ↓ war is ↑ often ↓
150.31	may be foiled.] <are defeated.> ↑ may be foiled. ↓
150.32	clearer] <plainer>clearer
150.35	by larger] ↑ by ↓ <with> larger
150.35	age.] age. [new page] <We have been disabused of many illusions England has been a stepmother>
151.1	manhood, the] manhood [new page] [new line]

<America the Paradise of the Third Class, of the
Middle Interest, ↑ home of the poor; of mankind
in their shirtsleeves ↓ the day of the omnibus, of
third person plural.> [new line] the

151.5	change! We] change! <These> We
151.6	climate] <Jo> climate
151.6	us] <them> ↑ us ↓
151.11	England . . . world.] ↑ England . . . world. ↓
151.12	threatens] threatens <inevitably>
151.13	India . . . Pacific] India <&> ↑ if she keeps it &
	to ↓ China, <if she keep them>by the Pacific
151.14	the London] <that> the London
151.17	suffers] <utters> suffers
151.19	independence] independence <And they will then
	be able to keep the Yankees>
151.21	it. The one] it. [new page] [paragraph] <In every
	crisis people look for the master of the situation,
	who is usually slow to appear. He does not come
	when he is called. We have found none in Amer-
	ica. But in England, which our politics im-
	mensely concern, they have found none.> The
	one
151.24	France,] France <Germ>
151.25	sympathize,] <sha> sympathize,
151.26	Then the] ↑ Then ↓ The
151.29	these.] these. <A mob has nothing to lose, & can
	afford to steal; but England & France not.>
151.31	as in France,] ↑ as ↓ in France,
151.32	like birds,] ↑ like birds, ↓
151.34	Christians,] <poets> Christians,
151.36	question.] ques ↑ tion. ↓
152.6	the House of Lords] <Lord Shaftesbury or the dot-
	age of Lord Brougham> ↑ the House of Lords ↓
152.8	a drunken Lord Soft?] ↑ a drunken ↓ Lord Soft,
	or the ↑ imbecility of <Lord Brougham?> ↓
152.10	not go] not <to> go
152.14	think] think <of>
152.15	motive,] motive <which they cannot hide of the
	venom,>

152.17	I believe] <Now> I believe
152.24	usefulness,] usefulness, <& diffusion, let these wonders work>
152.25	carpets,] <[unrecovered]>carpets,
152.27–28	for justice . . . the last found, is] for justice . . . < ↑ [unrecovered] ↓ >the last found, is
153.4	will be,—that] will ↑ be ↓ ,—that
153.10	nature.] nature. <"Before Abraham was, I am.">
153.10	work. And] work. <But nothing that has occurred but has been a surprise, & as much to the leaders, as to the hindmost.> ↑ And ↓
153.12	did it.] did it. <Tis the fly in the coach again.>
153.31	guiding] <natural> guiding
153.31	facts, is] facts, i<n>s
153.34	North] <the> North
154.1	traffic] <trade> traffic
154.2	foisted] <clandestinely> ↑ <shipped> foisted ↓
154.5–7	disorganization. . . . for] disorganization. [new page] <In seeing this guidance of events, in seeing this felicity without example, that has rested on the Union thus far,—I find new confidence for> ↑ In seeing this guidance of events, in seeing this felicity without example, that has rested on the Union thus far,—I find new confidence ↓ ↑ for ↓
154.9	active] ↑ active ↓

EMENDATIONS

137.4	[paragraph] It] Read before the Parker [new line] Fraternity December, 1863. / [paragraph] It
137.14	Wedgwood] Wedgewood
138.3	mathematical] mathematicia<n>l
139.11	possibility. At] possibility. *America.* At *See* Textual Notes
139.20	it is proved] ↑ it ↑ as ↓ is ↓ <best> proved
139.32	Religion. "The] Religion. [new page] be called to pass, without alarm. "The *See* Textual Notes
140.10–11	in the present . . . terms.] ↑ <in the present attitude

of the war> ↓ to <short & hasty peace, on any
terms—> *See* Textual Notes

140.16   Comines] Commines

140.17   Louis] Lewis

141.11   Frederick] Frederic

142.11–12   weak. [paragraph] There] weak. [paragraph] France itself [new page] [paragraph] <England is gross & fa-
tal But> there

142.30   4th] 4

142.31   nations. When] nations. <A Waterloo in the air.>
[paragraph] Tis when men <in earnest> ↑ with religious convictions ↓ are behind ↑ <with religion> ↓
the cannon [new page] [paragraph] When

143.11   we."] we." [new line] AC 274

143.32   Saadi] Sadi

144.2   circumstance is here.] circumstance here.

144.3   are girt] girt

143.4   legislature heard] legislature listened ↑ heard ↓

145.16–17   foundation. [paragraph] My] foundation. [new page]
<There . . . ahead.> [paragraph] "The integrity of
more principles is of more consequence than the interests of nations." [new line] *De Stael* [new page]
[paragraph] <There . . . one> [new page] [para-
graph] My *See* Alterations in the Manuscript

145.22   circumstance.] circumstance. <War, I know, is a potent alternative,> [new page] <<wha> tonic, mag-
netiser,—reinforces manly power a hundred & a
thousand times. I see it come as a frosty October,
which shall restore intellectual & moral <power>
↑ vigor ↓ to these languid & dissipated populations.> [new page] ↑ <built on gunpowder> ↓
[new line] For it is not the plants or the animals,
innumerable as they are, nor the whole magazine of
material nature, that can give the sum of power; but
the infinite applicability of these things in the hands
of thinking man. ↑ every new application being
equivalent to a new material. ↓ <The world stands
on that> [new page] <forces. [paragraph] The class
of which I speak defy this condition, & make them-

selves merry without duties. They sit in ↑ deco-
rated ↓ clubs in the cities, & burn tobacco, & play
whist <o>in the country, they sit idle <[unrecov-
ered]> [new line] & reckons Greeks & Romans &
middle ages little better than Indians, & bow-arrow
times; & tomorrow, the> [new page] ↑ are ↓ turning the globe into a brain. Over it, & under it, are
laid nerves & straps, which throb across seas & territories, and, at each city & town in the course an
operation plays on the elemental forces as on the
keys of a piano.

146.7 two stones.] two stones. We, <are> by civilization &
ideas, [new page] Why need I recall the proud catalogue of your mechanical arts?

146.9 McCormick's] McCormicks

146.21 terror, passing] terror, passing ↑ ed ↓

147.1 hypocrites have] hypocrites has

147.8 care of sick] ↑ care ↓ & <the> of <its> sick

147.32 to praise] to <try to get> up <a sentiment of
cosmic> praise

148.3 uniform.] uniform. [new page] [paragraph] speed of
growth. [new line] A land is covered with <camps
of> settlers' camps; then, presently, with log-cabins;
then, soon after, with white wooden towns, <&>
which look to the European eye as slight & perish-
able as the emigrant camps they succeeded: but, almost as quickly, these yield to solid blocks of brick
& <stone> ↑ granite, ↓ which, anywhere [new line]
↑ 127 Salem ↓ [new page] else would last for centuries, but will give place very soon to marble architecture. Our white wooden towns are like the paper
kite which Mr Ellet the engineer flew across the Niagara River, and let it fall on the other side. <b>By
means of the kite string, a stronger cord was drawn,
& then a rope, a cable, & then [new page] an iron
chain, & then a light bridge, &, <then> ↑ in good
time, ↓ the huge Suspension Bridge. So here the
squatters' little town is presently a stone city with
two hundred thousand men, like Chicago & San

Francisco. [paragraph] It is not the fault of Nature if the healthy man has not bread for himself & his household. [new line] ↑ 129 Salem ↓ *See* Textual Notes

148.28   Pierce,] Pierce, [new line] Our politics were at an extreme pass. Battle cut the knot which no wisdom could untie, & showed you how to destroy slavery, which was harming the white nation more than it was harming the black.

149.8–9   works, politics,] works, of politics,

149.33   poise: he] poise:

150.10   done? This] done? [new page] Diligent adroit & bold [new line] This

151.1–2   the new man,] the new man [new line] the complemental man

151.15   selling Exchange] selling in all markets Exchange *See* Textual Notes

152.7   Punch's] Punchs

152.8   Soft?] Soft, or the ↑ imbecility of <Lord Brougham?> ↓

152.12–13   Gortchakoff] Gortaschoff *See* Textual Notes

152.19   liberty like] liberty [new line] like) [new page] Liberty, like

TEXTUAL NOTES

139.11   possibility. At] The term *America.* is used as a header for a new page and is clearly not intended to be a part of the text.

139.32   religion. "The] The restored passages have been canceled in pencil, leaving no possible transition to the next paragraph.

143.36   ball.] ball. ↑ 2 ↓ We have ample domain,—& thence facility of living. <a homestead for every child of Adam> ↑ 1 ↓ We have repealed the old abuses.

148.3   uniform.] The deleted pages may have been used when Emerson delivered the lecture in Salem. At any rate, they clearly do not fit here.

151.5–10   What . . . gift.] 'They . . . gift.' is at the top of the

	page, preceded by 'A 2' and a hand pointing down, separated by a line from 'What . . . John' at the bottom of the page, preceded by 'A 1'.
151.15	selling Exchange] The phrase 'in all markets' is at the end of a line. Emerson probably changed his train of thought and wrote 'Exchange' at the beginning of the next line, forgetting to delete the now unnecessary phrase.
152.12–13	Gortchakoff] In a later journal entry, Emerson wrote 'Gortachoff', similar to his spelling here, then changed it to the correct 'Gortchakoff', which we have adopted as our reading (see *JMN*, 15:393).
154.14	men.] There are other leaves following this in the manuscript folder at Harvard, but they are clearly earlier versions of some passages in the final lecture, or unrelated to it, and are not printed.

NOTES

Historical Background

1. *The Collected Works of Ralph Waldo Emerson*, ed. Alfred R. Ferguson et al., 4 vols. to date (Cambridge, Mass.: Harvard University Press, 1971–), 1:156. All subsequent references to this edition of Emerson's work appear parenthetically as *CW*.
2. *The Letters of Ralph Waldo Emerson*, ed. Ralph L. Rusk and Eleanor M. Tilton, 8 vols. to date (New York: Columbia University Press, 1939; 1990–), 1:194. All subsequent references to this edition of Emerson's letters will appear parenthetically as *L*.
3. *Slavery*, vol. 2 of *The Works of William Ellery Channing*, 6 vols. (Boston: James Munroe, 1848).
4. *The Journals and Miscellaneous Notebooks of Ralph Waldo Emerson*, ed. William H. Gilman et al., 16 vols. (Cambridge, Mass.: Harvard University Press, 1960–1982), 5:150. All subsequent references to this edition of Emerson's journals appear parenthetically as *JMN*.
5. Channing, *Slavery*, pp. 107, 115, 11.
6. Quoted in Daniel Walker Howe, *The Unitarian Conscience: Harvard Moral Philosophy, 1805–1861* (Cambridge, Mass.: Harvard University Press, 1970), p. 277.
7. Ralph L. Rusk, *The Life of Ralph Waldo Emerson* (New York: Charles Scribner's Sons, 1949), p. 153.
8. Gerald Sorin, *Abolitionism: A New Perspective* (New York: Praeger, 1972), p. 33.

9. Merton L. Dillon, *The Abolitionists: The Growth of a Dissenting Minority* (New York: W. W. Norton, 1974), p. 6.

10. Henry Steele Commager, *The Era of Reform, 1830–1860* (New York: D. Van Nostrand, 1960), p. 10. See also Alice Felt Tyler, *Freedom's Ferment: Phases of American Social History from the Colonial Period to the Outbreak of the Civil War* (New York: Harper and Row, 1944), for comprehensive discussions of the many reform movements of the time.

11. Dillon, *Abolitionists*, p. 39.

12. John L. Thomas, *The Liberator: William Lloyd Garrison, A Biography* (Boston: Little, Brown, 1963), pp. 178ff.; Leonard L. Richards, *"Gentlemen of Property and Standing": Anti-Abolition Mobs in Jacksonian America* (New York: Oxford University Press, 1970).

13. Dillon, *Abolitionists*, p. 114.

14. Franklin Sanborn, "The Women of Concord," *Critic*, May 1906, p. 409; Ellen Tucker Emerson, *The Life of Lidian Jackson Emerson*, ed. Delores Bird Carpenter (Boston: Twayne, 1980), pp. 64, 83–84.

15. Thomas, *Garrison*, pp. 304ff.

16. Richards, *Anti-Abolition Mobs*, p. 12.

17. Sorin, *Abolitionism*, p. 91.

18. Channing, "Address to the Citizens of Boston," *Yeoman's Gazette* (Concord, Mass.), 9 December 1837, p. 2.

19. James Elliot Cabot, *A Memoir of Ralph Waldo Emerson*, 2 vols. (Boston: Houghton Mifflin, 1887), 2:425–426.

20. Cabot, *Emerson*, 2:426.

21. *The Selected Letters of Lidian Jackson Emerson*, ed. Delores Bird Carpenter (Columbia: University of Missouri Press, 1987), p. 74.

22. Lidian Emerson, *Letters*, pp. 74, 308.

23. For examples of this concern, see *JMN*, 7:393, 12:152.

24. *The Complete Works of Ralph Waldo Emerson*, ed. Edward Waldo Emerson, 12 vols. (Boston: Houghton Mifflin, 1903–1904), 11:61. All subsequent references to this edition of Emerson's works appear parenthetically as *W*.

25. *The Early Lectures of Ralph Waldo Emerson*, ed. Stephen E. Whicher, Robert E. Spiller, and Wallace E. Williams, 3 vols. (Cambridge, Mass.: Harvard University Press, 1961–1972), 3:91. Subsequent references to this edition of Emerson's lectures appear parenthetically as *EL*.

26. Ellis Gray Loring to Emerson, 16 March 1838, Houghton Library, Harvard University; quoted with permission.

27. Maria Weston Chapman, draft article on Emerson, 1844, Boston Public Library; quoted with permission.

28. For a discussion of abolitionism in the Emerson family and in Concord, see Len Gougeon, *Virtue's Hero: Emerson, Antislavery, and Reform* (Athens: University of Georgia Press, 1990), pp. 24–40.

29. I thank Robert A. Gross for his generosity in providing me with information regarding these and other Concord petitions from the Massachusetts State Archives and the National Archives.

30. For further information on Emerson's extensive preparation of this important speech, see Gougeon, *Virtue's Hero*, pp. 73–75, 88–91.

31. *Herald of Freedom*, 16 August 1844; Martha L. Berg and Alice De V. Perry, "'The Impulses of Human Nature': Margaret Fuller's Journal from June through October 1844," *Proceedings of the Massachusetts Historical Society* 102 (1990): 107; George William Curtis, manuscript account, 4 August 1844, Archives of the Paulist Fathers, New York City.

32. John Greenleaf Whittier to Emerson, 12 September 1844, *The Letters of John Greenleaf Whittier*, ed. John B. Pickard, 3 vols. (Cambridge, Mass.: Harvard University Press, 1975), 1:648.

33. Quoted in Rusk, *Emerson*, p. 360.

34. W. J. Potter, "Emerson and the Abolitionists," *Index*, 3 December 1885.

35. For an interesting and informative discussion of the history of this "lost journal," see John C. Broderick, "Emerson and Moorfield Story: A Lost Journal Found," *American Literature* 38 (May 1966): 177–186.

36. Harold Schwartz, "Fugitive Slave Days in Boston," *New England Quarterly* 27 (March 1954): 191–212.

37. Ellen Emerson, *Lidian Emerson*, p. 125.

38. Walter Harding, *The Days of Henry Thoreau* (New York: Alfred A. Knopf, 1962), p. 318.

39. John Hope Franklin, *From Slavery to Freedom* (New York: Alfred A. Knopf, 1947), p. 268.

40. Some Transcendentalists—Thoreau, Alcott, Theodore Parker, William Henry Furness, William Henry Channing, James Freeman Clarke, Moncure Daniel Conway, Margaret Fuller, and later Thomas Wentworth Higginson—came to support the abolition movement to a greater or lesser degree. Parker and Channing were undoubtedly the most active contributors of this group. Other Transcendentalists and their sympathizers, however—George Ripley and Frederic Henry Hedge, and George William Curtis and Orestes A. Brownson among them—objected to the abolitionists on a variety of grounds. Overall, it is difficult to generalize about the relationship between Transcendentalists and abolitionists since much depends on the individuals involved and the period under consideration.

41. Michael Meyer, "Discord in Concord on the Day of John Brown's Hanging," *Thoreau Society Bulletin* 146 (Winter 1979):1–3.
42. For a discussion of this confrontation, see Gougeon, *Virtue's Hero*, pp. 253–256.
43. *Atlantic Monthly* 9 (April 1862): 509.
44. For a discussion of Emerson's reaction to British conduct during the war, see Len Gougeon, "Emerson, Carlyle, and the Civil War," *New England Quarterly* 62 (September 1989):403–423.

Letter to Martin van Buren

1. Emerson was prompted to send this letter to President Van Buren by his Concord neighbors and friends, who organized a protest meeting on Sunday, 22 April 1838. At that meeting, according to Lidian, Emerson first delivered his "Appeal of the Cherokees." A draft of this letter appears in *JMN*, 12:25–29, and an edited version of the draft appears in *L*, 7:303–306.
2. The Cherokees made considerable progress in cultural and social arts, adopting an alphabet of eighty-five characters, publishing a newspaper, establishing a representative type of government, and forming a public school system.
3. *"Note by a friend of the writer.—* The fact that few Cherokees who made the treaty were not authorized to make it, was known to the Executive at the time, not afterwards discovered, as supposed by Mr. Emerson." [Printed in the *Daily National Intelligencer*.]
4. The policy of Indian removal began under Pres. Andrew Jackson (1829–1837). In May 1850 Congress passed an act that provided for the removal of Indians to territories west of the Mississippi, even though as early as 1791 the Cherokees, in a series of treaties with the U.S. government, were recognized as a nation with their own laws and customs. On 29 December 1835 the Cherokees presumably surrendered all their lands west of the Mississippi in return for land in western Indian territory, transportation costs, and a payment of $5 million. Many sympathizers, including Lidian Emerson, saw this treaty as a fraud. There was armed resistance on the part of some Indians to this policy. Despite Emerson's letter, and other such protests, the Cherokees were eventually removed.

"An Address on the Emancipation"

1. Emerson was invited to give this address in Concord by the Women's Anti-Slavery Society. In addition to Emerson, who was "the orator of

the day," Samuel Joseph May and Frederick Douglass, among others, delivered lectures.

2. This view was common at the time. Josiah C. Nott, in *Types of Mankind, or Ethnological Researches* (Philadelphia, 1854), states that "the monuments of Egypt prove, the *Negro* races have not, during 4000 years at least, been able to make one solitary step, in Negroland, from their savage state" (p. 95). Louis Agassiz, Harvard professor of natural history and Emerson's friend, also published an essay, "Sketch of the Natural Provinces of the Animal World and Their Relation to the Different Types of Man," in this volume.

   Herodotus (d. ca. 424), Greek historian sometimes referred to as the father of history. Troglodytes, the name given by Greeks to various primitive tribes known for crude and uncivilized behavior.

3. Charms or fetishes, here used to mean "Obeah men" or witch doctors.

4. Disparaging term used by blacks for those of predominantly white blood.

5. Granville Sharp (1735–1813), philanthropist, pamphleteer, and scholar.

6. William Sharp (1805–1896), physician.

7. William Murray (1705–1793), chief justice of the King's Bench of Great Britain (1756–1788).

8. Charles Talbot (1685–1737) and Philip Yorke (1690–1764), jurists who ruled in a slave case in 1729 that a slave did not become free by coming to England or by baptism, and that any master might compel his slave to return with him to the West Indies.

9. Identified variously as James Somerset, Sommerset, Somersett, or Summerset.

10. Emerson apparently felt a continuing interest in Mansfield. He refers to his decision in the Somerset case again in a journal entry from 1850 (*JMN*, 11:281), in a passage that he would use a year later in the Fugitive Slave Law address at Concord.

11. These six Quakers are usually credited with launching the British abolition movement in 1783. They were later joined by Granville Sharp and Thomas Clarkson (see n. 13 below).

12. John Woolman (1720–1772), American Quaker and early advocate of the abolition of slavery, wrote *Some Considerations on the Keeping of Negroes* (1754).

13. Thomas Clarkson (1760–1846), British philanthropist, wrote his prize essay against slavery in 1786.

14. William Wilberforce (1759–1833), philanthropist and member of Parliament.

15. William Pitt (the Younger) (1759–1806), prime minister of England (1784–1801); Charles James Fox (1749–1806), member of Parliament who supported the abolition of the slave trade.

16. The American Colonization Society was founded in 1817.

17. William Carey (1761–1834) and William Ward (1769–1823), Baptist missionaries noted especially for their work in the East Indies.

18. Edward George Stanley (1799–1869), fourteenth earl of Derby.

19. A praedial is a slave attached to an estate.

20. Henry Peter, Lord Brougham (1778–1868), member of Parliament, a founder of the *Edinburgh Review*.

21. William Ellery Channing (1780–1842), influential Boston Unitarian minister and early antislavery advocate much admired by Emerson, published his controversial work *Slavery* in 1835.

22. "'Emancipation in the West Indies: a Six Months Tour in Antigua, Barbadoes, and Jamaica, in the year 1837. By J. A. Thome and J. H. Kimball. New York, 1838.'—pp. 146, 147." [Emerson's note.]

23. George Hamilton Gordon, fourth earl of Aberdeen (1784–1860); Sir George Grey (1799–1882), under secretary for the Colonies (1834, 1835–1839).

24. Lord Belmore, lieutenant governor of Jamaica from 1829 to 1832, arrived at a time when the slavery question was being hotly debated, and he was recalled after a rebellion broke out; Lionel Smith (1778–1842) was the first British governor-general of the Windward Islands and, nominally, of British Guiana, Trinidad, and Saint Lucia.

25. Thomas Fowell Buxton (1786–1845), member of Parliament and philanthropist, advocated prison reforms, repression of the slave trade, and the abolition of slavery in British dominions.

26. Charles Metcalfe (1785–1846), governor of Jamaica (1839–1842).

27. Sparta, also called Lacedaemon, was an ancient Greek city whose citizens were noted for their severe militaristic discipline. The Dorians were one of the three principal peoples of ancient Greece from whom the Spartans were presumed to have descended.

28. English cities known as manufacturing centers.

29. George N. Briggs (1796–1861), governor of Massachusetts (1844–1851).

30. Robert Henley, first earl of Northington (1708–1772), made the remark in a British slave case, *Shanley v. Harvey*, in 1762.

31. Edmund Burke (1729–1797), Richard Grenville (1776–1839), Charles Grey (1764–1845), and George Canning (1770–1827) were all members of Parliament who sought to abolish the slave trade and slavery.

32. William Cowper (1731–1800).

33. *Edinburgh Review,* British quarterly periodical published from 1802 to 1929.
34. Mr. Huddleston is unidentified.
35. In this famous case 133 slaves who had grown ill were cast into the sea by Capt. Luke Collingwood. Only one survived. The insurance arrangement provided that if the slaves died a natural death the loss would fall on the owners of the ship and the captain, but if they were thrown alive into the sea, on any pretext of necessity for the safety of the ship, it would be the underwriters' loss. See F. O. Shyllon, *Black Slaves in Britain* (London: Oxford University Press, 1974), pp. 184–209.
36. Joseph Sturge (1793–1859) published *The West Indies* (1837) to document the abuses of slaves and apprentices in the West Indies. Joseph John Gurney (1788–1847), Quaker philanthropist, wrote *Winter in the West Indies* (1840). The Reverend James Phillippo (1798–1879), British Baptist missionary to the West Indies, published *Jamaica: Its Past and Present State,* which was issued in a second edition in 1843.
37. Scythians is the name applied by the Greeks to barbarous nomadic tribes of southeastern Europe. Caraibs are black beetles. Feejees are inhabitants of the Fiji Islands.
38. Pierre Dominique Toussaint L'Overture (1743–1803), soldier, statesman, and liberator of Haiti.

Anniversary of West Indian Emancipation

1. The gathering at Waltham, like the other annual celebrations of West Indian emancipation, was sponsored by the Massachusetts Anti-Slavery Society. Contemporary accounts indicate that the event was attended by "large delegations from Boston and Concord" as well as other places.
2. This paragraph is from the *Liberator,* 8 August 1845, p. 126.
3. The Fitchburg Railroad was only minutes from the location of this antislavery gathering. Emerson was a longtime shareholder in the company (see *L,* 4:122).
4. See *JMN,* 9:100, 195, for similar statements.
5. The concept of Negro racial inferiority was pervasive in the nineteenth century, even among some abolitionists. In 1836 the abolitionist Theodore Weld estimated that "at least 3/5th of the northerners *now* believe the blacks are an *inferior* race"; see Merton M. Dillon, *The Abolitionists: The Growth of a Dissenting Minority* (New York: W. W. Norton, 1974), p. 67.

6. Arguments against Negro inferiority were plentiful and were often based on the evidence of social progress following emancipation in the British West Indies and Haiti. Several such accounts appeared in Emerson's hometown newspapers, the *Yeoman's Gazette* and the *Concord Freeman*, in the late 1830s and early 1840s.

7. See *JMN*, 9:124, for echoes of this passage.

Letter to William Rotch

1. The New Bedford Lyceum voted to exclude blacks from full membership in October 1845. When he was invited to speak at the lyceum in November, Emerson refused to lecture before the group and provided this letter of protest. He later allowed for its publication in the *Liberator*.

   For further correspondence on this matter, see *L*, 3:322–323. Charles Sumner (1811–1874), an ardent abolitionist who later served as senator from Massachusetts (1851–1874), also refused to lecture at the New Bedford Lyceum at this time. His letter of refusal appeared with Emerson's in the *Liberator*. For a comprehensive discussion of the entire New Bedford affair, see Len Gougeon, *Virtue's Hero: Emerson, Antislavery, and Reform* (Athens: University of Georgia Press, 1990), pp. 101–107.

Antislavery Speech at Dedham

1. Emerson gave this lecture at a combined picnic celebration and fair sponsored by the Massachusetts Anti-Slavery Society as a fund-raiser for the organization. Contemporary accounts indicate that the crowd was large, "numbering several thousands of both sexes." Other speakers for the day were William Henry Channing, James Freeman Clarke, William Lloyd Garrison, and Wendell Phillips.

2. Among other things, Emerson is here reacting to the recent declaration of war on Mexico (13 May 1846), a consequence of the annexation of Texas as a slave state in December 1845.

3. John Randolph (1773–1833), senator from Virginia (1825–1827).

4. Algerine, a native of Algiers; Sikh, an adherent of Sikhism, a monotheistic Hindu religious sect founded in the sixteenth century; Seminoles, a tribe of Indians located primarily in Florida. These, along with the Mexicans, had all experienced aggression by France, England, and the United States (see *JMN*, 9:425).

5. Despite protests throughout the state, Gov. George N. Briggs eventually supported the war with Mexico.

6. Emerson's extensive essay on Napoleon appears in *Representative Men* (1850).

Letter to the Kidnapping Committee

1. Samuel Gridley Howe (1801–1876), a champion of people laboring under disability, founded a school for the blind and was a staunch opponent of slavery. Emerson was invited by Howe, Samuel Sewall, Charles Sumner, Theodore Parker, and the Committee on Arrangements to participate in the Faneuil Hall meeting to protest the return of a runaway slave who had arrived in Boston as a stowaway on the *Ottoman*. Sumner, Parker, and Wendell Phillips all spoke at the meeting.
2. John Quincy Adams (1767–1848), sixth president of the United States (1825–1829) and later congressman from Massachusetts (1831–1848), was an early opponent of slavery and presided at the Faneuil Hall meeting.

Antislavery Remarks at Worcester

1. Emerson delivered this address at an antislavery gathering in Worcester, Massachusetts, which was held under the auspices of the Massachusetts Anti-Slavery Society on 3 August 1849. The third was chosen rather than the traditional first of August because Pres. Zachary Taylor had named the first a day of national fasting and prayer due to a cholera epidemic; the abolitionists saw this designation as an act of false piety on the president's part. Wendell Phillips and William Lloyd Garrison also addressed the meeting.
2. See *The Conduct of Life* (*W*, 6:36) for the relation of freedom and fate.
3. Emerson learned of the evolutionary development of fruit trees in Andrew Jackson Dowling's *Fruits and Fruit Trees of America* (1846) and saw this phenomenon as symbolically significant; see Edward Emerson's comment in this regard in *W*, 5:336.
4. Emerson states in *English Traits* (1856) that "the Heinskringla, or Sagas of the Kings of Norway, collected by Snorro Sturleson, is the Iliad and Odyssey of English history" (*W*, 5:57).
5. Emerson derived this notion about Columbus and slavery from his reading of Arthur Helps, *The Conquerers of the New World and Their Bondsmen* (1848–1852); see *JMN*, 11:77.
6. David Wilmot (1814–1868), congressman from Pennsylvania, proposed the Wilmot Proviso in 1846, which sought to exclude slavery from any territories acquired as a result of the Mexican War. The measure was passed by the House but defeated in the Senate.
7. See *The Conduct of Life* (*W*, 6:49) and *JMN*, 11:15, 161, for Emerson's concept of the "beautiful necessity."

8. Emerson uses this couplet in "Illusions," in *The Conduct of Life* (*W*, 6:325).

Letter to Mary Merrick Brooks

1. After the Fugitive Slave Law passed in September 1850, there were two unsuccessful attempts to enforce it in Massachusetts, in the fall of 1850 and spring of 1851. These events convinced Emerson that federal officials fully intended to enforce the law, at whatever cost. He provided this letter to be read at the annual meeting of the Middlesex Anti-Slavery Society, held in Concord on 3 April 1851.

   The "friend" is undoubtedly Mary Merrick Brooks (1801–1868), a member of the society's Executive Committee, who had encouraged Emerson's abolition activity on several earlier occasions. Sophia Thoreau, Henry's sister, was also a committee member at this time.
2. Emerson was lecturing in Philadelphia at the time of the society's annual meeting.
3. Mammon, the personification of riches, greed, and worldly sin in the New Testament.

"Address to the Citizens of Concord"

1. Emerson was invited to deliver this address by thirty-five of his fellow male citizens of Concord. In their letter of invitation (26 April 1851), the subscribers indicate that they are "very desirous of hearing your opinions upon the Fugitive Slave Law, & upon the aspects of the times" (Houghton Library, Harvard Univesity, bMS Am 1280 [675]).

   Emerson first gave the speech on 3 May 1851 in Concord. The *Liberator* (9 May 1851) later reported that it was well received and "is said to have been one of the ablest and most forcible of that distinguished gentleman's productions." Eventually Emerson was prevailed upon to repeat the speech on at least nine occasions throughout the Middlesex district in an effort to elect John Gorham Palfrey, a Free Soiler, to the U.S. Congress. Emerson notes in a letter to Theodore Parker (9 May 1851) that he is to read the lecture in "Lexington, in Fitchburg, & it is asked for in Cambridge & in Waltham also. . . . which . . . you see, is stumping Palfrey's district" (*L*, 8:277).
2. Publication of the ten-volume *Works of John Adams* (1850–1856), ed. Charles Francis Adams, had just begun.
3. The escaped slave Shadrach (Fredric Jenkins, or Wilkins) had been rescued from custody in Boston on 15 February 1851, an early attempt to prevent the implementation of the Fugitive Slave Law.

4. The battles of Lexington and Concord were fought on 19 April 1775; the Battle of Bunker Hill was waged in Boston on 17 June 1775.

5. One hundred guns were fired on the Boston Common after the bill's passage.

6. Hugo Grotius (1583–1645), Dutch jurist who wrote on the rights and duties of states; Edward Coke (1552–1634), English lawyer and attorney general; William Blackstone (1723–1780), English lawyer and author of *Commentaries on the Laws of England* (1765–1769); Jean-Jacques Burlamaqui (1694–1748), Swiss jurist; Emmerich de Vattel (1714–1767), Swiss jurist and author of *Law of Nations* (1758); James Mackintosh (1765–1832), Scottish philosopher and lawyer.

7. English chief justices Henry Hobart (d. 1625), John Holt (1642–1710), and William Murray.

8. In August 1572 Charles IX of France, in response to the Saint Bartholomew's Day Massacre of up to ten thousand Huguenots in Paris, wrote to his provincial governors ordering them to put to death Huguenots who attempted any form of assembly. Several governors refused to obey this edict. There is no hard evidence to confirm the story of Viscount d'Orthe's response, as reported by Vattel, which may be apocryphal, though in fact no massacre took place in Bayonne (see Robert Kingdon, *Myths about the St. Bartholomew's Day Massacres, 1572–1576* [Cambridge, Mass.: Harvard University Press, 1988], and Vattel, *The Law of Nations; or, Principles of the Law of Nature* [Northampton, Mass.: Simeon Butler, 1820], book 1, chapter 4, p. 77). Vattel is given as the source for this story in the manuscript, and, indeed, much of it was taken directly from the book, a copy of which is in Emerson's library.

9. See ll. 626–627 of Sophocles' *Electra*.

10. James Mason (1798–1871), senator from Virginia, drafted the Fugitive Slave Law.

11. On 2 March 1807 Congress passed a law prohibiting the African slave trade and the importation of slaves into America after 1 January 1808.

12. Emerson is referring to such sympathetic editorials as "Fugitive Slave Agitation" from the *Boston Daily Advertiser:* "The senseless excitement which was raised at New Bedford on Sunday last, by the active circulation of a false report, shows how ready a portion of the public are to become the dupes of a few designing men. . . . This transaction is a most unfortunate one, from the impression which it must produce abroad of the character of our community and the fidelity of our people to the Constitution" (20 March 1851, p. 2).

13. Probably Isaac Hill (1789–1851), New Hampshire editor and politician who opposed the abolitionists; Benjamin Franklin Hallet (1797–1862), editor of the *Boston Post*, who supported the slavery advocate Franklin Pierce for president in 1852 and was rewarded with the post of district attorney of Boston.

14. Prince Metternich of Austria (1773–1859), foreign minister and chancellor for nearly forty years; Charles-Maurice de Périgord-Talleyrand (1754–1838), French diplomat.

15. Phrenology, a popular pseudoscience holding that a person's character could be "read" by examining the bumps on the head, which were thought to correspond to areas of "influence" in the brain.

16. Henry Clay (1777–1852), Kentucky politician and American secretary of state, was instrumental in preparing the legislation that included the Fugitive Slave Law.

17. The African nation of Liberia had been founded in 1822 by blacks funded by the American Colonization Society and was declared a republic in 1847. A number of reformers suggested black emigration to Liberia as a solution to the slavery crisis.

18. William Parsons (1570?–1650), lord justice of Ireland.

The Fugitive Slave Law

1. Emerson delivered this, his second speech on the Fugitive Slave Law, as part of a series of antislavery lectures at the Tabernacle in New York City. At least partially in response to the recent passage of the Kansas-Nebraska Act, the presentation elicited various critiques. The *National Anti-Slavery Standard* (18 March 1854) reprinted a commentary from *Mitchel's Citizen*, which described the speech as "a tame repetition of Parker and Phillips, nay, a dilution of [Henry Ward] Beecher and a *rechauffée* of Miss Lucy." A reporter for the *Boston Transcript*, however, in an article reprinted in the *Liberator* (17 March 1854), indicated that, while some had entered the hall "thinking that the speaker would find no new form in which to exhibit his hackneyed subject . . . they found that, in the hands of the master, the old theme wears a new beauty when clothed with the graces of his thought."

   Emerson himself felt that the speech was somewhat unfinished and noted in a letter to William Henry Furness that he "had to carry to New York a makeshift instead of an oracle" (*L*, 8:397).

2. The Pilgrims' landing at Plymouth in December 1620 was usually commemorated on the twenty-second, which is also the anniversary day of the New-England Society.

3. On Webster's appearance at Bunker Hill at the dedication of the monument on 17 June 1843, see *JMN*, 8:425, and *L*, 3:180–181, both of which use some of the language employed in this passage.

4. The speeches supporting his position on the Fugitive Slave Law are: 7 March 1850, *Speech of the Hon. Daniel Webster on the Subject of Slavery* (1850; also published in 1850 as *Speech of Hon. Daniel Webster on Mr. Clay's Resolutions*); the speeches in New York State in May 1851, *Mr. Webster's Speeches at Buffalo, Syracuse, and Albany* (1851; delivered 22, 26, and 28 May, respectively; the last one was published separately as *Speech of Hon. Daniel Webster, to the Young Men of Albany* [1851]); and 20 April 1850 in Boston.

5. The English jurist Baron George Jeffreys (1648–1689). On Talbot and Yorke, see n. 8 to the emancipation address of 1844. On Lord Mansfield (William Murray), see n. 7 to the same speech.

6. *Vera pro gratis* ("truth rather than pleasantness") appeared as part of a Latin passage included in the preface to Webster's publication of his speech in pamphlet form. Claude Moore Fuess reports that Webster insisted these words be printed in capitals, "a fact which proves that he was conscious of the storm which he was about to raise" (*Daniel Webster*, 2 vols. [Boston: Little, Brown, 1930], 2:222–223).

7. Edward Waldo Emerson writes that the passage is from the Greek historian Dio Cassius (ca. 163–164 to ca. 235), gives the Greek original, and provides a translation and commentary. To Edward, it "seems very doubtful whence the Greek verses came" (*Miscellanies* [1904], p. 590).

8. "Just ten years earlier, Hon. Samuel Hoar, the Commissioner of Massachusetts, sent to Charleston, South Carolina, in the interests of our colored citizens there constantly imprisoned and ill used, had been expelled from that state with a show of force" (Edward Waldo Emerson's note, *Miscellanies* [1904], p. 590). Ralph Waldo Emerson comments on this event at length in his sketch "Samuel Hoar," in *Lectures and Biographical Sketches* (1884).

9. Webster had died on 24 October 1852.

10. "The sending back of Onesimus by Paul was a precedent precious in the eyes of the pro-slavery preachers, North and South, in those days, ignoring, however, Paul's message, 'Not now as a servant, but above a servant, a brother beloved, specially to me, but how much more unto thee, both in the flesh and in the Lord. If thou count me therefore a partner, receive him as myself' (*Epistle of Paul to Philemon*, i, 16, 17)"— Edward Waldo Emerson's note, *Miscellanies* (1904), p. 590.

11. Oliver Cromwell (1599–1658), lord protector of England.

12. Emerson was fond of this phrase from Mahomet (ca. 570–632), prophet of Islam, writing it in his journal (see *JMN*, 6:388, 7:401) and using it as the epigraph to "Heroism," in *Essays: Second Series* (1844).

13. The Persian poet Muslih-uh-Din Saadi (ca. 1200–ca. 1292), a longtime favorite of Emerson, who wrote a preface to an 1865 edition of *The Gulistan, or Rose Garden*. Emerson copied this sentiment into his journal (*JMN*, 9:39) and also used it in "Ethnical Scriptures," *Dial* 4 (January 1844): 404.

14. Louis Napoleon (1808–1873) ruled France as Napoleon III from 1852 to 1871.

15. Emerson also used this passage in "The Sovereignty of Ethics," in *Lectures and Biographical Sketches* (1884), pp. 184–185, and in his lectures on slavery in May 1854.

16. Unidentified.

17. Unidentified.

18. Unidentified.

19. Schleswig-Holstein, a province of Prussia, had recently engaged in a war with Denmark (1848–1850).

20. This could be either Earl Charles Grey (1764–1845), English statesman, or Earl Henry George Grey (1802–1894), English politician.

21. Castalia, a fountain on Mount Parnasuss in ancient Greece sacred to the Muses and Apollo.

22. Edward Emerson notes that the "occasion alluded to was Hon. Robert C. Winthrop's speech to the alumni of Harvard College on Commencement Day in 1852. What follows is not an abstract, but Mr. Emerson's rendering of the spirit of his address" (*Miscellanies* [1904], p. 592). Actually, much of this passage is based on Emerson's contemporaneous account in *JMN*, 13:71–73, regarding Robert Charles Winthrop (1809–1894), congressman and senator from Massachusetts.

23. Francis Bacon (1561–1626) was befriended early in his career by the courtier Robert Devereux, second earl of Essex (1567–1601), but later served as a witness for the prosecution in Essex's trial for treason.

24. Demosthenes (ca. 384–322 B.C.), Athenian statesman; Martin Luther (1483–1546), theologian; William Wallace (ca. 1270–1305), Scottish national hero; George Fox (1624–1691), founder of the Society of Friends, or Quakers.

25. In the Greek legend, Cassandra was given the gift of prophesy by Apollo, but when she refused his advances, he cursed her by having no one believe her predictions.

Lecture on Slavery

1. In May 1854 Anthony Burns, a fugitive slave, was arrested in Boston and returned to slavery. Emerson and other abolitionists were outraged by the event, and in response he began work on another antislavery address. In September he indicated in a letter to Thomas Wentworth Higginson that he was ready to schedule presentations of the piece (*L*, 8:411–412). The first occurred on 25 January 1855 in Boston, at the Tremont Temple.
2. The White Mountains of New Hampshire; Mount Katahdin in Maine; Mount Hoosac in the Berkshires of western Massachusetts.
3. *Nolumus mutari:* "we are unwilling to be changed."
4. The well-known hotels, the Astor in New York, the Tremont in Boston, and the Girard in Philadelphia.
5. The Parthenon, the temple of Athena on the Acropolis in Athens; between 1801 and 1803, Thomas Bruce, seventh earl of Elgin (1766–1841), brought most of the marble frieze of the Parthenon back to England, where it is now in the British Museum. Apollo Belvedere (a life-size Roman statue) and Torso Belvedere (an Athenian statue of Hercules in a sitting position) are both in the Vatican.
6. The Stoics, members of a philosophical school founded in 308 B.C., known for their belief in submitting to necessity. Alfred the Great (849–899), king of Wessex and half of England.
7. Emerson also used this example in other writings, including his 1854 address on the Fugitive Slave Law; see note 15 to that lecture.
8. The Laws of Menu (or Manu), Indian commentaries on religious laws and social obligations, compiled between 200 B.C. and 200 A.D.; Lycurgus (fl. 800 B.C.), Spartan statesman; Emperor Justinian of Byzantium (483–565); Henri-François d'Aguesseau (1668–1751), French jurist whose surname was originally Daguesseau.
9. John Selden (1584–1654), English jurist; Richard Hooker (1554?–1600), English theological writer.
10. Emerson may be referring to one of the four governors of Massachusetts during this period: George N. Briggs (1796–1861), governor 1844–1851; George S. Boutell (1818–1905), governor 1851–1853; John H. Clifford (1809–1876), governor 1853–1854; and Emory Washburn (1800–1877), governor 1854–1855.
11. Arthur Wellesley, duke of Wellington (1769–1852), English soldier.
12. Charles Fourier (1772–1837), French social thinker, believed it possible to distribute the functions of daily life among a group of people, who together would add up to a completed whole.

13. Horatio Nelson (1758–1805), English admiral.
14. The "Father of his country" is George Washington; the cornerstone for the obelisk-shaped monument to him in the nation's capital was laid in 1848, but the completed structure was not dedicated until 1885.
15. John Lowell, Jr. (1799–1836), left $250,000 in his will to the city of Boston for establishing a free public lecture series; George Peabody (1795–1869) established the educationally minded Peabody Institute in Baltimore in 1857 and gave $1,400,000 to it by the time of his death; Joshua Bates (1788–1864) gave $50,000 to the Boston Public Library in 1852; John Jacob Astor (1763–1848) built an impressive library that helped to form the New York Public Library. All were merchants or bankers.

Assault on Charles Sumner

1. After Sen. Charles Sumner was attacked and severely beaten in the Senate chamber by Preston Brooks, a congressman from South Carolina, Emerson and other supporters of Sumner expressed their outrage at a meeting in Concord on 26 May 1856, where Emerson delivered this address. Sumner later wrote Emerson to thank him for "that most beautiful speech of yours" (16 August 1856, *The Selected Letters of Charles Sumner*, ed. Beverly Wilson Palmer, 2 vols. [Boston: Northeastern University Press, 1990], 2:465).
2. Webster declined when John Randolph challenged him to a duel in 1816.
3. A reference to Brooks.
4. Emerson may be referring to either *Freedom National, Slavery Sectional* (1852) or *The Demands of Freedom: Speech of Hon. Charles Sumner . . . on His Motion to Repeal the Fugitive Slave Bill* (1855).
5. John Caldwell Calhoun (1782–1850), senator from South Carolina; William Pitt, earl of Chatham (1708–1778), English statesman.
6. Bishop Gilbert Burnet (1643–1715), Scottish prelate.

Kansas Relief Meeting

1. Several meetings were held in Concord and elsewhere to raise money for the defense of free-state immigrants in Kansas (see *JMN*, 14:96). Emerson delivered this speech at such a meeting in Cambridge on 10 September 1856.

   Emerson might be referring to Edmund B. Whitman, a friend and correspondent of John Brown who lived in Lawrence, Kansas.

2. The politicians are Franklin Pierce (1804–1869), fourteenth president of the United States (1853–1857), and senators Lewis Cass (1782–1866) from Michigan (1845–1847), Henry Sheffie Geyer (1790–1859) from Missouri (1851–1857), and Robert M. Hunter (1808–1887) from Virginia (1846–1861). All were noted for their strong proslavery political positions.

3. These individuals remain unidentified. All are from towns in Massachusetts and Connecticut.

4. On the Fourth of July 1856, Emerson, Thoreau, and several other citizens of Concord signed a letter addressed to "His Excellency, the Governor of Our Commonwealth." The letter expresses the belief that citizens of Massachusetts have been "unlawfully seized, robbed, and held as prisoners by citizens of the State of Missouri," and that the governor should "take such immediate action as may seem in your judgment best to protect our fellow citizens and the rights of Massachusetts" (see *L*, 8:493). The governor at the time was Henry J. Gardner (1819–1892).

5. Emerson may have developed this idea of "primary" government as early as 1835, when he composed his "Historical Discourse" on the history of Concord (see *W*, 11:46ff).

6. John Curtiss Underwood (1809–1873), lawyer and Free Soiler whose liberal views on slavery forced him to move from Virginia.

7. Emerson apparently always felt a strong antipathy toward Pierce, an occasional visitor of his close friend Nathaniel Hawthorne in Concord; see *JMN*, 15:60, for comments on "that paltry Franklin Pierce."

8. The "eminent man" is Daniel Webster; see *JMN*, 14:387.

9. On the Committee of Safety, see "Historical Discourse," *W*, 11:72.

Speech at a Meeting to Aid John Brown's Family

1. John Brown (1800–1859) was best known as a leader of the Free Soil forces in the Kansas conflict. His abortive raid on the federal arsenal at Harpers Ferry, Virginia, in October 1859 led to his arrest and execution for treason on 2 December 1859. Following the raid, Brown's supporters organized various gatherings to raise funds to support his indigent family. Emerson delivered this speech in Boston on 18 November 1859. The account in the *Boston Atlas and Daily Bee* (21 November 1859) indicates that "the Temple was thronged. A fee of 25 cents for admittance was asked, and the sum taken was large. These facts indicate a deep and wide-spread sympathy for the old hero and his

family." The meeting's chair was John A. Andrew (1813–1867), lawyer, legislator, antislavery advocate, and governor of Massachusetts (1861–1866).

2. Emerson could have learned these facts about Brown's family from a series of articles James Redpath published in October in the *Boston Atlas and Daily Bee*.

3. General William Hull (1753–1825), commander of American forces, surrendered Detroit to the British in the War of 1812.

4. Henry Alexander Wise (1806–1876), governor of Virginia (1860–1866). Emerson drafted a lengthy letter to Wise pleading for Brown; he apparently never sent it but instead used some of the material here; see *JMN*, 14:334.

5. On 1 May 1857 Comdr. Hiram Paulding (1797–1878) arrested William Walker, who had, with a group of twenty armed men, seized a town in Nicaragua as part of a filibustering expedition. After surrendering, Walker was paroled and, on reaching Washington, released. Paulding was rebuked for exceeding his authority in the matter, but his action was applauded by others, and eventually a congressional investigation ensued. The issue was debated in both the House and the Senate along sectional (North-South) lines.

6. As Edward Emerson notes, this acerbic statement undoubtedly refers to the trials of the fugitive slaves Shadrach, Sims, and Burns in Boston (see *W*, 11:601–602). Shadrach escaped from the courthouse and fled to Canada in 1851. Thomas Sims and Anthony Burns were returned to their owners in 1851 and 1854 despite strong protests from abolitionists and substantial efforts to defend them in the Massachusetts courts.

7. Titus Hutchinson (1771–1857), Vermont State Supreme Court justice (1826–1830) and chief justice (1830–1833).

8. A writ of habeas corpus requires that a person in custody be brought forth for a hearing to determine the legality of his detention. While normally used to protect a citizen's rights, at this time Emerson's neighbor Franklin Sanborn was under subpoena to appear before the commission investigating the Harpers Ferry raid. He refused to go because he feared for his personal safety. When federal marshals arrived in Concord to take Sanborn into custody, he was defended by a crowd of fellow citizens, including Emerson, who physically prevented his arrest.

John Brown

1. Emerson may have learned these facts from James Redpath's series of articles in the *Boston Atlas and Daily Bee*. Eventually Redpath published a formal biography, *The Public Life of Captain John Brown* (1860), which he dedicated to Wendell Phillips, Emerson, and Thoreau because they were "Defenders of the Faithful."

2. A reference to the presumed purpose of Brown's raid on the Harpers Ferry Arsenal.

3. Also called El Cid Campeador (ca. 1040–1099), Spanish soldier of fortune and hero of legend memorialized in the epic poem *Poema Del Cid*, written in the twelfth century, which depicts him as a romantic, chivalrous hero.

4. Mountains in northwest Virginia, bordering the Shenandoah Valley, not far from Harpers Ferry. Alfred the Great was noted for his interests in learning and law. Lycurgus (fl. 600s B.C.), traditionally the lawgiver who founded most of the institutions of ancient Sparta.

Attempted Speech

1. The occasion for this presentation was the annual meeting of the Massachusetts Anti-Slavery Society in the Tremont Temple, Boston, on 24 January 1861. The president of the Massachusetts Anti-Slavery Society at the time was Francis Jackson (1789–1861). The *Liberator* account (1 February 1861), reproduced here, gives the audience's responses as well as Emerson's remarks.

2. Reverend Cassie Waterston (1812–1893), Unitarian minister and a long-time social acquaintance of Emerson's.

3. Emerson was born on what was then Summer Street in Boston on 25 May 1803. He entered Boston Latin School in 1813 and Harvard College in 1817. He was graduated from Harvard in 1821 and subsequently entered the Divinity School there, being ordained a Unitarian minister in Boston on 11 March 1829.

4. Wendell Phillips invited Emerson to speak on this occasion (see *JMN*, 15:111).

5. Philip Henry Gosse (1810–1888), English zoologist who early in his career served as a schoolmaster in Dallas Township, Alabama. He wrote several scientific books, including *The Aquarium* (1854), which popularized collecting and preserving marine specimens. Emerson's reference here is to *Letters from Alabama (U.S.): Chiefly Relating to Natural History* (1859); see *JMN*, 14:298–299.

6. John Wilson (1785–1854), member of the editorial staff of *Blackwood's*

Magazine and author of several of the items in the "Noctes Ambrosiane" series.

"The President's Proclamation"

1. Lincoln issued the preliminary proclamation of emancipation on 22 September 1862. Emerson applauded the measure but was realistic in his assessment that the struggle was far from over. In his journal he observes, "It seems to promise an extension of the war. For there can be no durable peace, no sound Constitution, until we have fought this battle, & the rights of man are vindicated" (*JMN*, 15:293). Almost immediately he set about preparing this presentation, which he delivered on 12 October 1862 at the Music Hall in Boston and published in the *Atlantic Monthly* in November.

2. The Augsburg Confessions, read in 1530, formed the basis for the chief Lutheran creed; "the plantation of America" refers to the Pilgrim landing in 1620; Oliver Cromwell instituted a new Parliament in 1648, after capturing King Charles I; the Reform Bill of 1832 changed British voting practices and increased enfranchisement; the Corn Laws, which regulated foreign and domestic trade of grain, were repealed in 1846; a telegraph line between Ireland and Newfoundland was laid in 1858 but lasted only twenty-seven days—one laid in 1865 and completed in 1866 stayed in place; the Homestead Bill was passed by Congress on 20 May 1862 and gave any head of a family, aged twenty-one or older, the right to purchase up to 120 acres at $1.25 per acre after he or she had settled on it for five years; Lincoln's proclamation in September was to take effect on 1 January 1863.

3. John Milton, "Comus" (1634), ll. 596–598.

4. On 27 September 1862 the Confederate Congress enlarged its conscription act to call up men aged thirty-five to forty-five into military service.

5. William Shakespeare, "Sonnet 107" (first published in 1609).

"Fortune of the Republic"

1. Throughout 1863 tensions between Great Britain and the United States were at an all-time high. British Confederate sympathies were well established and there was talk of intervention to bring about a cessation of hostilities in the American war. Many Americans, weary of the costly and protracted struggle, would undoubtedly have welcomed such a development. The same war-weariness also cast doubts on Lincoln's reelection, as the Copperheads (Northerners who opposed Lincoln's war policy) argued for a negotiated settlement of the war.

Emerson was appalled at the notion that the great struggle would be concluded without a Northern victory, especially after such enormous sacrifices had been made. He was also outraged at the British, especially their intellectual and cultural leaders, such as Carlyle, Tennyson, and Arnold, for their failure to support the North in its struggle against the dark forces of corruption and moral degradation represented by the slaveholding South. All of these concerns are expressed in the powerful address Emerson delivered on several occasions from December 1863 through February 1864.

2. Josiah Wedgwood (1730–1795), English potter; John Flaxman (1755–1826), English artist. Wedgwood moved his operations to Etruria in 1769.

3. The Roman gods Bacchus of wine and Ceres of grain and the harvest; Richard Arkwright (1732–1792), English inventor of the spinning frame for cotton; Eli Whitney (1765–1825), inventor of the cotton gin, which separated the fiber from the seed.

4. Roger Bacon (1220–1292), English inventor, and Bethold Schwarz or Schwartz (fl. 1400–1450), German monk and alchemist, were both erroneously credited as the inventors of gunpowder.

5. Napoleon Bonaparte.

6. Barthold Georg Niebuhr (1776–1831), German historian.

7. Philip de Comines (ca. 1447–1511), French historian; Charles the Bold of Burgundy (1433–1477), who eventually lost his war and life to King Louis XI of France (1423–1483).

8. Thomas Carlyle (1795–1881), Scottish author and Emerson's lifelong friend, published *The History of Frederick the Great* between 1858 and 1865.

9. In 1848 the French overthrew Louis-Phillipe and established a democratic republic.

10. Riots in Berlin in 1848 were followed by the establishment of a new Parliament at Frankfurt.

11. Napoleon Bonaparte's defeat at the Battle of Waterloo in 1815 marked the end of his public career.

12. Emerson may be thinking of either the Inquisition of the Roman Catholic church against heresies in the twelfth and thirteenth centuries or the Spanish Inquisition against Jews and Moors (1478–1835).

13. The houses of York and Lancaster fought the Wars of the Roses (1455–1487) for the throne of England; there were only twelve to thirteen weeks of actual fighting. Both sides failed when the House of Tudor succeeded to the throne.

14. On Clay's and Webster's support of Greece in its war against Turkey, see Claude Moore Fuess, *Daniel Webster*, 2 vols. (Boston: Little, Brown, 1930), 1:310–314.

15. The Marquis de Lafayette (1757–1834), a hero of the American Revolution, had been given use of the ship *Alliance* by Congress for return trips to France in 1781 and 1788. He made an enormously successful tour of the eastern states in 1824 and was deeded 11,520 acres of land near the Kentucky and Ohio rivers by Congress for his services to the United States.

16. Lajos Kossuth (1802–1894), Hungarian patriot, had been welcomed in Concord by Emerson, whose comments on that occasion were published in *Kossuth in New England* (1852) and reprinted in *Miscellanies* (1884).

17. Congress sent three ships of provisions to famine-struck Ireland and Scotland in March 1847.

18. The Know-Nothing or American party was violently anti-Catholic; it declined rapidly after unsuccessfully running Millard Filmore for president in 1856.

19. In a discarded manuscript leaf in the folder with this lecture, Emerson identifies him as Louis Agassiz (1807–1873), who founded the Museum of Comparative Zoology at Harvard University in 1859.

20. The Chartists were powerful between 1838 and 1849. In complaining that the Reform Bill of 1832 was too limited, they made the six proposals Emerson lists—universal male suffrage, vote by secret ballot, payment for members of Parliament, annual election of Parliament, equality of electoral district representation, and no property qualifications to hold a seat in Parliament.

21. Thomas Allen Jenckes (1818–1875), Rhode Island congressman whose civil-service reforms failed to win passage in 1865 and 1868.

22. Thomas Babington Macaulay (1800–1859), English author and historian.

23. Richard Hoe (1812–1886) developed the rotary press; Cyrus Hall McCormick (1809–1884) invented a version of the modern grain reaper; Merlin was the magician at Camelot in Arthurian times; Heinrich Cornelius Agrippa (1486–1535), a German philosopher, was interested in alchemy.

24. Horatio Seymour (1810–1886), governor of New York, sympathized with the South but supported the Union when war broke out; Clement Laird Vallandigham (1820–1871), Ohio congressman and a leader of the Copperheads, was arrested for pro-Confederacy speeches during

the Civil War; George Wood (1789–1860), New York jurist, argued for preserving the Union at all costs; Fernando Wood (1812–1881), mayor of New York and congressman, was a strong Southern sympathizer.

25. Niccoló di Bernardo dei Macchiavelli (1469–1527), Italian statesman and political strategist, known best for *The Prince* (1513).

26. The illustrated London satirical weekly *Punch* was started in 1841; "Lord Soft" is a generic reference to weak English lords.

27. Prince Mikhail Dmitrievitch Gortchakov (1795–1861), Russian soldier.

28. General Winfield Scott (1786–1866) commanded the U.S. Army during the Mexican War.

29. A gillot is a loose woman; "without restraint" is the meaning here.

30. Among Napoleon Bonaparte's military accomplishments in 1807 were forcing Russia and Prussia to sue for peace and invading Spain and Portugal.

31. John Clark Frémont (1813–1890), explorer and unsuccessful candidate for president in 1856, had been appointed by Lincoln as major general in charge of the West. In that capacity, he declared on 30 August 1861 that all slaves in Missouri were emancipated; Lincoln countermanded the order.

32. Giuseppe Mazzini (1805–1872), Italian patriot.

INDEX